WOMEN IN GREEK MYTH

WOMEN
IN GREEK MYTH

Second Edition

Mary R. Lefkowitz

The Johns Hopkins
University Press
Baltimore

© 1986, 2007 by Mary R. Lefkowitz
All rights reserved. Published 2007
Printed in the United States of America
on acid-free paper
2 4 6 8 9 7 5 3 1

The Johns Hopkins University Press
2715 North Charles Street
Baltimore, Maryland 21218-4363
www.press.jhu.edu

Library of Congress Cataloging-in-Publication Data
Lefkowitz, Mary R., 1935–
    Women in Greek myth / Mary R. Lefkowitz — 2nd ed.
    Includes bibliographical references and index.
    ISBN-13: 978-0-8018-8649-2 (hardcover : alk. paper)
    ISBN-13: 978-0-8018-8650-8 (pbk. : alk. paper)
    ISBN-10: 0-8018-8649-X (hardcover : alk. paper)
    ISBN-10: 0-8018-8650-3 (pbk. : alk. paper)
    1. Women—Mythology. 2. Mythology, Greek. I. Title.
    BL795.W65L44 2007
    292. 1'3082—dc22   2006037277

A catalog record for this book is available
from the British Library.

Dis Manibus
H.L.R.

Contents

Preface to the Second Edition

The subject of women in Greek mythology never ceases to intrigue us. How else could *Women in Greek Myth* have remained in print for more than twenty years and been translated into German and into modern Greek?[1] It was certainly not because the book pretended to be a comprehensive treatment of the subject, or anything, really, except a set of related essays about topics connected to Greek myths. It was not because the book received the unanimous endorsement of its reviewers or that what I said persuaded everyone that I was on the right track.[2] I suspect that one reason for the book's survival is that it was written without constant reference to the theoretical constructs into which so much recent writing about myth and literature has been set. Literary and anthropological theories can be useful in helping us to see aspects of experience that we might otherwise have overlooked, but they inevitably rest on less secure foundations than scientific theories, particularly in the case of the study of the ancient world, where the evidence to support them, or any other kind of theory, is so scattered and remote. In this book I tried to bring people directly into contact with the past, with as little mediation or intermediation as possible. I have suggested meanings that might be extracted from sets of data, but my first aim has always been to let my readers see what ancient writers themselves said.

Most likely, the main reason that this book is still being read has to do with the continuing power of the myths it discusses. Ancient Greek myths remain part of us, despite all the differences between our culture and theirs. I know that in my own case I should never have become interested in the lives of ancient women had I not been interested in the way in which women's roles have been defined in modern society.

Yet, that sense of community with ancient Greek women can be misleading. Often, when we seek to talk about the past, what we end up providing is a new portrait of ourselves and our own modern concerns. If in this book I have made any progress in trying to describe what happened in the past, it is only because I have tried, so far as possible, to get away from the modern world and its preoccupations.

Our natural tendency to concentrate upon ourselves often misleads us. It makes perfectly good sense for modern people to suppose that there was an ancient cult of the Great Goddess, because we have grown up in a world where monotheism is the norm. But in the ancient Greco-Roman world there were many gods and goddesses, and before the second century BC no worshipers of these deities supposed that Aphrodite and Artemis were different manifestations of the same being. The notion that matriarchy preceded patriarchy is as modern as the notion of a unitary Great Goddess. No ancient Greeks thought that women were in charge of the world in the Golden Age that had preceded the miserable Iron Age in which they found themselves. To them, communities of women like Amazons were an anomaly, an unwholesome exception to the rules of ordinary society, and in any case, no one had ever seen one. They were always on the other side of an ever-retreating border.

Ancient men and women might have been even more surprised by another modern assumption, which is that Greek men disliked or hated women, were afraid of women's sexuality, and were determined to exclude them from the world of culture and civilization. Modern scholars appear to suppose that women writers were actively discouraged, that women's advice was deliberately unheeded, and that women were never seen as positive models of human behavior. In this book I suggest that, on the contrary, women could play all these roles and more.

Although the essays in the first edition of this book were written at various times, they share a common approach and a common vision, a concentration on and appreciation of women's courage and moral reasoning. Those topics are frequently overlooked, because so many recent discussions have concentrated on what men do to women and on the negative aspects of women's existence. In the twenty years since the book was first published, I have kept coming back to the subject. One essay has led to another and/or suggested some new way of looking at the texts that I have been reading and teaching about for the whole of my career. Hence the second edition, with six additional essays, all written since the first edition was published.

Some of these essays respond, if not always directly, to issues raised by reviewers. I should have explained in the first edition why I have relied on literature to uncover and examine the nature of women's courage and moral force. Our other sources, for all their great value, allow us only to glimpse specific instances of what women said or did in relative isolation. We hear what they accomplished or see them in a room or parting from their families for one last time. It is only in literature that we can see women interacting with other people, both male and female, over time. Literature provides the context for the inscriptions, papyri, vase paintings, and occasional references to women in ancient books, many of which are included in *Women's Life in Greece and Rome*, the collection of source materials that Maureen Fant and I have co-edited.[3]

As at least one reviewer observed, in the book I interpret myths (whenever possible) by reference to real life, rather than try to use the myths as documents that by themselves reveal the actual patterns of women's lives.[4] My readers will look in vain for an attempt to decipher hidden meanings in the myths or to wrest from them meanings that the ancients themselves did not make explicit. I have not examined theoretical power relationships, because it is so obvious that women were always under the supervision of men. Rather, the question seems to me to be one of intention. Did the possession of the power to rule, or indeed the power not to get pregnant, mean that ancient Greek men always despised all ancient women and sought to disparage them? As Richard Hawley has observed, "misogyny is an emotive word" that does not accurately describe the attitude of most ancient men towards most ancient women.[5] Protectionism is an aspect of patriarchal control, but the evidence suggests that its intention was more often kindly than repressive.[6]

When modern readers call attention to more animated attacks on women in ancient sources, they too often seem to forget that they are hearing the words not of Athenian society or of Euripides but of a character in a play by Euripides who is speaking for a particular dramatic purpose. In wishing that one could simply purchase children and dispense with women altogether, Hippolytus is speaking for himself. So is Iphigenia: When she urges her father to sacrifice her to Artemis by arguing that it is better for one man to live than ten thousand women (Euripides, *Iphigenia at Aulis* 1394), she is indulging in hyperbole.[7] Her father and other men were hardly eager to sacrifice her, and at the time, human sacrifice was regarded with horror. One can insist, with Jane Cahill, that the lines "*must* be taken as evidence of Greek misogyny," but to do so is to fail to take account of the demands of religion. The sacrifice is demanded by a powerful goddess.[8] Today we do not believe that Artemis exists, and certainly some of Euripides' contemporaries also had their doubts that she would have demanded such a sacrifice. But most people at the time and long afterwards did believe in those very gods, who did not seem to place much value on the lives of most particular individual mortals.

The new material in this second edition of *Women in Greek Myth* is included as chapters 2, 3, 5, 6, 7, and 8, interspersed in the rough chronology represented in the old chapters, which I have revised and updated. After the first, programmatic chapter about how easy it is for us to misunderstand Greek mythology, the book now begins with the portrayal of women in early epic and ends with a comparative discussion of misogyny in pagan and Christian contexts. The newer essays fill in some of the gaps in the first edition, but even in its expanded form the book can hardly claim to be anything other than an introduction to some of what can be learned from thinking about women in the myths.

The second chapter, "The Powers of the Primeval Goddesses," considers the roles played by females in the ancient Greek creation epic, Hesiod's *Theogony*. There the goddesses try to find ways to end the fighting and brutality perpetrated by the male gods. The third chapter, "The Heroic Women of Greek Epic," shows how mortal women play an analogous role in the *Iliad* and *Odyssey*, though without the goddesses' power to bring about the changes they desire.

In "Chosen Women," now the fourth chapter, I had begun to consider the influential myths in which gods intervene in human life by what appears to be sexual exploitation. Although these stories have seemed to some modern critics to exemplify the ways in which Greek males brutalized women, I argue that what is happening in the myths is not rape in the modern sense but, in most cases, a romantic abduction that confers some benefit on the mortal "victim." The mortals, men and women, are often terrified or puzzled by these encounters; but in the end they understand that their relationship with the gods, however impermanent, has brought them distinction and made them the parents of famous children. Chapter 5, "Seduction and Rape," describes the gods' methods in more detail and suggests why it is that in the end the women are not ashamed of their encounters with the gods. One can understand the fate of the chosen women more clearly when it is contrasted with that of males "raped" by goddesses. The male mortals who are abducted by goddesses derive fewer benefits from their experiences, or so Athenian vase painters appear to indicate, as I suggest in Chapter 6, "'Predatory' Goddesses."

Chapter 7, "The Last Hours of the *Parthenos*," deals with stories of young women (*parthenoi*) being offered as human sacrifices. Yet, in the hands of the poets, even these brutal practices can serve as vehicles for women to distinguish themselves in ways that ancient readers would admire. Along with the accounts of divine abduction, these myths reminded their audiences of the terrifying power of the gods and of how hard it is for mortals to understand or come to terms with their demands. Women as well as men needed to do all they could to accommodate and appease these deities. The eighth chapter, "Women in the Panathenaic and Other Festivals," seeks to describe the important role played by ancient women in stories about the two most important Athenian cults, and to show how the survival of the city depended upon them.

Both men and women realized that the participation of women was essential to the functioning of their communities, not just because of their roles as mothers and companions, but also because of their service to the gods. Even in the myths that describe how women were seduced and abducted by gods, the women were chosen because they displayed qualities of courage, enterprise, and intelligence that made them stand out from other women. They become the founding mothers of Greek heroes and great families, an important role in a society which paid particular honor to mothers.

Women in the ancient world were better understood and appreciated than modern readers at first might suppose, and pagan religions gave them responsibilities and freedoms that were later denied to them under Christianity.[9] Although only a few women ever got a chance to govern or play some direct role in politics, ancient writers nonetheless show them as having views and opinions that men ignored to their peril. It is certainly true that women kept the house and worked in wool, and that more of them would have been able to write poems or even novels had not their time been taken up with their responsibilities within the home, or had so many of them not died young or been maimed in various ways by the demands of childbearing. If severe limits were imposed on them by the nature of their lives and the restrictions of ancient societies, it does not necessarily follow that all women were always merely chattels, silent, repressed, and unappreciated.

In the preparation of both editions of the book, my thanks, as always, go to Sir Hugh Lloyd-Jones for many improvements and corrections, and also to Geneva Robinson for her technical assistance. My father, who always read everything I wrote, urged me to write a book about women and myth accessible to nonspecialist readers; I wish that I had been able to complete it in time for him to see it.

Preface to the First Edition

The Greeks' most important legacy is not, as we would like to think, democracy; it is their *mythology*. Even though in the first century AD it was announced that the god Pan was dead and mysterious voices were heard lamenting him,[1] the Greek gods and many obscure and irrational stories about them lived on in the imaginations of artists and writers, no matter how often or in how many different ways Christians and philosophers tried to dismiss the myths as frivolous or harmful. And even now, when man has acquired greater power than ever before to alter the natural world, the old myths continue to haunt us, not just in the form of nymphs and shepherds on vases and garden statuary, but in many common assumptions about the shape of human experience. The notions—now presumably obsolete—that a man should be active and aggressive, a woman passive and subject to the control of the men in her family, are expressed in virtually every Greek myth, even the ones in which the women seek to gain control of their own lives. That the most important phase of a woman's life is the period immediately preceding her marriage (or remarriage) is preserved in the plot of many novels, as is the notion that virginity, or at least celibacy, offers women a kind of freedom that they are no longer entitled to when they become involved with a man.

In this book I wish not only to describe how the Greeks portrayed female experience in myth, but also to suggest why, in the hands of the great poets, the narrative patterns were not as restrictive as I have made them sound. I believe that it is possible to show that the Greeks at least attributed to women a capacity for understanding that we do not always find in the other great mythological tradition that has influenced Western thought, namely, the Old and New Testaments.

There are two main reasons why we give the Greeks too little credit for their relatively balanced view of women's abilities. The first is that most of us encounter Greek mythology only in a condensed and filtered form, at best in a translation of some work of literature but more often as stories retold in a modern handbook. In the process of condensation and translation, the original meaning can easily get lost. For example, it is very hard to know what is to be deduced from the prophet Tiresias' famous statement that women get more pleasure out of the sexual act than do men. The story was first told in an epic poem of the sixth century BC, now lost, the Hesiodic *Melampodia*; only two lines of it survive: "Of ten shares the man enjoys one, the woman by enjoying ten satisfies her mind (*noema*)" (fr. 275 M-W). According to the outline of the original version that writers of the third century BC give us, Tiresias, who had been both a man and a woman, was asked by Zeus to say whether women or men got more pleasure out of intercourse; and because of his answer, Hera blinded him and Zeus then, in compensation, gave him the power of prophecy. How are we to interpret this story? Did Hera blind him because he revealed some mystery? Does the story imply that because women were said to enjoy intercourse more they were more eager for it and had to be watched more carefully? Or is it, as comparative anthropology would suggest, intended as an explanation of why bards often behaved and dressed in a female manner, and indeed had to understand both male and female experience in order to be able to prophesy accurately? Transvestism in ritual often marks a critical change, as from puberty to adulthood; it can also, as in the case of Pentheus in the *Bacchae*, mark one for destruction. In either case it helps the one who changes to acquire a privileged, otherwise inaccessible knowledge.[2] Thus, while it is possible to say that the story of Tiresias puts female sexuality in a bad light, it may also be possible to say that the story affirms that there were some benefits to be derived from acquiring female identity.

The second, and more insidious, reason why myth tends to be misunderstood derives from the concerns and beliefs of our own society. Even when myths about women are preserved in surviving works of ancient literature, so that we can have some idea of how the authors at least meant them to be understood, our own assumptions about what myth ought to mean can lead us to place undue emphasis on factors the ancients themselves were not aware of. We tend to assume that human nature has for all time remained basically the same, and we therefore conclude that the ancients were preoccupied with much the same problems as we are, in particular, sex, and the definition and role of the sexes. But it is another question whether the ancients themselves would have understood or accepted interpretations that place primary emphasis on the role of desire and incest. The text of Sophocles' *Oedipus Tyrannus* gives no indication that Oedipus was sexually attracted to Jocasta; he married her because marriage to the king's widow was the reward for ridding Thebes of the Sphinx. Similarly, I think, Thyestes has intercourse with his daughter not because he is in love with her but because the Delphic oracle told him that the son born from this union would take revenge on Thyestes' brother, Atreus, for murdering Thyestes' other children. The son, Aegisthus, seduces Clytemnestra and murders Atreus' son Agamemnon, and so gets back his own father's kingdom; in each generation inheritance and power are more compelling motives than sex.

Nonetheless, in looking at the myths, some scholars have tended to think in polar opposite ways that organize experience into certain restricted channels, much as a language might forbid some particular grammatical usages in favor of ones that are inherently no more worthy than those it has excluded. So the *Oedipus Tyrannus* can be understood as being primarily concerned with incest, or an excessive endogamy that ends in sterility and the extinction of the family.[3] But was that Sophocles' message? It is true that in this myth incest leads to destruction. Oedipus' sons by his mother Jocasta, Eteocles and Polynices, kill each other in single combat; his daughter Antigone dies because she seeks, against her uncle Creon's orders, to bury her brother Polynices' body. But in the *Antigone* Sophocles speaks only about the inexorable progress of the family curse, from which no generation can free itself, which he calls "folly in speech and a fury in the mind." Other critics, looking at the same myth and concentrating on references in it to lameness and maiming, have suggested instead that the story of Oedipus' family concerns the question of the origin of man—whether born from woman, or from the earth, like plants?[4]

But where modern critics would emphasize either sexual or social issues, the poet himself speaks of *perceptual* and *ethical* problems: will man know what is right, and even if he does, will he do it? Sophocles' answer is unequivocally negative:

> Hope in its many wanderings is a help to some men, but to others it is the deception that comes from vain passions. It comes on a man who knows nothing until he burns his foot in the hot fire. In wisdom once—from some unknown person—a famous statement came to light: "evil seems good to the person whose wits the god is leading towards delusion (ate); he acts only for the shortest time apart from delusion." (615–25)

The chorus does not say specifically that these lines apply to any particular character in the play, but since they concern the house of Oedipus it is natural to assume that they refer to Antigone, though it soon turns out that they apply equally well to Creon, the king who has condemned her to death for trying to bury her brother against his orders; his decision will cause the death of *his* family as well. At least so far as the Greeks themselves were concerned, it is not so much gender as the human condition that causes the problems that both men and women are bound to experience, especially if they try to accomplish something out of the ordinary.

In this book I suggest that it may not be profitable to regard the myths as a kind of code that could be reliably deciphered were we to apply the right modern methodology. Whatever the story of Oedipus may have meant when it was first told (whenever that was), by the time the poems of Homer were composed, it and virtually every other myth were presumed to belong to a distant past. The myths had become a kind of history, and they were retold both for entertainment and for instruction, often with conclusion first, since everyone knew how the story would end: even an extraordinarily long narrative, like the *Odyssey*, begins by stating that Odysseus returned home after wandering and learning much but having lost his companions because of their own folly. Modern critics may discern in Odysseus' adventures a covert description of the development of the human psyche, but the Greeks themselves understood it first as a moral tale in which the evil suitors were defeated by the courage and intelligence not only of Odysseus but also of his wife Penelope, to whom he was eager to return, in spite of an offer of immortality from the goddess Calypso.

Before I begin, I should make explicit two aspects of my approach to myth. (1) It must be stressed that the Greeks, unlike certain storytellers in cultures without developed literary traditions, have admirably spoken for themselves, and that we are therefore not easily justified in assuming that they meant something other than, or beyond, what they actually said. For that reason, in the discussion that follows, I am not going to try to interpret myths that survive only in summary or quotation, where we cannot know or recover the emphasis in the original. (2) I shall also try to distinguish, whenever possible, between literal and mythical meaning. We should not immediately assume that everyday action is what is described in myth or that normal relations between the sexes are always represented. When these stories are told in epic or in drama, they are set either in a remote past or a remote place; the characters are not ordinary people but heroes and heroines. When these stories are enacted in ritual, clear lines of demarcation are observed. In certain myths connected with Dionysus, such as the story of King Lycurgus in *Iliad* 6, a man pursues a group of women with intent to harm them, but they escape (130–40). But in the festival of Agrionia in Boeotia, when the priest Zoilus, carried away by excitement during the performance of the ritual, kills one of the maidens he was pursuing, he falls ill and dies, and the town is subsequently beset by lawsuits; so the priesthood was taken away from his family (Plutarch, *Moralia* 299e–300a = *WLGR*[3] 390). For reasons that are not explained here or in other accounts of myth and rituals involving Dionysus, it is the pursuit that matters; and bloodshed, while threatened, is better avoided.[5] In the myths that involve the pursuit of women by a man, the women are described as "maddened" and have left their normal occupations of weaving and child care to wander in the wilderness. The male pursues them and threatens to punish them, and in cases where he does not manage to kill the women (or the women kill him or someone else), the women contrive to return to their homes. The pattern of pursuit in myth does not necessarily imply the existence of an abiding hostility between the sexes.[6] By contrast, it may only suggest that the Greeks knew how to describe basic human sexual instincts, both male aggression and female submission, and believed that these must be recognized but also controlled if human beings of both sexes are to live together in harmony and understanding.

I have not tried in this book to give a comprehensive account of what happened to all women in Greek myth or to describe every aspect of women's life that the myths describe. Instead I have concentrated on those aspects of women's experience which have been most frequently misunderstood in recent literature. I consider the notions of matriarchy and the Amazons, women's life when they were away from men, marriage, women's role in politics, the degree of repression expressed in women's martyrdom, and finally, the nature of Greek misogyny. If my account of women's experience in myth and men's attitude towards women seems less negative than that given by other women scholars about the ancient world, it is not because I wish to be an apologist for the past, which I am delighted not to be living in myself, but because I am trying not to read into it the standards and preoccupations of the present.

WOMEN IN GREEK MYTH

1

Princess Ida and the Amazons

No Greek myths about women have claimed so much attention in recent times as those that concern matriarchy. These myths became a subject of interest in the mid-nineteenth century, when the question of women's education began seriously to be debated. Tennyson's poem "The Princess" (1847–51) describes the creation and demise of a woman's college; the story was parodied by Gilbert and Sullivan in the comic operetta *Princess Ida* a generation after Tennyson's poem was published. In the original "Princess," Tennyson described a "university for maidens," modeled along the lines of an Oxbridge college but run entirely for and by women—a vision that was to become a reality in 1869 with the founding of what was to become Girton College. In the poem, only the founder of the college, Princess Ida, is strong enough to abide by the rules of celibacy and withdrawal that she has set, and in the end, even she is called back to the normal role of wife and mother, not by brute male force but by what Tennyson saw as a natural dependency on men and an instinctive female desire to nurture. Tennyson portrays the princess's vision with great sympathy and complexity. Feminist writers today have returned to the poem because the founders of the great women's colleges in both America and England knew it and because Tennyson describes with such clarity the principal problems of feminism, not only in his own time, but in ours as well.[1]

Princess Ida seeks first to have an environment that expresses the ideals of her institution. The statues in the great hall of her women's college are

> —not of those that men desire,
> Sleek Odalisques nor oracles of mode,
> Nor stunted squaws of West or East, but she
> That taught the Sabine how to rule, and she
> The foundress of the Babylonian wall,
> The Carian Artemisia strong in war,
> The Rhodope that built the pyramid,

I

Clelia, Cornelia, with the Palmyrene
That fought Aurelian, and the Roman brows of
Agrippina. Dwell with these, and lose
Convention, since to look on noble forms
Makes noble thro' the sensuous organism that
Which is higher. O lift your natures up;
Embrace our aims! Work out your freedom! (ii. 62–75)

To judge by the library of Wellesley College, a university for women founded in 1875, the princess's choice of statuary is most unconventional. In 1913, doors were chosen for the library with figures representing Wisdom (Sapientia), rather oddly, a bearded old man with a book, and Charity (Caritas), represented by a woman comforting a naked child. These doors were (and still are) flanked by matronly statues of Athena and Hestia, "so that the goddess of wisdom was balanced by the goddess of the hearth."[2] The princess, by contrast, picked women of accomplishment—rulers, builders, the general-like Artemisia (Herodotus 8. 87–88), the intrepid Cloelia who swam the Tiber (Livy 2. 13. 6–9), Cornelia, who educated her sons the Gracchi (Plutarch, *Tiberius and Gaius Gracchus* 1. 7–2. 1; WLGR[3] 52), and the elder Agrippina, who stood up to the emperor Tiberius (Tacitus, *Annals* 4. 35). But the princess's speech describing them shows a certain obliviousness: Rhodope, who built the pyramid, made her fortune as a courtesan, if indeed she built the pyramid, which Herodotus denies (2. 134).

Tennyson's narrator, Prince Hilarion in female disguise, does not comment on such inconsistencies; he is much more impressed by the beauty of the students than by the statues. But he manages to summarize a lecture that might serve as a syllabus for a present-day popular survey of women's history. The lesson begins with a Darwinian account of human evolution (omitting God and Adam), starting with the cave man "crushing down his mate." Then the lecturer, Lady Psyche

Glanced at the legendary Amazon
As emblematic of a nobler age;
Appraised the Lycian custom, spoke of those
That lay at wine with Lar and Lucumo (ii. 110–13)

before briefly characterizing and criticizing more recent civilizations, and finally prophesying a future in which men and women would work together. As in the case of the statues, the most positive models are drawn from the

Greco-Roman past: the Amazons who ruled themselves and fought wars like men; the Lycians, who were said to be known by their mother's rather than their father's name and whose citizenship was determined by their mother's status (Herodotus 1. 173); and finally Cloelia (again), the girl who swam the Tiber and was praised even by her enemy Lars Porsenna, and Tanaquil, the domineering wife of Rome's fifth king, the Etruscan Lucumo or Tarquinius.

Of these legendary and mythical role models, only the Amazons have been taken seriously by feminist scholars, probably because they represent a whole society and not just the singular achievement of an extraordinary individual. For example, Phyllis Chesler has suggested in her best-selling book *Women and Madness* that "Amazon society was probably better for the development of women's bodies and emotions than any male-dominated society has ever been."[3] The source for this information appears to have been a single book, Helen Diner's *Mothers and Amazons: The First Feminine History of Culture*, a work first circulated in English in the 1930s under the pseudonym Sir Galahad. Diner claims that she consulted the ancient sources, but the way she refers to ancient historians shows that she has no notion of when they lived or whether their works still survive.[4] Her reconstruction of Amazon society appears to have been inspired primarily by the Swiss jurist Johann Jacob Bachofen's influential treatise, *Mother Right: An Investigation of the Religious and Juridical Character of Matriarchy in the Ancient World*, first published in 1861. Bachofen argued that women had been the first governors of ancient societies, on the basis of the scattered references in the ancient sources to Amazons and to matrilinear societies (in which descent and property rights follow the female line).[5]

At first sight there appears to be some evidence for Bachofen's theory: Herodotus in the fifth century BC speaks of an Amazon society, the Sauromatae, in Scythia, where women hunt on horseback alongside men, often wear men's clothing, and even fight in wars (4. 116); a woman in this society is not allowed to marry until she has killed a man in battle (4. 117). The Greek medical treatise in the Hippocratic corpus *Airs, Waters, Places*, which may be as early as the late fifth century BC, offers a slightly different description of the Amazon tribe Sauromatae: Women ride to hunt and fight in battles so long as they are virgins, but rarely after their marriage; they must kill three men before they can marry. They have no right breast; these are removed by their mothers when they are babies, by cauterization with a special bronze instrument, so that all the strength and bulk of the removed breast are directed to the right shoulder and arm (ch. xvii, CMG I 12). In the treatise *Articulations* (on the joints of the body), we are told that some authorities relate that the Amazons disjoint the lower extremities of male infants in order to render them lame (53, L iv 232). A commentary on Homer that has its origins in the third century BC adds that the Amazons fed their babies with tortoises, lizards, and snakes, since they did not use their breasts (schol. *Iliad* 3. 189). Diner was able to deduce from this kind of information that Amazons not only did not nurse their children but did not raise them, and that retaining the left breast was an affirmation of feminine strength, since the ancients believed that girls were conceived on the left and boys on the right.[6] Even though no ancient source said anything about it, Diner was also able to conclude that Amazon women did not make class distinctions among themselves but had equal access to power and opportunity.

In the treatise on matriarchy on which Diner based her reconstruction of Amazon society, Bachofen[7] started from the premise that mythology and legend preserve at least a nucleus of historical fact or, to put it another way, that in spite of certain fanciful elements in one or another account, some record of an actual past is preserved therein. But this was to assume that the first narrators of ancient myth were interested in recording history or facts (as we think of them), rather than describing attitudes or similitudes or drawing moral lessons. In practice, it did not matter to most ancient writers whether they had actually seen or had access to an eyewitness account; they were concerned much more with describing enduring characteristics and establishing general truths about human experience. In *Airs, Waters, Places*, the information about the Amazons' life is included among a series of anecdotes that explain why Asians are weaker, or more effeminate, than Greeks: climate is one factor, environment another, since the Asians are generally ruled by despots; then follows the description of the Amazons and of the strange customs of the other Scythians. Herodotus puts his account of the Amazons into a general description of Scythia, "a country no part of which is cultivated, and in which there is not a single inhabited city" (4. 97), a land beyond the pale, with strange, interesting and occasionally admirable customs that are in general demonstrably inferior to those of the Greeks. It is important to note that in Herodotus' account every feature of Amazonian society has a direct antithesis in ordinary Greek practice. In ancient Greece, women did not hunt or go to war; women's initiation rites did not involve exposure to physical danger; women nursed their children and stayed at home.[8]

Only two aspects of Amazon life are not inversions of Greek ordinary practice, and they are rather grotesque exaggerations of character derived from crude etymologies of names. The Greeks preferred to explain foreign loan words in their own language, even at the cost of straining credibility. For example, the story of being born from the sea foam (*aphros*) explains the name Aphrodite (Hesiod, *Theogony* 195–96); her son is called *Aeneas* because she had terrible (*ainos*) grief because of him (*Homeric Hymn* 5. 198–99).[9] Accordingly, Amazon was explained as *a-* (un- or no) *mazos* (breast); hence the story that their right breast was removed. The tribal name Sauromatae was derived from *sauros*, the Greek word for lizard; hence the idea that Amazon mothers fed their babies not on milk but on lizard juice. However, no ancient artist ever saw or even imagined these practices, because the Amazons represented in art always have both breasts.

Whatever we now might think of the merits of Amazons, the Greeks treated them as negative illustrations of what might happen if warrior women were in control, as a means of avoiding a dangerous hypothetical situation the potential for which in fact did not exist. I say warrior women rather than simply women because in myth and art their power receives more emphasis than their sex. Several heroes fight against them: Bellerophontes (on Pegasus) and the young Priam; one of Heracles' labors was to bring back the girdle of the queen of the Amazons (Euripides, *Heracles* 408–18). Athenian vase painters, when depicting this expedition, gave more credit to their own city's hero Theseus than to Heracles. Theseus was often depicted repelling an invasion of Attica by Amazons, who had come to claim their sister Antiope (or Hippolyte), who had been carried off by Theseus.[10]

For all their strength and skill, the Amazons tend to lose their battles against male heroes, especially if they are Greeks.[11] The Trojans have high hopes for Penthesilea and her friends, who arrived in Troy just at the time when the *Iliad* ends, but Achilles kills her on her very first day in the field (*Aethiopis* F 1/Q.S.I). Phidias' statue of Athena Parthenos on the Athenian Acropolis (now lost) had on the outer surface of its shield a relief of the battle of the Greeks against Amazons, and on the inside the battle of the gods against the giants (Pliny, *Natural History* 36. 18, Pausanias 1. 17. 2). On the metopes of the Parthenon a battle of Greeks against Amazons was paired with the battle of Greeks against the monstrous Centaurs. On the temple of Apollo Epikourios at Bassae in Arcadia a frieze of Heracles fighting the Amazons was matched by a frieze of the Thessalian Lapiths fighting the Centaurs.

In each case the Amazons are classified with the established enemies of law and order. In virtually every pictorial representation of conflict, the Amazons are shown being defeated; significantly, in Attic vase paintings after 480 BC, they are often shown in Persian costume, as if representing the great empire twice defeated by the Athenians.[12]

How historical were other ancient matriarchal societies? The evidence for their existence is equally unreliable.[13] In "The Princess" Lady Psyche in her history lesson also praises the "Lycian custom" (according to Herodotus unique in the world) of taking the mother's rather than the father's name and status (1. 173). But Herodotus' account of the Lycians is not an eyewitness record; it simply represents the opposite of the standard practice of the Greeks. The same can be said about his description of the marvels of Egypt, where "the people, in most of their manners and customs, exactly reverse the common practice of mankind. Women do the marketing [in fifth-century Athens men or male slaves did the shopping]; men work the loom; women urinate standing up, men sitting down; daughters must support their parents; they write letters from right to left" (2. 35). Here too he is not reporting the literal truth, but attempting to illustrate the foreignness of Egypt.[14] Also, the other evidence we have suggests that for the Lycians maternity was no more significant than for other peoples. In the earliest reference we have to the Lycians, the Lycian Glaucus explains who he is by tracing the male lines of his ancestry (*Iliad* 6. 196–210). His cousin Sarpedon is chief of the Lycians at Troy, rather than Glaucus himself, not because Sarpedon was the son of Bellerophontes' daughter, while Glaucus was son of his son, but because Sarpedon was the son of the king of the gods, Zeus.[15] Inscriptions from Lycia have recently been found that also reveal no trace whatever of a matrilinear system of descent.[16]

Aristotle states explicitly that the "Lycian custom" that Lady Psyche praises would have been interpreted by the Greeks as a sign of decadence; to Aristotle, the rule of women (or *gynaikokratia*) was a sign of how democracies tended to turn into tyrannies; women get out of hand, wives are permitted to inform against (i.e., get political power over) their husbands (*Politics* 1269b40, 1313b32). The Lycians, declares a summary of Aristotle's account of their government, "are all pirates. They have no written laws, only customs, and have long since been under the rule of women. They sell false witness together with their property" (Heraclides, *Politics* 15 = Aristotle, fr. 611. 43 Rose).[17] The third-century BC poet Apollonius of Rhodes states that the

Amazons also "do not respect the laws of the gods" (*themistes*, "Voyage of the Argo" 2. 987–88). Aristotle's pupil Clearchus (a contemporary of Apollonius) claimed that the Lydians could be considered decadent because they had been ruled by a woman, Omphale; she had been raped by Lydian men, and in revenge she forced respectable women to have intercourse with slaves (Athenaeus 12. 516a). This same Omphale was said to have purchased as a slave the greatest Greek hero, Heracles, and to have made him her lover (Scylax 709 *FGrHist* F21).[18]

Mythologies of matriarchy in other cultures serve a similar function. Joan Bamberger[19] has shown that myths about the rule of women from two culturally distinct areas are intended as negative examples. Both in Tierra del Fuego at the extreme southwest tip of South America and in the tropical forests of the northwest Amazon and central Brazil, women are said to have been the first to rule over the land and to have owned all the emblems of power, but they ruled without mercy and justice. Then, suddenly, in both myths the situation is reversed; the women are driven out, excluded from the secrets of power, and kept forever after subordinate. This changeover is also celebrated in ritual. The myths "constantly reiterate that women did not know how to handle power when they had it." They do not represent actual history but instead explain the way things are. "The Rule of Women," concludes Bamberger,[20] "instead of heralding a promising future, harks back to a past darkened with repeated failures. If, in fact, women are ever going to rule they must rid themselves of the myth that states they have been proved unworthy of leadership roles."[21]

Greek myths of matriarchy, like the South American, are didactic rather than historical. But it is easier to accept that the South American myths are unhistorical, because Greek authors present their material in such reasonable and rational form that it takes some time to realize how greatly their research methodology (if one can call it that) differs from ours. In the sixth century BC, Greeks traveled to Themiskyra and the Thermodon River, on the south shore of the Black Sea, the land that in seventh-century BC epic poetry had been inhabited by Amazons. When they found no Amazons there, they did not give up their belief in the Amazons' existence but, rather, thought of the Amazons as being located farther away, in the part of the world that had not been explored, namely the uncivilized land of Scythia; other accounts put them in Ethiopia or places they had heard of but where no one had actually been. But as Pierre Devambez has pointed out,[22] if the Amazons had existed, other cultures would have represented them in their art; in fact only the Greeks seem to have known about them. Nor have archaeologists uncovered the kind of empirical information that could confirm that Amazons, or female tribes like them, existed. The Spanish explorers of Brazil named the great river they discovered there the Amazon because they saw native women fighting alongside their men;[23] the discovery of fourth-century Sauromatian graves containing the skeletons of women and horses, with spears, may indicate that there were women warriors, but not that these women were independent of men, like the Amazons, or indeed matriarchal.[24]

Since we are accustomed to thinking of Herodotus as the founder of modern history, it is sometimes difficult to appreciate how different the Greek view of reality was from ours. They thought in terms of probability (what they called *eikos*, what is fitting or likely) and did not distinguish between the remote and recent past. Nor did they accord more credibility to what could be demonstrated empirically than to what could be vividly described (even at third hand). In relating an account of a past event, an author was free to remove or add details to render his story more probable.[25] This attitude has contributed greatly to modern confusion about the relationship of ancient myth to history.

For example, orators in fourth-century BC Athens spoke of the story of the Amazons' invasion of Attica as if it were as historical (in our terms) as the Persian invasion of 480. Athens' victory over the Amazons came to be regarded as her first major civic achievement. The orator Lysias in a speech honoring the war dead in 389 (2.4–6) depicts the Amazons as formidable enemies. They were the first to wear iron armor and to ride on horseback; they had conquered all their neighbors. But "when matched with our Athenian ancestors they appeared in all the natural timidity of their sex, and showed themselves less women in their external appearance than in their weakness and cowardice." All were killed on the spot. Other writers, less concerned with praising the state in general, described the battle in ways that explained the position of various monuments, such as the Amazoneum, various tombs, and a column outside the city gate near Phaleron commemorating the Amazon Antiope or Hippolyte (Theseus' consort), who according to some authorities was killed there but according to others lived on to establish the Amazoneum at Troezen. Precise strategic and topographical details of the battle were supplied by Cleidemus, author of an early history of Attica, from his own imagination.[26] Plutarch in his *Life of Theseus* (27) illustrates how an an-

cient author approaches his source material: he gives the most space to Cleidemus (323 *FGrHist* F18), because of the detail his account provides. Plutarch adds other information when it corresponds to existing monuments in
Athens and elsewhere; he copes with contradictions (such as when and where
Antiope/Hippolyte died) by giving both versions, and observes that "it is
hardly surprising that history should go astray when it has to deal with events
so remote as these."

Bachofen's approach to the evidence is no less eclectic than Plutarch's,
though his premises were more elaborate: he assumed that myth represented,
if not a precise record of specific institutions, then at least a general impression of cultural practice, enduring characteristics, and human psychology.[27]
Scholars in his day had become increasingly interested in discovering the
common grounds among civilizations of different times and places. Artists
like Wagner sought to recapture in their own language and customs impressions of their vanished heritage. Bachofen spoke of discovering in myth fixed
and recognizable laws, among them the notion that in primitive societies
woman could be seen to exert over man a powerful religious and moral influence, so that even though she was physically weaker, she was able to ensure
the continuity of her sense of social values. One suspects that his notion of
ancient realities was based on a contemporary appreciation of the role of
women in his own society, and that the fixed laws he saw in the confused and
contradictory record of the past were the patterns he most wanted to find.
His work had wide influence; Nietzsche was familiar with it, and Engels
adopted the idea of early matriarchy because it gave support to the notion
that the earliest (i.e., natural) form of human existence had been communal.[28]

Bachofen's theories would be of purely antiquarian interest were it not that
they continue to be taken seriously by scholars who are not familiar with the
methods of ancient historians.[29] The continuing appeal of his work results
from his putting the blame for women's loss of power onto male conspiracy,
envy, and ignorance. By implication, then, restoring women to their rightful
place first of all requires recognition of that conspiracy and emphasis on
whatever instances of female supremacy can be discovered in past history,
however remote in time or scattered in different cultures. In "The Princess,"
according to Tennyson's narrator, Lady Psyche presented "a bird's-eye view of
all the ungracious past" (ii. 109), a survey in which she described events in
summary and out of context: women's status in the Persian, Grecian, and Roman empires, "how far from just" (116); women in China, Islam, the Age of

Chivalry, and finally the present, when "commenced the dawn," and the future, with full equality for women (162). Emotion is involved in every aspect of academic discourse at Princess Ida's college: "O lift your natures up; / Embrace our aims; work out your freedom" (ii. 74–75); the faculty are more like clergy than professors in their desire to convert and to retain a group of faithful.

Tennyson also makes it clear that in the process of recovering events and of endowing them with a significance that they in fact never had, Lady Psyche and her followers seem to have assumed that because they are women they are competent to assess the fate of other women in all of history and all over the world. But better tools for the purpose, at least in the case of ancient Greece and Rome, are knowledge of the languages and of the methods and aims of ancient historical writers. Without this knowledge, scholars run the risk of imposing present values onto the past and of writing not history but a new mythology.

Let me offer a few examples of the kinds of distortion that result when scholars try to approach ancient literature directly, as if they were reading the works of a contemporary writer. Bachofen, relying in part on Aeschylus' *Eumenides*, claimed that the discovery of paternity was a key factor in the shift from matriarchy to patriarchy; he cites Apollo's famous lines which state that the real parent of the child is the father, while the mother is merely a vehicle for carrying the seed from which the child grows.[30] Kate Millett, in her attempt to write a universal history of the treatment of women in literature, not only recapitulates Bachofen's argument in her discussion of the *Oresteia* but uses a rather free translation that seems to her "closer in spirit to the original" because it puts special stress on Clytemnestra's sexuality.[31] But in the original the argument about paternity, which no one in the audience would have understood as a statement of general "law" or truth, wins the day only when the goddess Athena casts the deciding vote,[32] and in any case Clytemnestra is not just an ordinary woman but a murderer by treachery, "who slew her husband, the watcher of the house" (*Eumenides* 740). The female Furies, who demand vengeance against Orestes for his having killed his mother, are not simply vanquished by a new "male" order; they are persuaded by the goddess Athena to play a more positive role in the administration of justice by an offer of great honor (*timē*), which included material recompense in the form of sacrifice and powers, the sort of thing the Judeo-Christian divinities did not always care about but which no Greek god would ever disdain.[33] Far from being suppressed, as Bachofen supposed, the Furies' great strength is recognized, since it is only with their support that Athens will maintain her judicial system and her political and economic importance.[34]

But, the assumption that women in antiquity were deprived of their original powers by a conspiracy on the part of men, and kept powerless because of men's fear that they would naturally try to reassert themselves, gives increased emphasis to the role of gender in myth, and such an emphasis seems even more plausible in light of the importance given to the role of sexuality in the psychological theories of Freud. It has been argued that, when Orestes in the *Eumenides* is purified by pig's blood, the pig's blood represents a rebirth that breaks the original bond between the child Orestes and his mother Clytemnestra.[35] The various words for pig were also slang for the female genitalia. *Delphax,* a word for young pig, is cognate with the root-*delph,* signifying "womb" and probably also with the place-name Delphi.[36] But in actual practice, outside the "world" of this particular drama, pig's blood was used at Delphi to cleanse any murderer, not just matricides, of blood guilt.[37] In those many cases when the victim was not the murderer's mother, how could pig's blood have symbolized a rebirth that breaks the bond between the murderer and his victim?

Similarly, it is possible to view the myths of Amazons and other wild and destructive women who oppose men, like the women of Thebes in Euripides' *Bacchae,* as expressions of the psychological conflict imposed by the customary segregation of the sexes in Athenian society and men's apprehensions about female sexuality.[38] But myths telling of these conflicts, and rituals enacting them, existed long before and continued long after respectable women in Athens ceased to be confined primarily to their homes; and it is significant that in these myths, not only the women, but the men who attack and pursue them suffer in the end from their violent behavior. Nor does the defeat of the Amazons primarily represent the triumph of the male hierarchy over women or express male sexual domination simply because the Amazons are portrayed as young, attractive women whom the men stab with their swords.[39] If it can be argued of the Parthenon's metopes, which depict Theseus fighting the Amazons in conjunction with the battle of the Lapiths against the Centaurs, that the "masculinized" Amazons represent *all* ordinary women, then the half-equine Centaurs must be understood as representatives of *all* ordinary horses and the metopes must thus advocate the Athenian suppression of horses, animals that in reality were, of course, highly prized and well-treated.

Since the Greeks were perfectly capable of expressing complex meanings in both literature and art, there is no need to believe that if they wanted to say something about male domination of Greek females they could not have done so directly, without employing an "ethnographical code."[40] The Amazons and other mythical women who attack men are destructive to themselves as well as to the rest of society; the myths' "message" is directed both to women and to men and warns that anyone who withdraws from or hates ordinary family life becomes dangerous to society as a whole. The Greeks, male and female, would have been surprised that Lady Psyche for her women's college chose the Amazons as "emblematic of a nobler age," since to them the Amazons represented one of the best arguments for retaining a status quo in which groups composed exclusively of either sex were not permitted continuously to segregate themselves.

In the end, interpretations such as Lady Psyche's tell us more about ourselves than they do about the cultures that they purport to describe, rather like the anthropologists who failed to understand the purpose of the myths of the Trobriand Islanders and so deduced that the natives did not know where babies came from. Imagine what those natives might conclude about our notion of sexual intercourse from a literal interpretation of the story of the Annunciation.[41] How then should modern feminists try to approach the past, so that—to use Henry James' Olive Chancellor's phrase— "men shouldn't taunt them with being superficial"?[42] We should, to begin with, make a clear distinction between rewriting mythology, or, as Carolyn Heilbrun called it, *Reinventing Womanhood*,[43] and reporting history. In the latter case, we need to get beyond the stage of reaction, past Bachofen, Jane Harrison, and all the recent revivals of their work, and back to the full texts of the sources they cite only partially, back also to the kind of documentation Bachofen and his modern followers have not considered.[44]

The social documents that will tell us most about the real status of women are to be found in places that few standard ancient history courses until quite recently considered: gravestones, boundary markers, wills, marriage contracts. The information is found mostly on inscriptions and papyri; most are untranslated, most require special training to read; and much cataloguing still needs to be completed. Studies of these documents show that it is dangerous to derive our picture of the ancient world exclusively from literary documents, especially from dramas or legal orations, which often portray the breakdown of normal life rather than its routine. However, epic and drama themselves have much to tell us about normal relationships, if we look closely at what the characters say rather than simply at the main lines of mythic conflict. In the fifth and fourth centuries BC, members of Athenian families wished to be buried near each other, even if it necessitated moving established graves; in the fourth century, details of their affection and relationship began to be described.[45] Strong ties existed not only between mother and daughter but between husband and wife. Upper-class women in all periods and places in the Greek world had the opportunity to be educated.[46] If they did not voice dissatisfaction even in Rome, where women owned and managed property, perhaps they saw certain advantages in the status quo, such as protection and mutual trust. Lower-class women and female slaves lived in many respects the same kind of life as men of the same station, with set occupations, some of which were sex-segregated, but fewer than we might have expected.

Women's status has not been as easy to explain as Bachofen thought, and it may take several generations seriously to describe it accurately, even for one small portion of the world's history, like that of ancient Greece and Rome. In order properly to evaluate these new findings, comparison must constantly be made with the status of men in the same period and country and equivalent social class. If I were asked what statues to put in front of the Wellesley College Library, I would not choose goddesses like Hestia and Athena, because it is impossible for a mortal to emulate beings who are immortal, ageless, and infinitely powerful; nor would I pick Amazons or the equally nonexistent Lycian matriarchs, or even the swimmer Cloelia from Rome's legendary past. I would begin with some ancient women Lady Psyche had apparently never heard of, who won in their time the respect of their contemporaries, men and women both: the poet Erinna, composer of the epic poem *The Distaff*, about the death of a female friend;[47] Hipparchia the philosopher, who traveled around lecturing with her husband Crates (Diogenes *Laertius* 6. 96–98[48]); Menophila of Sardis, who was honored by her city for being clever (she is shown with a book) and for being a leader;[49] the philosopher Hypatia of Alexandria.[50] Certainly they were unusual, but they did exist—which we might not have guessed had we considered only the accounts of women in myth.

The Powers of the Primeval Goddesses

In the Greek myths that describe the creation of the world and the hierarchy of the gods, goddesses play a prominent role, either as wives or mothers or as permanent (and powerful) young virgins. According to the poet Hesiod in the *Theogony,* his epic about the genealogy of the gods, the divinity who first emerges from the primeval void (Chaos) is not an omnipotent male deity, like the "Lord God" in the first chapter of Genesis, but the goddess Earth. She is the mother of the god Heaven, who becomes her consort and the father of most of her children, initially, the mountains, the sea, and the river Ocean who surrounds the sea. But Earth comes first not because the goddesses had some ancient priority over the (male) gods; rather, as the Greeks themselves understood the story, it seemed more natural to imagine that a female rather than a male would conceive and give birth. Motherhood conveyed certain privileges and some limited powers, but in all the myths it is assumed that the universe will be controlled by the (male) gods.

What then are the powers of the goddesses? The first, and in many ways the most sinister, is the ability to conceive without male intervention. This power, even in a world dominated by male gods, can be used for destructive or retaliatory purposes. For example, Night, like Earth the fatherless daughter of the grammatically genderless Void, "bore Doom and dark Fate and Death; she bore Sleep and the race of Dreams; secondly black Night bore Blame and miserable Woe, having slept with none of the gods" (*Theog.* 211–14). And this, according to the eighth-century BC poet Hesiod, is just the beginning of a long list of her baneful and fatherless children. The anonymous author of the *Homeric Hymn to Apollo* (composed perhaps in the seventh century BC), makes Hera, Zeus' sister and last wife, the mother of Typhaon, the monster Hesiod also calls Typhoeus. In the hymn Hera gets angry at her husband because he swallowed Athena's mother, Intelligence (Metis), and gave birth to Athena without her, while Hera had been able to bear only a puny and crippled son, Hephaestus. So Hera asks: "Can't I give birth by myself? Even though *she* (Athena) will be called *your* child exclusively by the immortals that live in wide heaven! Watch out; I may plan something evil for you in the future" (324–25a). She then promises to bear a child of her own, without committing adultery or having intercourse with Zeus. She then leaves the company of the gods, strikes the earth with her hands and prays to Earth and Heaven and the other Titan gods beneath the earth to give her a "child apart from Zeus, in no way less powerful than Zeus himself" (337–38). This child turns out to be a monster, "unlike gods or mortals, fearful, harsh Typhaon, the scourge of mortals" (351–52).

The author of the Homeric hymn does not need to explain in detail who Typhaon is because the Greek audience for this hymn would have known about him from Hesiod's *Theogony*, or "Genealogy of the Gods." Since Hesiod was regarded by the ancients themselves as the ultimate authority, he is not only the earliest, but probably the most reliable source for understanding how the Greeks themselves understood the myths of creation. Unlike us, the Greeks (men and women both) learned their myths from texts by individual authors, not from books about mythology, at least until the Hellenistic age, when Greek culture was adopted by peoples whose first language was not Greek. In the account in the *Theogony*, Zeus defeated Typhaon after a long struggle, and only with the aid of the thunder and lightning made for him by the Cyclopes, the sons of Earth and Heaven. Zeus threw Typhaon's burned and battered body into the depths of Tartarus, but because Typhaon is immortal, he still causes trouble: "from Typhaon come the strong wet winds" that cause storms, unlike the favoring winds that the gods send to help men (861–63).

The myth of Typhaon indicates that although Hera can make trouble for Zeus and the other gods by using her powers of unassisted conception, she cannot defeat Zeus and his established patriarchal rule. Nor could her grandmother Earth, in her time, assume power, even though she had come into being before her son and consort Heaven. Earth bore "starry Heaven equal to herself, so that he might cover her everywhere, and be the home of the blessed gods, always secure" (124–26). "Equal" here means equal in size; in other respects, Heaven seems to have the power, which he uses to keep his children from replacing him. As Earth's consort, he begets children later known as the Titans, "all of whom were the most dreadful of children, and their father hated them from the beginning" (156–57).

Heaven's youngest son Cronus, the most dreadful of these most dreadful children (137–38), hates his father in return, not out of some instinctive adolescent tendency towards rebellion (since adolescence hadn't yet been invented as a stage in human life), but rather because of Heaven's brutality: "as soon as one of them was born, Heaven used to hide them away in the depths of Earth and not send them up to the light, and he rejoiced in his evil work" (154–59).

Earth, who is compressed by having her children stored within her, and moaning with pain, thinks of a plan of revenge. Using her powers of unassisted conception, she gives birth to the element Hesiod calls "grey adamant" (a metal like steel that is used only by the gods) and fashions a great sickle (161–62). But then, rather than trying to use the weapon in her own defense, she employs the second of the powers peculiar to goddesses: the loyalty owed by children to their mother. She asks her offspring: "children of mine and of an evil father, please listen to me; we could take revenge on your father's evil outrage; he was the first to devise shameful deeds" (164–66). What we do see here is not the command of a matriarchal entity that could control her offspring by force, but a female who uses persuasion and rudimentary moral reasoning to get her *sons* to help her punish her husband. She speaks of Heaven's cruelty to her and her children as a crime. It is because of this wrongdoing that her son Cronus promises to help her, echoing her words: "I don't care about my father—who doesn't deserve the name; for he was the first to devise evil deeds" (170–72).

Cronus is eager to do what his mother wants, since it is the only way he can come "into the light," a term that usually means "be born," instead of being hidden inside his mother. In order to imagine the scene, it is necessary to think of these gods as being at the same time disembodied forces and anthropomorphic, and of the children of Heaven and Earth as being full-grown, even though they have not yet been born. Their peculiar situation dictates the form of revenge Earth chooses: since Heaven is immortal, they can't kill him, even if they could somehow get out. Under the circumstances, castration (during intercourse) provides the most practical solution. Nothing the poet says indicates that he had in mind Freudian notions of father-son rivalry, mother-son incestuous desires, or a mental anguish that derives from female "impotence."

Earth, delighted with her son's promise to help, hides him, sets him in ambush, puts the sharp sickle into his hands, and explains the whole plot to him. Significantly, it is she, not Cronus, who thinks of the plot:

> Great Heaven came bringing on Night and longing for love, lay himself on Earth and spread out everywhere. Cronus reached out from his ambush with his left hand, and in his right took the huge sickle, long and sharp, and swiftly lopped off his father's genitals, and threw them so that they fell behind him. (176–82)

This last action indicates that Cronus knows he is committing a crime, because he tries to put the evidence out of sight where he cannot see its pollution.

Earth does not win control over Heaven or the other gods as a result of Cronus' attack. The bloody drops that fall on her make her pregnant, this time with the Furies, the Giants, and the Melian nymphs; from the genitals themselves the love goddess Aphrodite is born. Cronus takes over as ruler of the gods, though Heaven promises to get revenge for the crime committed against him. For a time, "history" seems to repeat itself. Cronus marries his sister Rhea, and she bears Hestia, Demeter, Hera, Hades, Poseidon, and Zeus.

> And Cronus swallowed them up, as soon as each came to her knees from her holy womb, with this in mind, that no one else of the proud sons of Heaven might have the honor of kingship among the immortals. For he had learned from Earth and starry Heaven that it was fated for him, strong as he was, to be overthrown by his own son, through the plans of great Zeus. So he kept a sharp watch, and swallowed up his children, and he had unending sorrow. (459–67)

Once again, the children's mother, this time Rhea, asks for help to avenge the crime Cronus committed against his father and against her own children, and she gets it, first from her mother and father, Earth and Heaven, and also from her youngest child, Zeus, who, with the collusion of her parents, is hidden away. A rock is given to Cronus to swallow up in his place. Earth had planned the overthrow of her husband, Heaven; now she has a scheme to overthrow their son Cronus. As soon as Zeus is grown, which takes only a year, Earth tricks Cronus into releasing his children, and Zeus subdues him with thunder and lightning that his Titan uncles give him, because he set them free.

I have summarized and quoted Hesiod at such length in order to show how when a Greek poet tells the story of the birth of the gods, there is never any question of females taking charge, neither at the beginning nor at any other time. In a brief modern summary of the story, Earth might seem to possess some independent authority, but in Hesiod's account, her role is first to bear children and then to maintain, through her advice, general standards of justice that none of the male gods seem to want to abide by, at least until Zeus takes over the command. Earth and her daughter Rhea, not the male gods, are the first to demand justice and to plan how justice might be done. Perhaps because they are unwilling to take aggressive action, it is they, rather than the male gods, who wish to maintain order and balance. Since any religion reflects the moral attitudes of its adherents, it is possible to see in the characterization of these goddesses some reflection of the roles of mortal women in archaic Greece. The women in the *Iliad* also advise restraint on the part of their men and encourage alternatives to the code of honor that leads the male heroes into increasing danger.[1] It is primarily the women who are able to understand the full consequences of war for its survivors, on both the winning and the losing side.

It has often been observed that the Greek succession myth follows the general pattern of the ancient Near Eastern creation myth.[2] The Babylonian creation epic, which is known in Akkadian as *Enuma Eliš*, was probably composed about a thousand years before the *Theogony*. This epic was recited every year on the fourth day of their New Year's festival; like the *Theogony*, it celebrates the triumph of the present ruler of the gods, in this case, Marduk.[3] The world had first been ruled by the primordial oceans, the goddess Tiamat and her husband Apsu. They quarreled with the subsequent generations of gods, and Apsu was killed (in the Akkadian religion gods could die) by Ea the god of wisdom. Tiamat seeks revenge for the crime, and Marduk fights her in single combat and kills her. Because she fights on her own, challenges Marduk, and is willing to engage in single combat, she appears to be stronger than Earth in the Greek myth. Tiamat flies into a rage, she recites a charm, casts a spell, and, as Marduk attacks with his net and the evil winds, she tries to swallow him, but then he shoots an arrow into her stomach and kills her.

In the Greek epic, by contrast, Earth survives to remain a power among the gods. Hesiod tells us that even after Zeus took over, Earth gave birth (with her brother Tartarus as father) to Zeus' most formidable opponent, the monster Typhoeus. In the Homeric hymn to Apollo, as we have seen, Typhoeus (alias Typhaon) was the fatherless son whom Hera bore to get even with Zeus for giving birth to Athena. Hesiod does not say why Earth, who in his account had helped Zeus overcome Cronus, later produced Typhoeus to plague him. But her action provides yet another example of the most elemental way in which goddesses can assert themselves in the Greek patriarchal system. In the *Theogony* Earth also proves to be more impartial and impersonal than Tiamat in her revenge. When Heaven wrongs her she gets Cronus to attack him; when Cronus wrongs Rhea and their children, she contrives to preserve Zeus so that he can replace Cronus as the ruler of the gods.

A fragment survives of a Hurrian creation epic that also has affinities with the *Theogony*. The myth is preserved in a Hittite text now known as "The Song of Kumarbi."[4] It tells of the defeat of Anu, the king of heaven, by the god Kumarbi, who bites off Anu's "manhood." This action makes Kumarbi pregnant with a number of important gods, but before they are born the fragmentary text becomes hard to read. Apparently the gods in Kumarbi's interior discuss with him through which opening in his body they should be born, a practical problem that is solved more discreetly in Greek myths by having Athena be born from Zeus' head (after he swallows her mother) and Dionysus from his thigh (after he rescues the embryo from his mother's charred body). In the Hittite myth, Kumarbi combines in a single act the separate accomplishments of Cronus when he castrated Heaven and of Zeus when he swallowed the goddess Intelligence. But most significantly for the purposes of comparison with Greek epic, goddesses like Earth (and Intelligence) play no role in the Hittite narrative; females aren't needed either to give advice or for generation.

How and why did Hesiod's contemporaries worship the goddesses? The poet mentions and in some cases briefly describes the mothers, daughters, aunts, and wives of the principal gods; but he tells us in some detail about the cult of only one particular goddess, Hecate, daughter of the otherwise obscure god Perses and of the goddess Asteria, sister of Leto, who was the mother by Zeus of Apollo and Artemis (404–13). In recent times scholars have been puzzled by the disproportionate amount of space Hesiod devoted to Hecate, a goddess who received far less attention from other ancient writers and (so far as we know) from cults either in Hesiod's homeland or elsewhere in mainland Greece during the archaic period. It has been suggested that the lines were inserted into Hesiod's text by some later writer. Others assume that Hesiod was partial to Hecate because she was important in a local cult that may have been brought to his home in Boeotia from Asia Minor by Hesiod's father. Certainly the cult as he describes it is different from what we know about her worship in later times, when Hecate was associated with witchcraft, magic, and the underworld. But whether or not Hesiod had particular personal reasons for including her, the description of Hecate is not out of place in his genealogy, or in his poem, since it provides yet another instance of the new (to the world at that time) and constructive justice of Zeus. And even if the lines were added to Hesiod's text by some later worshiper, they still show what importance a goddess can have in a basically patriarchal theology.

Hesiod includes Hecate and lists her powers at the end of his description of the children and grandchildren of Pontos, the Sea. Some of these he mentions only by name, but he says more about others, like Styx, daughter of Ocean, the "fearful" goddess who enforces the oaths of the gods, and Leto, who (in contrast to Styx) is "always kind, mild to men and the immortal gods, kind from the start, gentlest of the gods on Olympus." Leto is the maternal aunt of Hecate, and Hecate's father Perses, remarkable for his intelligence, is another descendant of the Sea. Zeus honored Styx, giving her large gifts and making her the power by which the gods swore their oaths, because she was the first of the old gods to move to Olympus and cooperate with him. He honors Hecate more than all the gods and gives her "shining gifts and a share of earth and of barren sea"; she also has "honor from starry Heaven, and is honored especially among the immortal gods" (412–16). Zeus' favoritism towards Hecate does not indicate that he was, so to speak, compensating in some small way for having taken over her once universal powers, any more than his honoring Styx means that she had been an independent force before he came along. Styx merely moved from a minor position under Cronus' rule to a major one under Zeus.' Zeus also wishes to secure the loyalty of Hecate, who was born under the rule of Cronus, though, as Hesiod tells the story, only just before Rhea gave birth to Zeus' siblings and Zeus himself.

From Hesiod's description, it seems that Hecate's honors consist in large measure of what results from her dominion over men:

> Even now, when a mortal man offers fine sacrifices and propitiates her according to custom, he prays to Hecate, and great honor comes to him easily, and the goddess gladly answers his prayers, and gives him prosperity, since she has the power. (416–20)

The poet is careful to add that Hecate has this power as a result of the respect of the other Titan gods who, like Styx, went along with Zeus, and because of the beneficence (once again) of Zeus. Rather than give her a smaller share of honor and gifts because she was an only child, and thus presumably had no brother to protect her, Zeus in fact increased her share (421–28). As a result, Hecate can, *if she wants to*, help kings administer justice, and, *if she wants to*, assist orators in the marketplace; she can bring victory in battle; she helps cavalrymen and also athletes in competitions. Fishermen pray to her and to Poseidon: "the renowned goddess can easily grant a large catch, and can easily take it away again once it appears, *if she wants to*." Along with Hermes, she helps herdsmen, whether of cattle, goats, or sheep; *if she wishes*, she can make a small flock grow large and a large flock small. And finally, Zeus made her fosterer of all the human young who were born after she came into the world (429–52).

Of the honors given to her by men because of her power over so many important aspects of their lives, only this last, being fosterer of the young (*kourotrophos*) would seem to us to belong more naturally to the domain of a female divinity. Not that she uses it only to sustain, because she can also withdraw her support. Because the nurturing of children was so essential and precarious, the first and best portions of sacrifices were offered to the female divinities designated as "fosterers of the young" in other cults. Presumably it is this privilege that makes Zeus' gift to her of the title *kourotrophos* especially honorific.

Of Hecate's other original powers, only two are shared with male gods. With Poseidon, she can help or hinder the work of fishermen, and with Hermes, the work of herdsmen. Of the rest—justice, rhetoric, war, cavalry, athletic competitions—she seems to have sole charge. Why are no male gods involved? The answer may be that there is little point for a mortal man to pray to the war god Ares for success in battle, or even to Zeus himself, since they are not, for the most part, directly concerned with men's daily affairs, however much they might govern the general course of war or history. In the *Iliad* Zeus does not intervene on the battlefield, even to save the life of his son Sarpedon, although he wants to. Aphrodite, however, rushes down to rescue her son Aeneas, and in the process even gets wounded.

There is a difference also in the nature of the powers wielded by goddesses and male gods. Hecate can help man or not help him, as she wishes, but she does not actively harm him; she "sits beside" kings while they administer justice, but she does not help them enforce that justice. Zeus, although he is the ultimate source of men's success or failure in many of the same areas of life, is both less susceptible to entreaty and less whimsical in his dispensations. He not only has more power, but he uses it actively to enforce his justice. We can compare to Hesiod's characterization of Hecate his description of Zeus, at the beginning of his other long epic poem, known to us as the *Works and Days*:

> Because of Zeus men are mentioned or not mentioned, spoken of and not spoken of, on account of great Zeus. For easily he makes a man flourish, and easily he strikes a flourishing man down; easily he diminishes the distinguished man and enlarges the inconspicuous man. Easily he makes the crooked straight and withers the proud man, Zeus the high thunderer who lives in halls on high. (2–8)

Both Hecate and Zeus, because they are gods, do what is impossible or difficult for mortals "easily"; but that is the nature of divinity, as Achilles says in the last book of the *Iliad*: "that is what the gods have spun as the fate of miserable mortals, to live in sorrow, while they themselves are without cares" (Homer, *Iliad* 24. 525–26). Hecate at least seems to *listen* when a prayer is addressed to her by a mortal, whether or not she wishes to grant it.

Although we may never know exactly why Hesiod chose to describe in detail the powers of this particular goddess among all the gods and goddesses of the generation before Zeus, the passage does show us how and why men as well as women would want to worship a goddess, even though the divine cosmos, like the human world, is ruled by males. She is somehow closer to humankind, and while she does not have final authority (which is reserved of course for Zeus), she has the potential to help. Like the Virgin Mary in some modern Christian cults, she has motherly qualities but without sexuality, and she can be appealed to for help in a wide variety of human activities.[5]

The gods in Hesiod respect those goddesses who, like Hecate and Athena, have elected not to marry and those who, having had children, thereafter remain celibate, like Styx, who comes with her children to live with Zeus, and like Leto, Demeter, and Earth herself (after Heaven has been castrated). Goddesses are dangerous or destructive to gods when they are sexually active, as when Earth sets Cronus in ambush against Heaven, when he embraces her "longing for love," or the goddess Intelligence (Metis) while she is bearing children to Zeus, or Hera in the *Iliad*, because she is still able to seduce Zeus in order to deceive him, so that he forgets his resolve to help the Trojans (14. 159–65). Aphrodite, the goddess who (in *Theogony* 190–98) was born from the severed genitals of Heaven, is always suspect, because she is so beautiful and "genial" (*philommeides*—the poet is making a pun on *mēdea*, "genitals"):

> Passion followed her and fair Desire when she was born and first went to the company of the gods. Such is the honor she has from the beginning and the lot she has obtained among men and immortal gods, the chatter of girls and smiles and deception and delicious pleasure and sweet love. (201–6)

Sexuality is regarded as dangerous not because it is physically unclean or polluting (as in Leviticus) but because of its ability to deceive; it affects the mind and warps judgment. Heaven, longing for love, did not suspect the ambush laid for him by Earth and Cronus; in the *Iliad*, Zeus is on one occasion so attracted to Hera that for a short time he allows himself to forget the Trojan War.

Because sexuality is so closely linked to deception, Zeus sees that he can use it as a punishment. Zeus had hidden fire from men, but the god Prometheus stole fire and gave it back to men. So Zeus devised another disadvantage for men, "the likeness of a modest maiden," whom the gods bring to life and dress up and adorn with a golden crown, "a beautiful evil in return for a good":[6]

> Both immortal gods and mortal men were seized with wonder when they saw this precipitous trap, which men could not escape. For from her is descended the race of women, a great pain to mortals, who dwell with men, and do not bear with them in cruel Poverty, but only in Plenty. (588–93)

Hesiod compares the women to drones in a beehive, who live off the work of other bees and do nothing themselves; they are "conspirators in causing hardship." Once man has been deceived by sexual attraction, so that he eagerly accepts the gift of woman, he must work even harder than he has in the past, in order to feed not only himself but his family.

Hesiod's portrait of this creature is so full of negative detail that as humans we can easily fail to see that being female can have a positive side, even in the male-dominated world of the *Theogony*. Certainly Earth, Aphrodite, Rhea, and Hecate never have primary responsibility for the conquest of enemies, nor do they arrange the distribution of honors that the gods and goddesses receive. The gods who offer resistance to change and who are capable of overcoming adversaries by force are all male: Heaven, Cronus, Zeus, Prometheus, Typhoeus. But in the course of his narrative, Hesiod does not let us forget that without the intervention of the female deities, nothing at all might have happened, or events might have come out differently. In fact, there might have been no world as we know it if Earth had not intervened to stop Heaven from hiding his children away, if Rhea had not asked her parents to help her find a way to stop Cronus from eating his children, and if Styx did not enforce her oath among the gods. The goddesses can encourage, discourage, and direct the actions of the gods, even though they may not always take physical part in them. Their sexual attraction allows them to get their way without force, by deception so potent that Zeus can use it as an instrument of punishment, adding new hardship to human life. Once we remember not only *what* happened, but *why* it happened, we can begin to understand the power of the goddesses, even under patriarchy.

3

The Heroic Women
of Greek Epic

Since the poetry of Homer formed the basis of Greek education, the *Iliad* and *Odyssey* continued to be read and recited long after many people had ceased to worship the gods described in them. All educated persons in antiquity (which would have included some women), from the sixth century BC to the fourth century AD, knew by heart the details of the *Iliad* and *Odyssey*, and many other men and women seem to have been familiar with the names of the principal characters and the outline of the story of the fall of Troy and the return of Odysseus. In the seventh and sixth centuries BC, poets who wrote about Helen, Andromache, and Hector, used Homeric language to remind their audiences of epic situations and values. The human characters in the Homeric epics and their stories became the subject of later epics and of the fifth-century Athenian dramas that were performed in repertory for many centuries. So any discussion of the status of women in the world of ancient Greece must begin with Homer, even though we do not know when he lived or exactly how his poems were recorded or anything about the background or life of the poet (or poets!).

It is a popular assumption that the Greeks, especially the Athenians in the fifth and fourth centuries BC, were misogynistic. It is true that in Athens women not only could not vote but could not own property and that their movements were restricted. In the Homeric epics women seem to have little independence; they are always under the guardianship of a man, whether a husband, a father, or even a son. Wives must live in their husbands' cities; women like Chryseis and Briseis, who have been captured in raids, become slaves and are completely subject to their masters. Thus, while the legal rights even of free women appear to have been severely limited, because women can speak, and because the poet allows them frequently to comment on the action of his epics, Homer's women still manage to exert a significant moral force.

Scholars who study the role of women in antiquity have not always attributed much importance to what Homeric women say, because the methodologies on which scholars tend to rely concentrate primarily on plot lines and on questions of economic and legal status. But epics, for all the information about social history that they may contain, are not legal codes; and, while it is possible to learn from the poems some of the practical details of the lives and status of the world described by the poet, it is important to remember that the epics were written primarily to entertain and instruct. Also, since epics are made up of words, a commodity to which even Greek women had legal right, one must in any discussion of women's role pay particular attention to what women say, even if it has no direct effect on the action and does not change the outcome of the events the women witness.

One might begin by asking what both epics, the *Iliad* and the *Odyssey*, would be like if there were no women in them. In the first place, neither story would have happened. The Trojan War would not have been fought, and Odysseus (assuming he had gone to Troy in the first place) would not have bothered to return home. Helen, the woman for whom Troy was destroyed, does not appear until Book 3 of the *Iliad*, but the epic opens with a description of the plague that was caused as the result of the capture, in a raid, of another woman, Chryseis, the daughter of the priest Chryses. After capture, Chryseis is assigned to Agamemnon; her father offers Agamemnon a ransom, and the other Greeks urge Agamemnon to respect Chryses because he is the priest of Apollo. Agamemnon refuses to give Chryseis back to her father, saying, "Before that old age will come upon her in my house, in Argos, far from her fatherland, working at the loom and attending my bed" and, later, "I prefer her to my own wife Clytemnestra, since she is in no way inferior to her, neither in body or stature, or in intelligence or in any way in her work" (1. 29–31, 113–15).

But Chryseis' father, Apollo's priest, prays to the god, reminding Apollo of his services to him, and the god sends a plague on the Greeks. So Agamemnon is forced to return Chryseis and, as a result, demands that the Greeks give him another prize. When Achilles opposes him, Agamemnon demands Achilles' prize, the woman Briseis. Because Agamemnon is the commander of the army, Achilles must follow his orders, and heralds are sent to take her from Achilles' tent. During the course of the arguments about these women, no one asks *their* opinion, but the poet makes it clear that Chryseis' father wants to get his daughter back. Even Agamemnon values her for something more than her looks (he mentions intelligence and work as well). Briseis is reluctant to leave Achilles. Achilles himself weeps, because he is deeply attached to her. As Achilles says later, "The sons of Atreus are not the only men who love their wives; every good and sensible man loves and cares about his own wife; and I loved [Briseis] from my heart, even though she was a war captive" (9. 341–43). So Achilles refuses to join in the fighting, and as a result the Greek side suffers severe setbacks in the war. A quarrel over a woman, which involves men's honor and status but also human ties of affection, causes not only the war but the anger (*mēnis*) that leads to the death of Achilles' companion Patroclus and of the principal heroes of the epic, Hector and Achilles himself.

When Helen appears in person, in Book 3, she is in the main room (*megaron*) of her house, weaving at her great loom, "a double cloth, purple, and she sprinkled in many trials of the horse-taming Trojans and the bronze-clad Achaeans, which they suffered on her account at the hands of Ares" (3. 125–28). The goddess Iris, the messenger of the gods, appears to her, disguised as her sister-in-law, to tell her that her two husbands, Menelaus and Paris, are about to fight each other over her, while the rest of the army looks on, and that she shall be called the wife of the winner. Helen's feelings at this point are not ambivalent; Iris puts in Helen's heart a longing for her first husband, Menelaus, and her city and parents; Helen dresses in white (as if for a ritual), "sheds a tender tear," and leaves the house accompanied by two maidservants (3. 142–45) (a woman does not go outside of her house alone in Homer, or generally in the ancient Greek world).

As Helen goes to join her father-in-law Priam on the wall, the Trojan elders say to one another:

> No one could think it wrong for the Trojans and the well-greaved Achaeans to suffer hardship for so long a time on behalf of such a woman; for in appearance she is dreadfully like the immortal goddesses. But still, even though she is so beautiful, let her go off in the ships, so that she does not bring sorrow to us and our children afterwards. (3. 156–60)

The whole dilemma of the Trojan War is expressed in this short speech. The elders comment on her beauty, because they have been looking at her, rather than talking to her; and, of course, it was because of this beauty that Aphrodite selected her for Paris. But Helen in the *Iliad* is more than just a pretty face. It is significant that Homer makes Helen constantly remind us by her words and by her actions that Paris has offended Zeus, the god of hospitality, and that the Trojans, by defending Paris, are ultimately in the wrong. Priam blames the gods rather than Helen for the war; but Helen also blames herself. As she says, if a god or some other force compels a human to do what is wrong, that person always has the option of suicide: "Would that cruel death had been acceptable to me when I followed your son here, leaving my bedchamber and my friends and my growing child, and companions of my own age. But that did not happen, and so I am wasted away by weeping" (3. 173–76).

Most mortals in Greek literature, when presented with a moral dilemma imposed on them by the gods, either take no action or are persuaded by their friends to take the wrong action. Phaedra in Euripides' *Hippolytus* tries to overcome her passion for her stepson Hippolytus and meanwhile wastes away with guilt and longing. Her old nurse, who came with her from her father's home in Crete, persuades Phaedra to confide in her and then declares that she has a remedy for her passion. It is only after Phaedra hears what the remedy is—the nurse has told Hippolytus that Phaedra wants to go to bed with him—and learned that Hippolytus is outraged by the suggestion that she decides to kill herself. Generally only the very young are ready to sacrifice themselves in response to oracles demanding self-sacrifice, like Iphigenia in Euripides' *Iphigenia at Aulis*.[1] Among adults, who have more opportunity to understand the value of human life, Alcestis is one of the very few who willingly decides to die when confronted with a choice between inaction and self-sacrifice. In most cases, as Phaedra says,

> it is not because of deficiencies in our intelligence that we take the worst course. Many people know what is right (*eu phronein*). But one must consider this: we understand what is good and we recognize it, but we do not struggle through with it to the end (*ekponoumen*), some on account of idleness (*argia*), others because they prefer some other pleasure to what is right. (377–81)

Helen is no exception to this rule. When Aphrodite comes to tell her that Paris has come back unharmed from the combat with Menelaus, even though the goddess is disguised as one of Helen's own slaves, Helen recognizes her and claims that it would be wrong for her to do what the goddess wants her to do—that is, return home and go to bed with Paris. Helen addresses Aphrodite:

> Strange divinity, why do you want to trick me like this? Is it that you will take me somewhere further away to some well-built city, either in Phrygia or in

lovely Maeonia, if you have there some other mortal man who is dear to you? Is it because now Menelaus has beaten bright Alexandros [Paris] in battle and wishes to take my hateful self home again, is it for that that you now stand near me trying to deceive me? Go now and sit beside him yourself, and abandon the path of the gods, and do not return on your feet to Olympus, but always suffer with him and look after him, until he can make you his wife or even his concubine. But I am not going there [to his bedroom]—even though it may anger you—to go to bed with him. Later all the Trojan women will blame me; I have sorrows innumerable in my heart. (3. 399–412)

Aphrodite replies by threatening Helen with an ignominious death:

Do not speak to me, wretched woman, lest I become angry at you and forsake you, and hate you as much as I now terribly love you, and devise cruel hatred against you in the midst of both forces, the Trojans and Danaans, and you may die an evil death. So she spoke, and Helen, daughter of Zeus was afraid. (3. 414–18)

Like most mortals, when confronted with the reality of death, Helen prefers to live, even though she is aware that what she is doing is wrong. She tells Paris that she wishes that he had been killed by Menelaus and urges him to return to the battle. As Phaedra says, most people know what is right, but cannot bring themselves to do it. In Helen's case, she hesitates because she is afraid of what Aphrodite may do to her; in Paris' case, it is because (to use Phaedra's words again) he "prefers some other pleasure to what is right" and persuades Helen to go to bed with him. As Helen says to Hector when he comes to get Paris to return to the fighting, "I ought to have been the wife of a better man, who understood the indignation and people's constant reproaches; but his wits are not steady nor will they ever be, and I think that he will pay the consequences" (6. 350–53).

Hector's wife, Andromache, is faced with a different moral dilemma. Her husband alone has been able to keep the Greeks from taking Troy, but, as she tells him, "Your courage will destroy you; you do not take pity on your little child and me in my distress, since I shall soon be your widow, for soon the Achaeans will kill you, all of them attacking together. But it would be better for me, once I have lost you, to go down under the earth" (6. 407–11). Andromache reminds him that, since Achilles has killed her father and brothers and her mother now is dead too, "You are my father and mother and brother, and you are my young husband" (6. 429–30). She advises him to stay with her on the tower and to station the army near the wild fig tree, where the city is most approachable and the wall can be overrun and where a group of Greek warriors has already tried to attack. Hector replies that he, too, is concerned about all this, but that he would be ashamed before the women and men of Troy if he avoided the fighting and that he has learned always to be brave and fight in the front lines. He admits that he knows that Troy will fall and that then his worst sorrow will not be for his mother or father or brothers—so many of whom have already fallen—but for her and the life she will lead as a slave.

> And you might be in Argos weaving at another woman's loom, or carrying water from the spring Messeis or Hypereia, much against your will, but strong necessity will compel you. And perhaps someone will say when he sees you weeping, "That is the wife of Hector, who was the best fighter among the horse-taming Trojans, when they were fighting around the walls of Troy." So someone will say, and new grief will come to you because you have lost the husband who could keep you from slavery. But may the earth cover me in death before I know anything of your cries when you are carried off. (6. 456–65)

In the end Hector deals with this dismal future by ignoring it; he prays that his son may be an even better fighter than he: "Let him kill his enemy and bring home the bloody spoils, and delight his mother's heart" (6. 480–81). As for himself, no man will die before his time, he tells Andromache, and says, "You go home and see to your work, the loom and the shuttle, and order your slaves to go to their work. The war will be the concern of the men—all the men of Troy, but particularly to me" (6. 490–93). Andromache does as he says, but the slave women start singing the lamentation for the dead for him, even though he is alive. The poet thus makes it clear that ignoring the problem does not make it go away; the women know better. They mourn his death and the sorrow and deprivation his death will bring to them.

Since ancient times, readers of the *Iliad* have realized that this passage is meant to set into vivid relief the conflicting demands of war. It is clear that here, as elsewhere in the *Iliad*, honor is more important than simple survival. Otherwise Hector, as he says, could take Andromache's advice to practice defensive tactics only. Homer also seems to be saying that, while nature (at least in the ancient world) dictates that the principal duty of women is to look after the household, women can and do express their views about what their men are doing, just as the men show concern for the fate of the women. As an ancient commentator noted, Andromache's advice makes perfect sense, if the goal is to preserve Hector's life: "This is an invention to keep her husband from the field; and that is why Hector does not answer it."[2] Instead, he simply explains why he cannot do what she requests. He does not object to her expressing herself or to her reasoning; it is only that his code of honor will not allow him to follow her advice, even though he knows that the consequences of his action will lead not only to his death but to a life of slavery for her. By his request that she return home to her loom, Hector indicates that he has been moved by what she has said to him. As another ancient commentator observed, "The poet most effectively makes Hector order her to stay at home, so that she will not appear on the wall and persuade him not to fight against Achilles."[3] Hector hopes that at home she can occupy herself with her work and not watch the battle, which is what she had been doing when he found her after he had first gone to look for her in their house.

By making Andromache remind Hector of the dangers involved in following his code of honor and having her point out a reasonable alternative course, Homer again shows that women not only understand what is happening in the male world of war but are, as the continuing victims of war, perhaps better able to judge its consequences. Confusion about the nature of women's role in the *Iliad* has led to some curious misinterpretations of this passage. In the third century BC, the Homeric scholar Aristarchus suggested that Homer did not write the lines where Andromache advises Hector to stay on the tower and station his men near the fig tree to guard the wall. Aristarchus reasoned that "the words are unsuited to Andromache; she is being general instead of Hector, and the advice is wrong."[4] Other ancient scholars understood Hector's request that Andromache return home to her loom and her shuttle to be a reminder that a woman's place is in the home: "He describes in brief the life and household of a proper lady."[5] This commentator makes a sharp distinction between the worlds of men and of women, or between the household and the home, *oikos* and *polis*. But, as yet another commentator saw, the characters in the *Iliad* do not always make such clear distinctions between the men's and women's roles. Speaking of Andromache's strategic advice, this commentator noted, "Even if the advice is not appropriate for a woman, it is appropriate for Andromache, since care of horses is not a woman's work, but Andromache (in 8. 186–90) gives Hector's horses grain and pours out wine for them, since because she loves her husband she is concerned even about the horses which transport him."[6] It has been suggested that Andromache's strategic advice may indicate that, at least in some cities in the area around Troy, women took some share in government.[7] But it is not necessary to infer that Andromache is doing anything that would be considered exceptional even in mainland Greece. Women in Greek drama frequently emerge from their households to take action in the world of politics.[8] Antigone in Sophocles' drama is perhaps the most familiar example: She finds a decision made on behalf of her city unjustified, and she not only expresses her dissent to her uncle the king but actively opposes that decision.

The focus of the next fifteen books of the *Iliad* is on the battle and on the question of Achilles' involvement in it. Even though Homer's concentration is on the war, he still reminds us of the losses that are borne by the women involved with the men. In the story of Meleager, which Phoenix tells to Achilles in order to urge him to rejoin the Greek forces, Meleager is finally persuaded to come to the aid of his city by his wife:

> She begged him, weeping, and told him all the sorrows which come to people when their city is taken; they kill the men, and they destroy the city with fire; other men lead from the house the children and the deep-girdled women; and the heart within him was roused when he heard of these evil deeds. (9. 591–95)

When Achilles finally decides to return to the fighting, because his friend Patroclus has been killed, his mother, the goddess Thetis, reminds him that if he returns he will die soon after he has killed Hector. But Achilles, like Hector, must think first of his honor and of the friend he has betrayed by not being there to protect him:

> Now let me win glory, and let me cause some Trojan or Dardanian woman to wipe away the tears from her soft cheeks with both hands in lamentation; let her know how long I have paused from the fighting. But do not try to keep me from the battle, even though you love me. You will not persuade me. (18. 121–26)

But, as Achilles knows, his mother will suffer as well. As Thetis says to Hephaestus when she goes to get Achilles' new armor:

> [Peleus] gave me a son to bear and to raise, the greatest of heroes, and he grew up like a sapling, and I raised him, like a vine-shoot in the best part of the vineyard, and sent him forth to Ilion in the beaked ships to fight the Trojans. But I will not welcome him again, when he returns home, to the house of Peleus. And now even while he lives and sees the light of the sun, he grieves, and I cannot come to his rescue. (18. 436–43)

The effect of war on women is even more poignantly expressed by Briseis, whom the poet lets speak for the first time when she sees Patroclus' dead body:

For me sorrow follows upon sorrow, always. I saw my husband, to whom my mother and father gave me, cut down by the sharp bronze in front of my city, and my three dear brothers, whom one mother bore along with me, all of whom went to their death on one day. But you [Patroclus] would not allow me to weep, when swift Achilles killed my husband and sacked the city of godlike Mynes, but you said that you would make me the bride of godlike Achilles, and take me in the ships to Phthia, and to give me a wedding feast among the Myrmidons. So because you are dead I weep unceasingly; you were always kind to me. (19. 290–300)

The poet adds: "So she spoke weeping, and the women joined in lamentation, openly for Patroclus, but each for her own sorrows," lest it seem that Briseis had accepted her new lot too easily (19. 302).

These passages, even though they are widely separated from one another and provide only brief interludes in the main course of the narrative, prepare us for the anguish expressed by Hector's parents when in Book 22 they see him waiting to engage Achilles in single combat. Hector's father Priam speaks of the loss of all of his other sons, of the even greater loss to Troy if Hector is killed, and of his own death at the hands of the Achaeans. Hector's mother, Hecuba, weeps and bares her breast to remind him of the *aidos*, or respect, that Hector owes to the mother who bore him (22. 79–80). We may compare how in Aeschylus' *Libation Bearers* Orestes is determined to kill his mother, Clytemnestra, until she makes the same gesture, at which he hesitates and asks his friend Pylades, "Shall I respect (*aidesthō*) my mother, and not kill her?" (899).

Hecuba reminds Hector that she nursed him herself and urges him to come within the walls, but unlike Meleager's wife she does not describe what will happen to her if her city falls. She concludes her speech by reflecting that when he dies neither she nor his wife will be able to weep for him on his bier, since "a long way from us beside the Argive ships the swift dogs will devour you" (22. 88–89). Her words anticipate what will happen—the death of Hector, and the defilement of his body by the angry Achilles. When she sees how Achilles is mistreating Hector's body, she tears out her hair and throws her veil aside and weeps loudly. The importance Hecuba attaches to proper burial is characteristic, however strange it may seem to us. In both archaic and classical times, carefully orchestrated ceremonies accompanied death, and in the laying out of the corpse (*prothesis*), the first phase of the ritual, women, and particularly the close female relations of the deceased, played the most prominent role, both in preparing the body for burial and in mourning.

As Priam weeps for his son and plans to try to ransom the body, Hecuba leads the formal lamentation, which Andromache hears from her house. Andromache is where we last saw her, as if no time had passed since Book 6, weaving at her loom in the interior of her high home. Like Helen in Book 3, Andromache is weaving a purple double cloth, but unlike Helen, who weaves the story of the contests endured by the Greeks and the Trojans in the course of the war, Andromache, as if now oblivious of the action that in Book 6 she had followed so closely, simply weaves in patterns of flowers. When she hears her mother-in-law's cry, she fears that Hector has been cut off alone by Achilles. She rushes to the wall like a maenad, and when she sees what has happened, darkness falls on her eyes, and she throws off the headdress that Aphrodite gave her on her wedding day. Finally she recovers enough to speak, but this time her speech concerns not herself but their son Astyanax. She fears (irrationally, since Hector has a large family) that because he will have no father to watch out for him, he will, as an orphan, be socially ostracized by other men.[9] Also she laments that the burial clothes she has made for Hector will never be used, since his body will be eaten by dogs and worms, far away from his parents. Significantly, it is with this speech about the loss of a father and husband, and not with Achilles' triumph and revenge, that this book describing the death of Hector comes to an end.

The final book of the *Iliad* has a similar narrative pattern. There is an encounter between two men, this time Priam and Achilles, and the book ends in Troy with the funeral of Hector and lamentations of the women in Hector's family. This time Andromache rather than Hecuba begins the lamentation. She fears for her son's future now that the great defender of all the women and children in Troy is dead:

> The women will be carried off in the hollow ships, and I along with them. And you, my child, either you might follow me, and there do work that will be disgraceful, toiling for a harsh master, or one of the Achaeans will take you by the hand and throw you from the tower, a cruel death, in anger because Hector has killed his brother or father or even his son, since many Achaeans bit the earth with their teeth at the hands of Hector. (24.731–38)

Andromache concludes her lament by wishing that she could have been with him when he died: "To me most of all you will have left cruel grief, for you did not reach out your hands to me when you died, nor did you speak to me words that I might always have remembered, for nights and days, as I wept" (24. 742–45). Her wish that she might have been with Hector when he was dying suggests how important it was for Greek families, through the rituals associated with death, to demonstrate a love for one another that would, at least through memory, survive even after burial. Performing the last rites for one's close relatives, as Sophocles demonstrates in *Antigone*, ensures that the survivors will be welcomed by their family when they, too, join the dead in Hades. In the play, Antigone pleads:

> I hope to come dear to you, my father, and most dear to you, mother, and dear to you, my brother, since with my own hand when you had died I washed you and arranged your clothing and poured libations on your tombs. (897–902)

It is significant that Andromache, a woman, does not wish to avoid witnessing the death of her husband, whereas Hector, who has seen so many deaths on the battlefield, does not even want to contemplate the thought of his wife's enslavement or the death of his son.

Hecuba's lamentation, by contrast, comments on the futility of revenge. Although Achilles took pity on some of Hecuba's sons and sent them away in exile, he killed Hector, because Hector had killed Patroclus; "but even so he did not bring [Patroclus] back to life" (24. 756). Hecuba is satisfied by the way Hector's body has been restored by the gods, so that he appears to have died a painless death: "You lie there like someone Apollo of the silver bow had approached and killed with his gentle arrows" (24. 758–59). This peaceful image provides a poignant reminder of what might have been had there been no Trojan War.

But we are quickly brought back to reality by Helen, the last woman to lead the lamentation. She recalls how Paris brought her to Troy, and again she exclaims, "Would that I had died before I came here!" (24. 764). During the twenty years that she has been in Troy, Hector was always kind to her, and he saw that her in-laws treated her well. "There was no one else in wide Troy so kind or friendly to me; all the rest were afraid of me" (24. 755).

The epic ends with the lighting of Hector's pyre and the burial of his remains: "Thus they carried out the burial of Hector, tamer of horses" (24. 804). But it is the women who speak the last important speeches in the epic, and it is their loss and prospect of further suffering that Homer's audience is left to contemplate, the last and certainly the most painful result of the wrath of Achilles.

If Homer had intended the *Iliad* simply to glorify war, he would have ended his epic with the fall of Troy and the triumph of the Achaeans. That he does not do so suggests that he meant his epic to describe *all* of the effects of Achilles' wrath, both victory and defeat; and it is in expressing the effects of defeat that the women play a crucial role. If there had been no women in the epic, or if the power of speech had been denied them, the progress of the war would still have occupied our attention. But Greek religion, in a fundamental sense, precludes contemplation of victory without defeat. Human life, as Achilles says, can never be all good: Zeus gives men a mixture from one of his two jars—good and evil or all evil (24. 527–33). Every victor must be prepared for eventual defeat. It is perhaps for this reason that Aeschylus' *Persians*, which describes the Greek victory at Salamis, is set not in the victorious city of Athens but in the palace of the defeated king, Xerxes, and is seen through the eyes of the king's mother.

The women who observe and comment on the consequences of war are not ordinary women; they are members of ruling families. Even Briseis, before she was captured by Achilles, was married to the king of Lyrnessus, a city in the Troad (2. 689–93). Much has been written about the nature of men's heroism, which is of course what the *Iliad* is primarily about; but we might also try to define some of the qualities of the women in their families. I have called them "heroic" in the title of this chapter, but in fact the Greek term *heros* applies only to men, and the female equivalent, *heroinē* is used for semidivine creatures, like springs and nymphs. Women by their very nature cannot be heroes, because heroes get their title by killing, destroying, or accomplishing something extraordinary, like founding a city.

Although not ordinary, the women of the *Iliad* follow recognizable standards of female behavior. They work the loom and design the patterns of the cloth they weave, and they lead the lamentations for the dead and consider themselves responsible for the details of the laying out of the dead body. They are excitable and emotional; they express fear and sorrow and grief without restraint. But, because they also understand the full consequences of what is going on around them, they can remind the men and the audience of where all of the fighting ultimately will lead them, and, thus, they provide a balance and a moral tone that would otherwise be missing.

In the end, the surviving men accept the women's view of the nature of war. Achilles plays the lyre that he captured when he sacked Eetion, the city of Andromache's father, and sings of the famous deeds of men (9. 186–89). But in Book 24, like Thetis when she speaks to Hephaestus about the armor or Andromache in her lamentation for Hector, Achilles concentrates on the suffering the war has caused his family and Priam:

> [My father Peleus] had only one son, doomed to an untimely death. I will not be able to look after [my father] as he grows old, since I sit in Troy, far away indeed from my fatherland, causing sorrow to you and to your children. And you, old man, we hear that you were once happy . . . that you were distinguished by your wealth and your sons; but the Uranian gods have brought this grief to you, and always about your city there are battles and slaughter. (24. 540–48)

Helen's story, compared to that of Andromache or Hecuba, has a relatively happy ending, but she is no exception to Achilles' rule that the best one can get in life from Zeus' two jars is a mixture of good and evil. When next we see Helen (in terms of the chronology of the myth), in Book 4 of the *Odyssey*, she is back with Menelaus in Sparta. Troy has fallen, and Agamemnon has been murdered on his return home, by Helen's sister Clytemnestra. Like Helen, Clytemnestra was seduced by another man, her husband's cousin Aegisthus, and she went to live with Aegisthus in his house. But Clytemnestra went off *willingly* and seems not to have regretted her action. As we have seen, once Helen is in Troy, she wishes that she had killed herself before Aphrodite had caused her to elope with Paris and leave her home and child and brought such sorrow to the Trojans. Her attitude in the *Odyssey* remains the same:

> The other Trojan women wept [when Odysseus secretly entered Troy and killed many Trojans], but I rejoiced, for already my heart had turned to go back home, and I lamented my delusion (*atē*), which Aphrodite gave me, when she led me there away from my dear homeland, and made me take myself from my child and my bridal chamber and my husband, who lacked nothing, neither in intelligence or appearance. (4. 259–64)

In the *Odyssey*, Helen's daughter Hermione and Menelaus' son by a slave girl, Megapenthes, are being married on the same day. In thus accepting and honoring Menelaus' son by a concubine, Helen shows herself to be a model wife. Once again a comparison with Clytemnestra is instructive. When Agamemnon returned home, Clytemnestra was present at the banquet where

Agamemnon and his men were slaughtered by Aegisthus. As the ghost of Agamemnon recalls it, she killed with her own hand the concubine whom
Agamemnon had brought home with him from Troy, Cassandra, said in the
Iliad to be the most beautiful of Priam's daughters (13. 365–66), as she sat next
to the dying Agamemnon (*Odyssey* 11. 421–23). Clytemnestra's resentment of
the beautiful young Cassandra would have seemed natural. Heracles' wife,
Deianeira, in Sophocles' *Women of Trachis*, feels similarly threatened by Iole,
whom Heracles sacked a city to obtain. But, as Euripides has Andromache say,
a wife is better advised to accept such behavior on her husband's part. As
the concubine of Achilles' son, Neoptolemus, she tells Neoptolemus' wife,
Hermione, that she went along with her husband in his love affairs (*synērōn*)
and nursed his bastard children, so that she might do nothing to displease
him (*Andromache* 222–25 = WLGR³ 30).[10]

In the *Odyssey* Book 4, Helen is said to resemble Artemis, which suggests
that she is still beautiful and, like the goddess, pure but nevertheless dangerous
(122). Whereas in the *Iliad* she was working at her loom with her female
slaves, in the *Odyssey* she is seen doing the sort of work one can do while entertaining company. Accompanied by her servants, Helen goes to join Menelaus
and his guests and begins to work in wool with a golden spindle and a beautiful silver basket. With the same acute intelligence that she showed in the *Iliad*
when she recognized Aphrodite even though the goddess was disguised as one
of her old servants, Helen identifies Telemachus immediately as Odysseus'
son. The whole company, including Helen, weeps at the thought of the Trojan
War and the losses it has brought to each of them, but Helen then uses her extraordinary intelligence to give Menelaus and his guests an elixir, to keep them
from weeping. This drug, which she had obtained in Egypt, is designed specifically to bring to an end grief and anger (*nepenthes t' acholon te*, the dominant
emotions of the *Iliad*), and causes one to forget one's sorrows: "Not for that
day would one shed a tear down one's cheeks, not if one's mother or father
died, nor if they slaughtered before one's eyes a brother or dear son" (4. 223–
26). Only after she has put the drug into the wine does she talk again about the
Trojan War and Telemachus' father, Odysseus, who is now missing.

This portrait of Helen in the fourth book of the *Odyssey* helps explain why,
after Troy was captured, Menelaus did not repudiate or punish the woman
for whom so many men had lost their lives—"hateful Helen," as Achilles calls
her—once he understands the full consequences of his wrath (*Iliad* 19. 325).
Because Athenian law required that a man divorce a wife who had committed

adultery willingly, Euripides, when writing for Athenian audiences in his *Helen*, told a version of the myth in which the real Helen was held in Egypt while the war was fought over a phantom, and in his *Trojan Women* he made Helen able by skillful rhetorical arguments to persuade Menelaus not to kill her. In Homer the idea of mandatory divorce never seems to come up. Aphrodite was primarily responsible for her actions, but in the *Iliad* Helen takes a share of the blame by saying that she did not kill herself when she had the choice (3. 173–75). Since in the *Odyssey* she is such an exemplary wife— beautiful, intelligent, sympathetic, and understanding—Homer allows us to see why Menelaus is content to have her once again as his wife and to sleep with her in the same bed. But perhaps the ultimate reason why she must remain alive is to tell others what she has learned and how much she has suffered. Men, like Achilles, sing of the famous deeds of men, but Helen, sitting at her loom in Troy, wove the story of trials the Trojans and Achaeans experienced on her behalf (*Il.* 3. 125–28). The principal female characters in Homeric epics understand and suffer; they survive to pass on their knowledge, even as slaves, to their new households. As Jasper Griffin observes, "Helen is a legendary figure not for her great achievements, not even for her womanly virtue, like Penelope, but for her guilt and suffering."[11]

If the Trojan War (the subject of the *Iliad*) was fought for Helen, the return of Odysseus (the subject of the *Odyssey*) was accomplished for Penelope. The goddess Calypso offers Odysseus immortality, and he admits that "wise Penelope is inferior to you to look upon, both in beauty and height," but he is willing to endure more suffering to return to her (5. 215–20). The suitors clearly are not interested in her solely for her wealth, though she would bring a dowry when she left Odysseus' house, nor for her youth, since she already has a son who is reaching manhood. The suitor Antinous says they admire her for her intelligence:

> She understands how to do beautiful work and has a fine intelligence, and wiles (*kerdea*), unlike any of the fair women of the past, Tyro [loved by Poseidon] or Alcmene [the mother of Heracles by Zeus] or Mycene [daughter of the river Inachus], none of these had an intelligence like Penelope's. (2. 117–22)

In the end, Penelope is admired and remembered for her faithfulness as well. As Agamemnon says after the souls of the suitors arrive in Hades:

> What sound intelligence (*agathai phrenes*) blameless Penelope had, the daughter of Icarius! How well she waited for Odysseus, her husband! So the fame of her

excellence (*aretē*) will never perish, and the immortals will make a delightful song to steadfast Penelope for mortal men. (24. 194–98)

The negative foil for her behavior is not Helen, who, as we have seen, behaved as well as humanly possible under the circumstances, but Clytemnestra:

> She did not plan evil deeds like the daughter of Tyndareus [Clytemnestra], and kill her husband. About her hateful song will come down to men, and she will give a bad name to all women, even if a woman does good deeds. (24. 199–202)

Clytemnestra, before she was seduced by Aegisthus, "had possession of a good intelligence" (3. 266). But, unlike Penelope, she did not use it to wait for her husband's return. What enables Penelope to wait is not simply her intelligence but a quality she shares with her husband, the ability to endure hardship. She has not, like Andromache, lost her husband in war, but, on the other hand, she does not know whether he is dead or alive:

> It soon will be time for sweet repose, for whoever can find sweet sleep, even though he is grieving. But to me the god has also given boundless grief, and I enjoy my days as I grieve and weep, as I look at my work and my servants' work in my house. But whenever night comes, and sleep overcomes everyone, I lie in my bed, and bitter cares throng around my heart. (19. 510–17)

She compares herself to the nightingale, who always mourns for the son she killed, and even when Odysseus returns and kills the suitors, she will have no long respite. She dreams that an eagle comes and slaughters the geese she has been fattening, which she has enjoyed looking upon. As it turns out, Odysseus' revenge will start another battle and lead to another journey. If Helen gains the respect of Greeks and Trojans alike for her awareness of her guilt and for her suffering, Penelope's fame also depends on her awareness of the pain her resistance will cause and on her sorrow.

Since ancient historians, with very few exceptions, do not record what ancient women thought of their lives, we cannot know for certain what ancient women learned from the portrayal of women in the *Iliad* and the *Odyssey*. The epics, of course, depict a heroic world that existed in an indefinite past time. But the conditions of life for Greek women did not change very much until the Hellenistic Age. It was still possible in the fifth century that if a city was captured, either by Greeks or by foreigners, the men would be put to death and the women and children sold into slavery. This is what the Athenians threatened to do to the city of Mytilene, and in fact did to the inhabitants of the island of Melos. Helen, Hecuba, and Andromache appear as characters in several surviving Greek dramas, each of which provides new reflections and comments on their experiences. At least we can say that women in Greek tragedy follow the pattern set by the women of Homer—understanding what is going on around them and trying to instruct others about what they see. It is also fair to say that in all these dramas the women, even Medea and, as we have seen, Phaedra, are capable of considering and expressing their thoughts on serious ethical questions, whether or not they decide in the end to do what is right.

If Athenian men regarded Athenian women simply as chattels or distrusted them completely because of their gender, they would not have continued to attribute to them such an important role in drama. We might contrast the articulate words of the women in Homer and in Athenian drama with the relative silence attributed to the female relatives and friends of Jesus at the time of his death. In the winter of 412 BC, just before the destruction of the Athenians' ambitious expedition to Sicily, which guaranteed their ultimate defeat in the Peloponnesian War, Euripides, in his play *Helen*, lets his chorus of Greek women make the following comment on Helen and the Trojan War:

> Mindless, all of you who achieve your excellence (*aretai*) in war and in conflicts of the mighty spear, senselessly trying to bring to an end the sufferings of mankind, for if conflict of blood decides [the winner], strife will never leave the cities of men. Strife would have left the bedchambers of Priam's land, Helen, had it been possible with *words* to settle the fighting over you. But now those men are in the charge of Hades, and the bright flame, as if from Zeus, has rushed over the walls [of Troy]; you bring sad sorrows upon sorrows, in pitiable disasters. (1151–64)

The lines are remarkable, not only because they were written by a dramatist who was at other times capable of voicing intense patriotism, but because they are put into the mouths of women. Knowing and saying what is right may not seem like a very rewarding role, especially if men (and some women) seem always to disregard what women say; but no one who heard those lines, at the time of their first performance or since, could fail to see that there was another kind of excellence to be won, without violence and with intelligence, and this was the excellence (or what we might now call heroism) of suffering and understanding that can be found in women.

Chosen Women

What would ancient Greek *women* have thought about Greek mythology? The ancients tell us very little about the process of women's education, and in general we only know what male writers tell us women thought, because there are so few female writers. But certainly everyone, men and women, free and slave, knew the stories. In Euripides' *Ion* a group of slave women who have been brought to Delphi eagerly identify, in the temple of Apollo, the representations of gods, heroes, and monsters, which they recognize from stories that were told to them as they worked at their looms (196–97). In Athens everyone attended the theatre; as Plato puts it, dramatic poetry was "a kind of rhetoric addressed to the general populace, including children, women and men, slave and free" (*Gorgias* 502d).[1] Not that any woman (or man) would have regarded the stories of Oedipus and Jocasta or Agamemnon and Clytemnestra as "norms," since they all belonged to a heroic past that no longer existed.

On the other hand, the myths place emphasis, although in idealized or exaggerated forms, on the kind of experiences and problems that most ancient women would encounter in the course of their lives. In myth, there were essentially two main courses of female existence: celibacy or involvement with males and (inevitably) childbearing. The two states of course were mutually exclusive, though a woman (or goddess) could return to celibacy after her children were born. For mortal women, involvement with males was the more usual, and probably the more promising, alternative, since virginity offered freedom only to goddesses like Athena and Artemis, who as goddesses had the power to defend themselves and by definition were ageless and immortal. Virgin goddesses like Hestia and Hecate were guaranteed protection and honor by Zeus. Other goddesses who had been wives or lovers of the gods could gain power temporarily by withdrawing from the males and by withholding something essential to men or to the gods; Demeter, for example, long estranged from Zeus, won their daughter Persephone back from Hades by keeping the seeds of grain within the earth, so that humans began to starve and the gods got no sacrifices (*Homeric Hymn* 2. 303–9). But to mortal women, who by definition as humans could be destroyed and would grow old, disengagement offered fewer rewards and posed greater dangers. Daphne refused to have sexual relations with Apollo and ended up fixed in one place, but as a laurel tree. Only in one respect does the existence experienced by the virgin goddesses correspond to that of mortal women. Although the virgin goddesses were worshipped for their power over many aspects of human life, in practice they acted only within limits defined by Zeus and with his approval or with the cooperation of another male deity. Hesiod, in a passage that describes and virtually advertises a local cult, explains how Zeus honored the virgin goddess Hecate beyond all others and gave her shining gifts (*Theogony* 411–12); he *permits* her to help or hinder kings, soldiers in battle, and athletes in competition; with the aid of the god Poseidon she can help the fisherman (440–43), or with the god Hermes the herdsman (444–47).

Myths about goddesses, and about women, concentrate on their relations with males, and most particularly on their first union with a male, which, in the case of ordinary mortals at least, was their marriage. Hesiod's *Theogony*, the great epic about the origin of the gods, is a chronological catalogue of divine unions, in which the virgin goddesses like Hecate and Athena appear as rare exceptions; virtually every other goddess is the mother of children. Earth, who with her husband Heaven is the ancestress of Zeus, of the most important gods, and of many primeval forces, asks her son Cronus to castrate his father because he hides all his children back in Earth as soon they are born, and she "groans because she is oppressed" (159–60). But Cronus, too, swallows his children as soon as they are born, and so his wife Rhea has to devise a means of keeping one son, Zeus, away from him, so that Zeus can drive him out of power by force and rule over the gods himself. Zeus prevents a recurrence of this cycle by having several wives and swallowing Metis, his first wife, so that he can bear Athena himself from his own head and thus keep her and her mother under his control (887–900). Then he has six other wives, the last of whom is Hera, and many temporary liaisons with both goddesses and women. Thus a patriarchal order is established, with both women and children kept subordinate, although with particular rights and responsibilities.

Hesiod does not say how Zeus tricked Metis ("Prudence") into letting him swallow her, nor does he note what she might have said when she discovered that she had been tricked, but Homer in the first book of the *Iliad* makes it clear that Hera very much resents Zeus' granting favors to other goddesses and opposing her plans without consulting her (552–59). Hesiod in the *Theogony* says nothing about the fate of Semele and Alcmena, the mortal women with whom Zeus had relations, but later poets would speak poignantly of both the perils and pleasures of intercourse with a god. Perhaps the most vivid description of a union of this type is spoken by Creusa in Euripides' *Ion*. Apollo had fallen in love with Creusa but immediately abandoned her; years later, as queen of Athens, yet unable to bear another child, she complains that she can neither ask for the god's help nor tell her story, because even associating with a woman who bore a bastard child might disgrace her. Like Persephone when she was carried off to the Lower World by Hades, or Europa when she was approached by a beautiful white bull who later turned out to be Zeus, Creusa was gathering flowers when Apollo, his hair glittering with gold, drew her into a cave, as she cried out in vain to her mother: "You brought me there in shamelessness as a favor to the Goddess of Love. And I in my misfortune bore you a son, and in fear of my mother I left him in the couch where you compelled me, in misfortune, in my sorrow, on a bed of sorrow" (895–901). When she speaks these lines she is angry at the god, who has (she believes) both abandoned her and failed to protect their son; it is only after she attempts and fails to kill him that she discovers that the boy her mortal husband thought to be his son is in fact her and Apollo's lost child, destined to be king of Athens. Similarly, in the *Prometheus Bound*, after hearing the story of Io's involvement with Zeus and seeing her head horned like a cow's, and listening to her hysterical ravings, that the female chorus exclaims that they would not want to "marry" one of the gods:[2] "Let my marriage be humble, may the passion of the powerful gods not cast on me an eye none can escape; that is a war I could not fight, a source of resourcelessness. I do not know who I would become. For I do not see how I could escape the mind of Zeus" (901–7). Their words make it clear that they are afraid not only of the gods' power, but of the physical changes in themselves which sexual union with a god might cause. A Hippocratic medical treatise asserts that girls in the first stages of puberty (the time when they would ordinarily be married off) become hysterical and suicidal, like Io; the prescription and cure for them is, as it was for her, pregnancy (*On the Diseases of Young Girls*, viii 468 Littré = WLGR[3] 349).[3] Also, neither Io nor the chorus can see that for her, as for Creusa, what she presumes to be misfortune will ultimately bring her fame and happiness: the birth of a son who will be the ancestor of a famous race, and whose descendants will include another son of Zeus, Heracles.

Like Antigone, Io and Creusa are victims of *atē*, "folly of speech and a fury in the mind," because they do not understand the consequences of their actions, and fear as a disaster what will ultimately bring them fame and guarantee them a place in history. Judged by standards of what Christianity promises to the good, at least after the Day of Judgment, the Greek reward for endurance may seem slight indeed. But in Greek religion no human being, male or female, could live entirely without sorrow; from Zeus' two jars—good and evil—a person can get either a mixed portion or *all evil*, but there is no possibility of *all good* (*Iliad* 24. 527–33). For women, the best available "mixture" would seem to be marriage—however temporary—and family, particularly if her children are heroes or the mothers of great men.

Perhaps because the life of any individual human being was perceived as being essentially temporary and fragile, the myths tend to emphasize the importance of the continuity of the race—not just of families, but of whole peoples. Creusa's son by Apollo is Ion, ancestor not only of the Athenians but of the Ionians in Asia Minor. Virtually every village and town claimed descent from a god, often through a hero for whom the town was named, as the Ionians were said to have been named after Ion. Hesiod's *Theogony* ends with a long catalogue of marriages and extramarital unions between gods and goddesses, gods and women, and goddesses and men, all of which result in the birth of gods, goddesses, heroes, or women who married heroes. Another epic attributed to Hesiod, the *Catalogue of Women*, described the unions that produced all the famous heroes, nations, and races; each new heroine was introduced with the words "And like her was . . ."

For centuries we possessed only short quotations from the *Catalogue* and some prose summaries that could give little impression of the shape of the original epic, but in the course of the twentieth century a number of long fragments were discovered on tattered strips of papyrus, and from these we can get at least a partial sense of the pacing and emphasis of the original narrative. Although Greek bards could describe brilliantly the excitement of sexual passion and the verbal and physical prelude to making love—the *Homeric Hymn to Aphrodite* is the best example—the *Catalogue of Women* seems to have been valued and recited, even in the Hellenistic Age, not for its power to engage the emotions, but as historical information, like the begats in Genesis or at the beginning of Matthew's Gospel, or the fascinating list of the different types of whales that interrupts the grim story of Melville's *Moby Dick*. The ancient Greeks seem to have been particularly fond of such catalogues: Book 2 of the *Iliad* contains a list of all the cities that sent ships and men to Troy.[4] But Hesiod's catalogue attributes to women a significant role in this formal history. Each "founding mother" is listed by name; none is merely an anonymous bearer of divine seed.

Like Hesiod's *Theogony*, the *Catalogue* is organized by genealogies, and within each family tree Hesiod concentrates on explaining why certain women captured the attention of gods or of heroes. In the first book, Demodice (about whom virtually nothing is said in any other surviving text), like Helen and Penelope, is wooed by numerous suitors because of her "unbounded beauty, but they didn't persuade her." She was holding out, apparently, for a god, and won Ares, by whom she became the mother of Thestius, father of Leda, who in turn was the mother of the most beautiful woman in the world, Helen (fr. 22 M-W). Mestra, daughter of Erysichthon, who had an insatiable appetite, was able to change into every type of animal; so each day her father sold her in exchange for food, and each night she changed back into human shape and returned to him, until Sisyphus bought her for his son and demanded arbitration when she ran away. But even then Sisyphus was not able to keep her, because "Poseidon broke her [*edamassato*—the same verb denotes both taming of animals and the taking of a virgin], far away from her father in sea-girt Cos, carrying her across the wine-faced sea, even though she was very clever" (*polïdris*, a term that always seems to imply, both for men and for women, that one is tricky or too clever for one's own good [fr. 43a. 55–57]). By Poseidon she became the mother of the great hero Bellerophon (fr. 43a. 82–83). Another fragment describes the contest for the athletic and beautiful Atalanta (fr. 73) from the point of view of her successful suitor, Hippomenes:

> The prize that awaited them both was not the same; swift-footed god-like Atalanta raced refusing the gifts of golden Aphrodite; for him the race was for his life, whether he should be captured [by Atalanta's father] or escape: and so he addressed her with crafty intention, "Daughter of Schoeneus, with your relentless heart, accept these shining gifts of golden Aphrodite..." [He threw an apple on the ground] and she snatched it swiftly like a harpy on delaying feet; but he threw a second apple to the ground ... then swift god-like Atalanta had two apples, and she was near the goal, but he threw a third to the ground, and with this he escaped death and dark fate. He stood there catching his breath ... (fr. 76)

In these, and in every other case, the males win, which could be interpreted as an illustration of the inferiority of women, if no struggle to capture them were involved and if, as in Atalanta's case, the woman's skill were not so obviously superior. The mother of a hero clearly must be more beautiful than other women, but she must also be cleverer or swifter than most men; and, in the end, she can be subdued only by or with the assistance of the gods. Perhaps the best example is Alcmena, the mother of Heracles, the greatest hero of all. Her brothers were all killed, and she "alone was left as a joy to her parents." The next lines immediately refer to Zeus, who wanted Alcmena to be the mother of his greatest mortal son, Heracles (fr. 193. 19–20). According to the epic *The Shield of Heracles*, another work attributed to Hesiod, but probably composed at least a century later than the *Catalogue of Women*, Alcmena was more beautiful, cleverer, and (in our terms) sexier than anyone, and also so faithful to her husband that Zeus had to pretend on her wedding night that he was her husband. That occasion had been postponed until Amphitryon had avenged the death of Alcmena's brothers, but "when [Amphitryon] had accomplished the great deed he returned to his home, and he did not go to his slaves or the shepherds in the fields until he had gone up to his wife's bed—such great desire ruled the heart of the leader of the army; and he lay with his wife all night rejoicing in the gifts of golden Aphrodite" (38–41, 46–47). No one need suppose[5] that Greek men got their sexual pleasure only from extramarital or homosexual relationships.

The moral superiority of women like Alcmena is significant, because the heroic age is brought to an end by the three daughters of Tyndareus, "twice and thrice married and leavers of husbands" (fr. 176 = 223 *PMGF*): Timandra, who left her husband Echemus for Phyleus; Clytemnestra, who "after she deserted her husband Agamemnon slept with Aegisthus and chose a worse husband[;] and then Helen disgraced the bed of fair-haired Menelaus." It is important to note that Helen, unlike Atalanta, is won not by the most daring man but by the man who offered the most gifts and who was not even present himself but rather was represented by his brother; the poet observes that "Menelaus could not have won Helen nor would any other mortal suitor, if swift Achilles returning home from Pelion had encountered her when she was a girl; but before that warlike Menelaus had her, and she bore fair-ankled Hermione in his halls—though the birth had been despaired of" (*aelpton*, fr. 204. 90–95 M-W). At this point the gods were divided by strife, and Zeus wanted to destroy the race of men; the Trojan War followed, and with it, a kind of *Heldendämmerung*: apparently, the race of heroes cannot exist without women of heroic caliber (95–103).[6]

Since Greek myth glorified the role of mother, it also tended to condemn to infamy those who in some way rebelled against it. A confirmed mortal virgin who resisted the advances of a god might get away simply with metamorphosis into a tree or flower, but women who consciously denied their femininity, like the Amazons, or who killed their husbands and fathers, like the women of Lemnos, were regarded as enemies and monsters (Aeschylus, *Libation Bearers* 632–38). The expected outcome of any sexual encounter between a mortal woman and a god was a notable child—as Poseidon reassures Tyro both in the *Odyssey* and in the Hesiodic *Catalogue*: "You will bear glorious children, since the embraces of a god are not fruitless" (fr. 31 M-W).[7] But in the *Catalogue*, when Poseidon had intercourse with the daughter of Elatus, king of the Lapiths in Thessaly, and promised to grant her any favor she wished, she asked to be turned into a man and to be made invulnerable (fr. 87). This man, Caeneus,[8] proved to be a threat to the gods, because he did not respect the limitations of his mortality, like Ixion, who tried to seduce Hera, or Tantalus, who stole nectar and ambrosia from the gods to try to make his friends immortal (Acusilaus 2*FGrHist*F22). Caeneus instead set up his spear in the marketplace and asked people to worship it, so that Zeus arranged to have Caeneus' father's old enemies, the Centaurs, drive Caeneus into the ground (fr. 88). According to the prose genealogy of Acusilaus, Poseidon allowed the sex change because "it wasn't holy for them to have children by him or by anyone else" (2 *FGrHist* F22 = 9B40a D-K). If we compare the story of Thetis, whose son was destined to be greater than his father and who was therefore married to a mortal man, or the story of Metis, whom Zeus swallowed in order to produce her offspring Athena from his own head, the notion seems to be that by completely preventing rather than only mitigating the outcome of her pregnancy, Poseidon makes Caeneus dangerous and undesirable.

Other mythical women who rebel against their traditional role as wife and mother come to a bad end. Coronis, who has intercourse with another of Elatus' sons, Ischys, while she is pregnant with Apollo's son (fr. 60 M-W = Acusilaus 9B39 D-K) is allowed to die, though the child, Asclepius, is saved, only to be killed when he too oversteps mortal boundaries. Medea, who kills her children to get revenge on their father, Jason, who has deserted her, gets away with her life but knows she will live unhappily ever after. Clytemnestra, who helped to murder her husband Agamemnon in order to live with her lover Aegisthus, is murdered by her son by Agamemnon, Orestes; throughout the *Odyssey* her evil actions are contrasted with the faithful Penelope's. Modern women[9] may admire these destructive women because they took action and used their great intelligence to right what they considered to be personal wrongs against themselves. But even the chorus of Corinthian women, who at first sympathize with Medea's desire to punish Jason for deserting her, condemn the form that her revenge takes.

Although few options in life seem to have been available to Greek women (or men), the Greeks did not hesitate to give "equal time" to description of the human dilemma as seen from a *woman's* point of view. We can tell from the titles of lost plays that women were the central figures of many tragedies, as they are in the ones that have come down to us. The poets, even though they were men and their plays were performed by male actors, allow their female characters to describe their predicaments in detail, which suggests that they had listened with a sympathetic ear to the complaints of women in their own families. Euripides shows with particular clarity how the conditions of ancient marriage could be both restrictive and frustrating. As Medea says, when a man is bored with his family, he can go out and put an end to his heartache, but a woman must stay behind, inside the house, and "look towards him alone" (Euripides, *Medea* 244–47). Phaedra complains of the aristocratic wife's dilemma of having too much time to think, and even of being with the man she loves but cannot have, because of the disgrace adultery would bring not only to her but to her children (Euripides, *Hippolytus* 373–430). Sophocles depicts the plight of Heracles' wife Deianeira no less sympathetically, abandoned year after year by her husband as he goes about his labors and sleeps with other women; Heracles sees his children "like a farmer who sees a distant field only at sowing-time and harvest" (Sophocles, *Trachiniae* 31–33). In a fragment of his lost play *Tereus* the king's deserted wife complains that women are happy only in their girlhood, in their father's house, after which they are "thrust out and sold to strangers or foreigners, in joyless or hostile houses—and all this once the first night has yoked us to our husband we are forced to praise and say that all is well" (fr. 583 *TGrF*).[10] Since Sophocles' and Euripides' dramas were produced, often in competition with one another, throughout the last decades of the fifth century BC, from the beginning until the disastrous end of the Peloponnesian War, during all this time their audiences were encouraged to reflect on how their customs and actions affected (or afflicted) women's lives.

It has been suggested[11] that the destruction of Athenian society was predicted in dramas: Euripides' *Bacchae*[12] describes how Pentheus, the king of Thebes, is murdered by his mother in a Bacchic frenzy; the Greeks are portrayed as being compelled by their habitual misogyny to seek the company and love of other men and to try to restrict and repress the females in their family. Euripides would then seem to be saying that if women are confined to "the loom and the shuttle" in the inside of their houses, women will rebel and tear apart not only the fabric of their own weaving but of the family and the state. Dionysiac ritual would then be providing a form of "socialization" that can keep the female under control.[13] But to judge from the emphasis in Euripides' text, I think it far more likely that both the poet and his audience saw in Pentheus' cruel death and in the disgrace and exile of his mother particularly vivid reminders of the universal power of *atē*, the deception which leads men to ignore the worship of the gods and of the vital forces in nature which they represent, and of the "folly in speech and fury in the mind" (Sophocles, *Antigone* 603) that will drive men to bring about their own destruction. Pentheus and his mother and aunts all refused to recognize the existence of the god Dionysus, and so the god whom they dishonor causes them to go mad and ultimately to destroy themselves. As in the *Antigone*, men and women are equally subject to *atē* and equally responsible for their actions. If the women abandon their homes and infant children, and the responsibility of caring for the family that is represented by the loom, Euripides suggests, they will harm not only others but themselves; he is not recommending that women enjoy the role that society has assigned to them but simply that they accept it as the least destructive possibility. Men too are compelled to play roles that they would not willingly choose: Cadmus, Pentheus' grandfather, had to abdicate his throne when he was too old to defend himself, and must with difficulty try to pretend that he is young again in the ritual required by the god; at the end of the play, although he is an old man and has done nothing himself to offend the god, he must leave the city he founded and end his days in the form of a snake.

Rather than insist that Greek men were misogynists because they did not give their women the "equal rights" that women have yet to acquire even in the most advanced democracies, I would suggest that they be regarded as pioneers in recognizing and describing with sympathy both the life and the central importance to their society of women. Women, to whom their society assigned the task of lamenting and burying the dead,[14] are very often in the position of being the last commentators on the war or murders described in an epic or a drama, and male poets did not hesitate to allow them to make articulate and poignant observations about the futility of all that their men had prized so highly. They assume an important role in drama because they are passive and are required to remain at home or away from the scene of the action, and thus are natural victims. As such, they are able to represent the human condition, man's true powerlessness before the gods and the fact of his own mortality.[15]

But even though male Greek writers of the fifth century BC were capable of such brilliant description of the problems of women's life, they were not equally good at offering solutions. Even the philosophers of the fourth century BC were better at explaining how the world worked than at proposing any practical changes. In the Hellenistic period, when the Macedonian conquests had imposed more efficient governance and caused Greek culture to come in contact with new ideas, the law, centuries behind the facts as always, granted women in name some of the rights they had already had in practice; but despite greater physical comfort and freedom of movement, women's basic role in life was unchanged,[16] and the old myths continued to be told and retold, even by the best and most sophisticated court poets in Alexandria. Medea, in Apollonius' epic *The Voyage of the Argo*, has the run of the palace and, with her handmaidens, of the city of Colchis; but she is still dependent on her father, and then on her lover Jason. The destructive powers of her magic and her selfish desires lead to her exile, the death of her brother, and unhappiness for both Jason and herself.

By stressing the importance of the family and of women's role within it as nurturers and continuers of the race, the Greeks at least attributed to women a vital function that the Church Fathers would later try to deny them, when they placed an even higher value on the state of celibacy and offered to virgins a new subservience rather than increased independence.[17] Comparison with narratives about women in the early Church reveals that however immoral the behavior in their tales, in the view of Christian ethics, the Greeks at least placed a higher value on women's initiative and intelligence. In Matthew's

Gospel, Mary is chosen to be the mother of God's son because she is a virgin, thus fulfilling the prophecy in Isaiah (7:14), quoted by Matthew, "Behold the maiden (*parthenos*) shall conceive in her womb and she shall bear a son, and they shall call his name Emmanuel."[18] We hear nothing about any of her other qualities, though she does, in the course of Luke's narrative, display both piety and common sense: "How can this be," she asks, "since I know no man?" (Luke 1:34). The sexual encounter that invariably marks the culmination of the episodes in Hesiod's *Catalogue* is of course missing in Luke, which emphasizes instead the power of God: "The Holy Spirit will come to you and the power of the highest will overshadow you" (1:35). The divine messenger goes on: "And behold, Elizabeth your kinswoman, she also has conceived a son, in her old age, and this is the sixth month for her who had been called barren," citing Genesis 18:14: "Because 'nothing at all will be impossible for God'" (1:36–37). In Greek mythology, by contrast, gods choose women because of exceptional qualities possessed by the women themselves. Io, for example, as the daughter of the river Inachus, has a distinguished genealogy. Cassandra was the "most beautiful of Priam's daughters" (*Iliad* 13. 365). Apollo admires Cyrene wrestling alone with a lion (Hesiod, *Catalogue* fr. 215).[19] Poseidon finally outwitted the "very clever" Mestra (fr. 43a. 55–57).

Of course I do not mean in any way to deny that from a modern point of view the patterns of women's experience described in Greek myth are severely limited; but then we cannot really blame them for not having been able to envisage the advantages for women that the industrial and scientific revolutions would bring. At the same time it would be foolish to claim that these old patterns have lost all their influence, or even appeal. Although some feminists have sought to concentrate instead on those relatively few myths and authors whose heroines assert themselves, even if only to hasten their own or others' deaths, the original myths, as ancient authors chose to tell them, also have something to teach us. *Atē* is still with us, and perhaps nowhere more obviously than in the belief that the ambitious career woman can "have it all," without divine intervention. The creation of new narrative patterns has helped at least to chart some of the crises other than marriage and childbearing that may arise for women as the result of a longer and more complex life.

In addition to reminding us of the limits of human vision, the ancient texts also emphasize the importance of "nature" as opposed to "nurture" in human life. Also, their concentration on certain critical moments reminds us that human existence is perceived episodically, even though it is lived chronologically. But perhaps the most important notion that Greek mythology has helped to fix in our minds is that women have not only the right but the power to comment on the events that shape their lives, even if they cannot control them; and because they have a voice, they are able to speak not only for themselves, but for humankind in general.

Seduction and Rape

In this chapter I challenge the common assumption that Greek mythology effectively validates the practice of rape and approves of the violent mistreatment of women, by ancient Greek standards as well as by ours cruel and unlawful acts. I shall argue that, in the case of unions of gods and goddesses with mortal men and women, we should talk about abduction or seduction rather than rape, because the gods see to it that the experience, however transient, is pleasant for the mortals. Moreover, the consequences of the unions usually bring glory to the families of the mortals involved, despite and even because of the suffering that individual members of the family may undergo.

Stories about abduction of women play a central role in the canon of ancient Greek literature: The Trojan War was fought to bring back Helen from Troy, after the Trojan prince Paris had abducted her from her husband's home in Sparta. The fifth-century Greek historian Herodotus begins his history of the dissension between the Greeks and the barbarians by recounting myths of how both sides abducted (*harpazein*) each other's women (1–2. 2).[1] According to these myths, after Phoenicians abducted (*harpasai*) Io, Greeks abducted the princess Medea from Colchis; then the Trojan prince Paris decided he could get away with abducting Helen from Sparta (3. 1). The Greeks showed that they took such matters seriously, by sending an expedition to Troy. But the Persians, although they acknowledged that abductions were "the work of unjust men," nonetheless refused to take action, because (as they said), "it's clear that the women wouldn't have been abducted if they hadn't been willing" (1. 4. 2).

As Herodotus makes clear, by contrasting the attitude of the Greeks towards abductions with that of the barbarians, Greeks, in responding to or avenging a case of rape, are not interested in whether or not the women gave their consent so much as with the question of *honor*.[2] The Greek attitude toward women is both more strictly moralistic and more protective: Persians adopt a laissez-faire attitude, letting the women do what they want, without attempting to get revenge; Greeks not only take revenge but (at least in the case of Helen) seek to retrieve the women. The difference emerges clearly in the case of the first of the abductions in Herodotus' list, that of Io. According to the traditional Greek version, which Herodotus does not tell, because his audience knew it (2. 1), Io's lover was the god Zeus. Herodotus first gives the Persian account of the story: that Io was carried off by Phoenician merchants.[3] A little later, Herodotus gives what he calls the Phoenician version: they agree that they took Io to Egypt, but they deny that they abducted her, claiming instead that she had had sexual relations with the captain of the merchant ship and decided to go away with the Phoenicians after discovering that she was pregnant, out of respect for her parents (5. 1–2)—in other words, they didn't bother to take revenge because she had consented to her "abduction."

In contrast to these pragmatic barbarian versions, the Greek accounts of these same abductions emphasize the involvement of the gods: Io was seduced by Zeus; in the *Iliad*, although Helen regretfully admits that she "followed" Paris to Troy (3. 174), she puts some of the blame for her seduction by Paris on the goddess Aphrodite, who brought her to Paris, in fulfillment of her vow to give him the most beautiful woman in the world.[4] Even though it is clear in the *Iliad* that Helen gave her consent and feels guilty about it (3. 172–76), the Greek generals, like the Greeks in Herodotus' account, insist on talking about it as if it were abduction or rape. Nestor says that the army cannot return to Greece "before one of us has slept with a Trojan man's wife, in order to avenge Helen's struggles and groans" (2. 356).[5] For rhetorical purposes, if not for the sake of Menelaus' honor (cf. 2. 590), the generals must imply that Helen was abducted by force, against her will, and that her abduction was a crime against her husband and his allies.

In Greek myth, apparently, seduction was also regarded as a serious crime, if (and this distinction is important) the seduction occurred in the house of the woman's husband or a male relative. Any seduction or abduction from the house was taken as seriously as murder; the relatives of the victim sought to kill the seducer. According to legend, the poet Hesiod was killed by two brothers who believed that Hesiod had seduced their sister while he was staying in their house; when the charge later proved to be false, the brothers themselves were sacrificed to the gods of hospitality and the sister hanged herself.[6]

But, if in myth and legend Greek men were determined to avenge abduction, and seduction from the woman's home, how can it be that the Greeks condoned or even applauded such behavior on the part of their gods? The difference seems to be that the gods do not rape mortal women or abduct or seduce them from their father's or husband's homes. Rather, the women are *seduced* by gods, usually outside of their homes; and the women give their consent, at least initially.

The distinction between rape or forcible abduction and voluntary seduction needs to be made with some care and emphasis, since these seductions by gods are often classified as rape in modern literature. Keuls in her provocative book *The Reign of the Phallus* speaks of male gods going on "raping expeditions."[7] Forbes Irving in his book on metamorphoses observes that "women are continually being punished in myth for being raped."[8] Zeitlin, in an interesting article on "Configurations of Rape in Greek Myth," includes in her discussion of rape the myths of erotic pursuit by the gods.[9] But, natural as it might seem in our own time to classify as rape all acts of sexual aggression by males (mortal or immortal) against females and younger males, the Greeks in their law codes distinguished between rape and seduction. As the founding myth of the court of the Areopagus suggests, rape provided sufficient justification for homicide: according to the story, it was there that the god Poseidon prosecuted the god Ares for the murder of his son Halirrhothius. Ares had killed Halirrhothius because he had raped Ares' daughter Alcippe, but the court acquitted Ares.[10]

Rape and seduction are regarded as equally serious crimes in Athenian law and in the Gortyn code.[11] In Lysias' speech about the murder of Eratosthenes, the defendant, Euphiletus, argues that seduction is the more serious crime; but this is a case of special pleading to help justify murder in the case of an adultery that took place with the wife's full consent.[12] Rape, as defined in the Gortyn code (ii. 4), explicitly involves the use of force (*kartos* or *kratos*).[13] The fine for rape of a free woman is the same as that for seduction in the house of her father, brother, or husband—100 staters—whereas the fine for seduction in another man's house is only 50 staters (ii. 21–24). The scale of fines in the code suggests that rape and seduction are equally serious crimes if the woman in question is married, but if she is not, the seriousness of the crime depends upon whether or not she gave her consent.[14]

But violence is not a characteristic of female mortals' encounters with the gods, at least in the heroic age; nor do gods tend to violate the laws of hospitality of a male relative's home; nor do they concern themselves with married women. Instead, the encounters between gods and mortal women usually take place in beautiful settings, outside of the woman's home, while she is unmarried. Even though the encounters between gods and mortal women are almost always of short duration, they have lasting consequences, not only for the females involved, but for civilization generally, since the children born from such unions are invariably remarkable, famous for their strength or intelligence or both. Whether we moderns choose to approve of it or not, most women in archaic Greek epic, perhaps because they believed that their gods existed and did not question the historicity of their mythology, tended to cooperate in their seduction.

The audiences of epics clearly enjoyed hearing genealogies of heroes and races that derived from the unions of a god with a mortal woman; naturally any descendant would boast of such an origin. Like Achilles himself, two of his captains have gods as fathers. The story of one of them is told in some detail in the *Iliad*:

> a girl's child (*parthenios*), whom Polymele bore, beautiful in the dance, the daughter of Phylas; strong Argeiphontes [i.e. Hermes] fell in love with her (*ērasato*) when he caught sight of her among the girls performing the choral dance to Artemis of the golden arrow, of the hunting cry, and straightway Hermes went into the women's quarters and slept with her in secret, and he gave her a glorious son Eudorus, an excellent runner and swift fighter. (*Iliad* 16. 180–86)

Polymele was not disgraced by her association with Hermes, even though the seduction took place in her father's house; on the contrary, after Eudorus was born, she was married to Echecles, who gave many wedding gifts for her, and her father raised Eudorus as his own child. It is significant that when the god falls in love with her "among the girls performing the choral dance—that is, at a time when she would be on display for mortal suitors—one of these in fact marries her after the birth of her son by the god.[15]

Homer does not say whether or not Polymele invited or eagerly received Hermes' attentions; the god "catches sight of her," literally, "sees her with his eyes," (182); did they exchange glances? On vase paintings, when gods are portrayed in pursuit of mortal women there is emphasis on the persuasive power of the god's glance; the woman moves away from him, but looks back, as if drawn to him.[16] Since there is no mention of violence, and Hermes and Polymele made love "in secret" in the women's quarters, the implication is that she did not strenuously resist the god's attentions. There is, however, an explicit case of eagerness on the part of the mortal woman in the catalogue of women in *Odyssey* 11; this is the story of Tyro, the first woman Odysseus sees after he speaks to his mother:

> She was said to be the daughter of blameless Salmoneus, and she said that she was the wife of Cretheus son of Aeolus. She fell in love with (*ērassato*) divine Enipeus, who was the most beautiful of rivers flowing on the earth, and she frequented the beautiful streams of Enipeus. But the Holder of the Earth, the Shaker of the Earth Poseidon made himself resemble Enipeus, and slept with her in the mouth of the eddying river. And a dark shining wave stood over them like a mountain, arched over them, and it hid the god and the mortal woman. And when the god had completed his acts of love (*philotēsia erga*) he took her hand and spoke and called her by name: "rejoice, lady, in our love (*philotēti*), and as the year comes round you will bear glorious children, since the beds of the gods are not infertile; and you must care for them and cherish them. Now go home and keep this to yourself and do not tell my name; but I am Poseidon the Shaker of the Earth." And with these words he went down under the swelling sea. And she became pregnant and bore Pelias and Neleus. (236–54)

Tyro in this story clearly feels intense physical passion (*ērassato*) for the god Enipeus and wants to attract his attention. But because she spends so much of her time beside him away from her home, where she would be protected, she attracts the attention of a more powerful god, Poseidon. Poseidon does not use force to compel her to have intercourse with him; rather, he assumes the form of the god whom she explicitly desires, Enipeus.[17] Then he takes her into the river's stream and creates a setting that offers not only privacy but a magical splendor, with a dark shining wave like a mountain.[18] He touches her hand, calls her by name, and speaks to her—the poet uses a formulaic line that introduces speech to a close associate (so Ares to Aphrodite in *Od.* 8. 291).[19] He tells her who he really is and that she will bear twin sons. Again, as in the case of Polymele's tryst with Hermes, Tyro's encounter with Poseidon brings no disgrace, because afterwards she is married to her uncle, the hero Cretheus.

In the cases of both Polymele and Tyro, the god has only this one encounter with the woman, and then disappears. This may seem heartless, but it is characteristic of every kind of encounter mortals have with gods, no matter how close their relationship. A god will send a dream; he/she will appear in disguise and give instructions to a mortal, as Aphrodite does to Helen in *Iliad* 3 and Athena to Telemachus in *Odyssey* 1. Even Thetis does not linger in conversation with her son Achilles. In Homer, the gods' female consorts do not complain that the gods behaved like gods. Even as a ghost in Hades, two generations after her death, when Tyro explains to Odysseus who she is, it is her brief encounter with the god that makes her remarkable. The next woman Odysseus sees is Antiope, "who boasted that she spent the night in the arms of Zeus, and bore two sons, Amphion and Zethos" (*Od.* 11. 261–62). Homer does not tell the rest of her story; but even though we know from other sources that she suffered great hardship because of her liaison with Zeus, what she boasts of to Odysseus is that one night she spent with the god, and the two sons she bore as a result of it (Apollodorus 3. 5. 5).

Liaisons between gods, heroes, and mortals appear to have been the subject of an entire epic, which was attributed to the poet Hesiod but was almost certainly written more than a century after his death. Only fragments of this poem survive, but we know that Tyro's story was told again in this *Catalogue of Women*, but with emphasis on Tyro's beauty and a much longer speech by Poseidon about her children and their descendants (frs. 30–42 M-W). A long papyrus fragment relates the story of another of Poseidon's liaisons, this one with Mestra, the daughter of Erysichthon; "the god took (*edamasse*) her in Cos" having brought her "far away from her father across the wine-dark sea" (fr. 43a. 55–57 M-W), despite her ability to turn herself into the shape of different animals. After she bears a son, she marries a mortal, Glaucus, and the catalogue of her descendants is given.

Nothing is said in the poem about whether Mestra consented or desired this union, though her life with her father could not have been easy: he had an insatiable appetite, and to pay for food, would sell Mestra in one of her animal forms, and then she would turn back into human form and escape (cf. fr. 43a. 31–33). Poseidon's attentions at least provide her with a means of transport to the east, where a husband awaited her, and with additional honor. But the gods have ways of making their approaches welcome.[20] A summary of a later section of the poem describes how Zeus fell in love with Europa while she was gathering flowers, and changed himself into a bull and "breathed from his mouth the scent of saffron" (fr. 140); thus he was able to deceive her and carry her off on his back to Crete, where he had intercourse with her. After that she had famous children and lived with the king of Crete.

In what survives of the Hesiodic catalogue, the poet does not describe how the women involved in these liaisons felt about the experiences.[21] But since the Athenian tragic poets gave their women characters ample opportunity to speak, we can at least know what the poets imagined the women might have said in retrospect about their encounters with gods, since of course no such incident could have been presented on the tragic stage. Only scraps of two plays about Sophocles' *Tyro* survive, but we have enough of the prologue of Aeschylus' *Kares* (or *Europa*) to see that Europa was very proud of her relationship with Zeus; she boasts of her fertility, since it is unusual for the women to give birth to triplets rather than to one child or a set of twins as the result of a single encounter with a god:[22]

> There was a flourishing meadow to welcome the bull; such was the trick that Zeus devised, by staying where he was, to steal me from my father without a struggle. And after that: I shall tell the whole story in a few words. A mortal woman united with a god, I exchanged the honored state of maidenhood, and was joined to the common owner of my children. In three travails I endured the pains of women, and the noble seed of the father could not reproach the field, that it refused to bring forth. I started with the greatest of these offspring, by giving birth to Minos. (Aeschylus *TGrF* fr. 99. 1–11)

Again, a meadow with flowers proves to be an irresistible attraction for a young girl, and again the god uses a deception (*klemma*, 2) in order to carry her off.

Although the philosopher Xenophanes complained that Homer and Hesiod sang about actions of the gods that were unlawful by human standards, their lying (*kleptein*), adultery, and deluding of one another (21 F 12 D-K), ordinarily people thought that when gods were involved, the ends justified the means. It would be a different—indeed, reprehensible—matter if a mortal used a ruse or disguise to deceive a young girl: he would be punished. An amusing example of such a case, perhaps based on the plot of a lost comedy, is preserved in a letter that purports to have been written by the fourth-century BC Athenian orator Aeschines but which was probably composed centuries later, possibly in the second century AD. Because in Troy at that time young women who were about to be married dedicated their virginity to the river Scamander, the protagonist of the story, Cimon, crowned himself with reeds and hid in a bush: when the girl he was after, Callirhoe, asked the river to receive her virginity, he jumped out of the bush and said, "I who am Scamander receive it with pleasure and take you, Callirhoe, in order to bestow great benefits on you." But when, the next day, Callirhoe's nurse discovered what had happened, Cimon had to leave town in a hurry.[23]

Why do the gods visit their mortal consorts only once and never return again, even to offer encouragement or comfort? It is this failure to return, to care about their mortal partners and mortal children, that a chorus of Athenian women complain about in Euripides' *Ion*, when their queen Creusa describes how she has been neglected by the god Apollo and has lost the son she bore to him, having had to abandon him many years before: "The son of Zeus [Apollo] shows that he does not remember, and did not beget the common fortune of children for my queen [Creusa] in her household, but produced a bastard child, doing Aphrodite another favor" (1099–1106). The *Ion* is the only extant play which explicitly scrutinizes, rather than simply accepts, the pattern of divine behavior towards mortal partners. Ion, before he discovers that he himself is Creusa's lost child by Apollo, raises the question of why gods are not held liable for seduction and adultery like mortal men:

> If—though it will not happen, but for the sake of argument—you gods paid the penalty to mortals for violating marriages, you and Poseidon and Zeus the ruler of heaven would empty your temples by paying the fines for your wrongdoing. (444–47)

Creusa makes the charge of irresponsibility even more explicit:

> To this light I shall speak in reproach against you, son of Leto. You came to me, with your hair shining with gold, when I was gathering saffron petals in the folds of my gown, to reflect the golden light in their flowering. You grasped the pale wrists of my arms and you led me to a bed in the cave, while I cried out "mother," a lover god granting a favor for shameless Cypris [Aphrodite]. And I in my misfortune bore you a son, and out of fear for my mother I threw him on your bed, where you had lain with me in my misfortune, in my sadness on our sad bed. Alas, and now he is gone, stolen, a feast for the birds, my child and yours, you wretch, and you play the lyre and sing your paeans. (885–902)

As mortals, we instinctively sympathize with Creusa. But before we criticize the god, we must be precise about the nature of his crime. First of all, he did not use force.[24] Like Europa, Creusa was away from home, in a meadow, gathering flowers. Like Poseidon when he appeared to Tyro, the god appears as the woman would like to see him, with his hair sparkling with the gold she has sought to collect in her lap with the petals of her flowers. The god takes her by the wrists, employing the gesture used in the marriage ceremony (*cheir' epi karpōi*) to lead away the bride.[25] Again, as Poseidon did for Tyro, Apollo takes Creusa to a private place.

Did Creusa give her consent? Certainly not at first, since she called out to her mother, though it is also true that she does not try to escape. But certainly afterwards she regrets the encounter; she calls herself unfortunate, sad; even their bed was "sad." But the reason for her sorrow is not regret that she had intercourse with the god but that he abandoned her and her son. The god behaved according to the epic pattern, except that he failed to inform his mortal partner fully of what would happen in the future to her child. In the *Odyssey* and in the *Catalogue* the god tells the women who their children will be and that they will be famous. Creusa discovers her child's fate and destiny only after many years, and then after much suffering and misapprehension of the facts.[26]

It would have been easier on Creusa if her father, like Polymele's, had been prepared to raise the god's son as his own.[27] But the god sees that all comes out well in the end, and Creusa, once she knows that Ion is her son and will be a famous hero, acknowledges that Apollo has not abandoned them (1609–10). Why didn't the god let her know what would happen? Because, as Creusa begins to realize at the end of the play, and the goddess Athena confirms, acting on Apollo's behalf, the god had planned to let her know her son's identity when they were safely back in Athens. Apollo does not appear himself *ex machina* at the end of the play, not because he is ashamed of his actions, but in order that "criticism not arise between them about what happened previously" (1558). Whatever Creusa's resentments against him, the god also has reason to complain of Creusa; after all, she nearly murdered his son, and ruined his first plans for the boy's future.[28]

So it seems that the encounters between mortal women and gods, however beautiful they seem at the moment and however attractive the attentions of the god, are not only brief and singular but often followed by suffering and neglect. Creusa has been childless for years, and she is certain that her son by Apollo is dead. When Zeus asked the maiden Marpessa to choose between the mortal Idas, who had abducted her, and Apollo, who wanted to kill Idas and carry her off himself, Marpessa chose the mortal, because Apollo would abandon her in her old age.[29] The other gods also do not treat their women well: Tyro was persecuted by her stepmother Sidero.[30] Antiope was forced to abandon her twin sons Zethus and Amphion; she married a mortal man, but he was murdered by her uncle, and she was persecuted by her uncle and his wife. Even Europa complains that she never sees two of her sons and lives in fear that she will lose "everything" if her son Sarpedon dies at Troy (*TGrF* fr. 99. 14, 23). As the old men in the chorus remind Antigone, "Danae suffered too . . . although she cherished the seed of Zeus that flowed in gold" (Sophocles, *Antigone* 944–50).[31] The moments of glory in these women's lives are memorable but brief: their seduction, the promise of their sons' fame, being reunited with their sons after a long separation. But that is the nature of human life as the ancient Greeks saw it: "in a moment delight flowers for mortals, and in a moment it falls to the ground, shaken by a stern decree"—so says Pindar of a (male) victor in the games (*Pythian Odes* 8. 92–94).[32]

Such flowers of delight, even if short-lived, are preferable for mortals to the alternative possibility, which is unrelieved suffering.[33] Why then do some mortal women resist the advances of the gods? In *Prometheus Bound*, the maiden Io refuses to obey dreams that tell her to go to the meadow where Zeus awaits her (645–54); then, for reasons that she does not explain but Prometheus attributes to Hera's jealous hatred (592), Io is turned into a cow and tormented by a gadfly. After the daughters of Oceanus have seen Io in her transformed and maddened state, they exclaim:

> Never, never, may you see me sharing a bed with Zeus; may I never be approached by a bridegroom who is one of the gods from heaven. I am terrified when I look at the male-hating maiden Io, tormented by Hera in cruel wanderings. (896–900)[34]

Since these fears are expressed by immortals, who by definition cannot die or grow old, they must be afraid not so much of male sexuality as of change: "I do not know who I shall turn into" (905).[35] Will they be persecuted by Hera and metamorphosed into cows? Will they marry and need to leave the familiar environment of their father's home for a strange and hostile place? It is displacement and separation from her mother that Persephone complains of when she is carried off by Hades on his chariot to his realm in the lower world.[36] Persephone went to pick a marvelous radiant narcissus, with a hundred blossoms and the sweetest scent (*Hom. Hymn* 2. 1–15), which Earth made to grow as a lure (*dolos*) for her. Modern scholars have suggested in various ways that the scene represents a rite of passage from girlhood to womanhood, or even a cruel perversion of the usual marriage ceremony.[37] But what the poet of the hymn has depicted is a particularly appealing setting for a divine encounter: as in the case of Europa, there is a meadow with flowers; like Creusa, Persephone was picking flowers, away from her mother; the narcissus has a scent that makes heaven and earth laugh for joy—Persephone tells her mother that it was like a *krokos*, the saffron flower (428), whose scent attracted Europa to the bull.[38]

But the goddess, unlike Tyro or even Creusa, is unwilling and weeping (19–21). She calls out first to her father; so long as she can see the earth and the sea and heaven—the familiar surroundings of this world—Persephone still hopes to see her mother and the other gods, and still cries out. When the narrative returns to her some time later, she is with her husband in his house but still "very reluctant, out of longing for her mother" (344). In obedience to Zeus' command, Hades allows Persephone to return to her mother; but he gives her a pomegranate seed to eat which he has secretly enchanted so that she will not stay with her mother permanently. The language suggests that what is involved is an act of ritual magic, rather than a euphemism for sexual intercourse. As in the case of love charms, or the apples that Hippomenes throws to Atalanta, the seed binds Persephone to Hades, since if one eats the food of the dead one must remain among them.[39] However, Persephone, in recounting the events to her mother, stresses that she was forced to eat it: "he secretly put the seed into my mouth, a sweet morsel, and forced me to eat it against my will" (413). Whether the seed represents a sacrament, or should be regarded as a euphemism for sexual intercourse is not so important as its meaning for Persephone, that she was compelled by force to eat it, so that she cannot remain with her mother but must spend a third of the year with her husband "in the gloomy darkness," away from her mother and the rest of the gods (464).

If the reason Persephone gives for her reluctance to marry Hades is that she must leave her mother and her normal surroundings, it may not be (despite modern theory) the sexual act per se but rather the change of ambience and status that makes females complain of the transition from girlhood to womanhood.[40] Mortal women married to mortal men complain instead of the transition from their childhood home to a new house and new family. In Euripides' drama, Medea complains of the enslavement of marriage, "taking a master (*despotēs*) for your body" (234), and of needing to be a prophetess when you arrive in a new environment with new customs, which you didn't learn at home. Unless you are in your own city, near your family, you have no protector if your husband mistreats you (238–40, 252–58). As Procne describes it, in Sophocles' lost play *Tereus*:

> Our lives are of all mortals the sweetest when we are young in our father's houses, for ignorance always keeps children safe and happy. But when we come of age and can understand, we are thrust out and sold away from our ancestral gods and from our parents. Some go to strange men's homes, others to foreigners', some to joyless houses, some to hostile. And all this when one night has yoked us, we are forced to praise and say that all is well. (Sophocles, *TGrF* fr. 583 = *WLGR*[3] 32)[41]

Since both Medea and Procne had reason to complain of their husbands, they cannot be taken to represent ordinary women who were happily married and well-treated. Procne, like most women in myth, was given in marriage to a man picked by her father, in this case a close military ally. In her opinion, she was "thrust out and sold."[42] But Medea, as the nurse says in the play's prologue, fell passionately in love with Jason (7). Apparently, even when the woman consents she cannot guarantee that for that reason her marriage will be happy. Whether the choice is deliberate or made on impulse, whether made by herself or her father or someone else, whoever makes the choice for the woman must begin by picking the right man.[43]

Because the Greeks believed that human beings do not usually understand what they are doing, they were able to enjoy stories about women who were seduced by the gods, where at least (like the victor in the games) the woman will have her moment of glory to remember, her honor to enjoy throughout her life, and her children to be proud of. In recent years, students of Greek mythology have tended to stress that the narrative pattern of myth suggests that marriage is (in effect) death for the individual female, either literally or figuratively.[44] But that, as we have seen, is only the first half of the story; if the choice of consort is right, even if the woman has not made the selection herself, even if she is only seduced or persuaded to accede to it, she can in fact be recognized and remembered as an individual, even apart from the accomplishments of her sons. That is also the message of the influential myth of Persephone's abduction: however unwilling Persephone has been to be led off by Hades and to remain for some part of the year in his home, through her marriage she gains a new importance and a kingdom of her own.[45]

The positive side of the pattern can perhaps most easily be seen in the many myths of abduction that serve as charters for new colonies. In an ode for a victor from Cyrene, the fifth-century lyric poet Pindar tells how Apollo admired the maiden Cyrene when he saw her in Thessaly wrestling with a lion without her weapons. He asks the centaur Chiron if it would be "permissible for me to lay my famous hand on her and to cull the sweet flowers of her bed" (*Pyth.* 9. 36–37). Chiron prophesies to Apollo (the god of prophecy) that he will carry her beyond the sea to the fine garden of Zeus in Libya, where she will be queen and will bear a son, Aristaeus. Pindar does not say, and Apollo does not ask, whether Cyrene approves of his plan; but he helps her deal with the lion, then gives her a city of her own to rule.

In another ode, Pindar describes how Zeus carried off Protogeneia, the daughter of the king of the city Opous in Elis, had intercourse with her in the mountains of Arcadia, then brought her to Italy to King Locrus, so that he would not die childless. Locrus was delighted that his wife was pregnant with the god's son, and he named the child Opous, for her father; it is this second Opous who became the eponymous hero of a new colony in Italy (*Olympian Odes* 9. 57–66). Again the poet says nothing about how the woman felt about these events. But what are the alternatives to marriage for an ancient Greek woman? She cannot be truly independent or self-sufficient but must remain under the protection of a male relative, in his household, which is run by his wife. At least if a woman has her own home, she might have children who would be loyal to her, defend her in case of trouble, and look after her in her old age. If she is seduced by a god, she will not only have children, but they will be strong and remarkable children, who could save her life, as Tyro's or Antiope's sons did; she will also have lasting fame, and perhaps have a city or colony named for her.

In many myths, the women chosen by the gods get another advantage: a special gift in return for consenting to the god's wishes. Amymone was rescued by Poseidon from the unwelcome attentions of a satyr; he also asked what wish she would like him to grant, and since she had been searching for water, she asked for a fountain (Apollodorus ii. i. 4).[46] But when Poseidon asked Caenis what he might do for her, she asked to be turned into a man and be made invulnerable. The god complied, and she became the hero Caeneus. In that way she was able to avoid giving birth to the god's child, but in the end her fate as a man seems to have been even less happy than it might have been had she followed the same course as Creusa or Tyro. Caeneus became arrogant, and eventually Zeus arranged that he should be driven into the ground by Centaurs pounding him with tree trunks; Caeneus could not be killed, since he was invulnerable ([Hes.], fr. 87–88; Acusilaus 2 *FGrHist* F 22).[47]

If these myths have any lesson to teach, it is simply what Pylades tells Orestes in Aeschylus' *Choephoroe*, when Orestes asks him if he must obey Apollo's command to kill his mother: "count all men your enemies rather than the god" (902). Given that life is by nature difficult for mortals, the gods will do what is best in the end, as Orestes and Creusa discovered. Another example is Cassandra, who refused to have intercourse with Apollo, although at first she had consented, when Apollo, while wrestling with her, "breathed grace" upon her. But then she "played him false" in regard to the "production of children" (*Agamemnon* 1206–8).[48] As a result of Cassandra's refusal, she lost both the prospect of famous children and her gift. The god had already given her what she asked for, the gift of prophetic power, and could not take it away again, but he fixed it so that she would not be believed.

It is significant that, despite the gods' undeniably greater power, they ask for the woman's consent and honor her right of refusal, even though that refusal may bring about her death, as it did for Cassandra and for Caenis, or transformation into a tree or fountain. The gods, at least as they are portrayed by the poets, wish to persuade mortals to carry out the gods' will, rather than make them comply by force. At the beginning of the *Odyssey*, Zeus sends Hermes to advise Aegisthus not to murder Agamemnon, and to warn him of the consequences of the action he intends. Opportunity for choice and human responsibility are distinctive (and often misunderstood) characteristics of Greek religion, and nowhere are they more evident than in these stories of seduction of women by gods.

Surprisingly, perhaps, the notion that these seductions are beneficial and honorific survives in later Greek literature. Plato's dialogue about the nature of love, the *Phaedrus*, takes place not far from the very spot on the banks of the Ilissus river where the god Boreas was said to have carried off Oreithyia.[49] Poems written far from mainland Greece in space and time describe love, both requited and unrequited, and are often, like Theocritus' idylls, set in attractive landscapes.

A short epyllion, or "mini-epic," written in Alexandria in Egypt in the second century BC by a pupil of the famous Homeric scholar Aristarchus, tells the old story of Zeus' seduction of Europa in much greater detail than even the Hesiodic catalogue would have allowed, and with a different focus: the poem, by Moschus, concentrates not on the god's predictions about the names and accomplishments Europa's progeny but on her own feelings.[50] It begins with a dream sent to her by Aphrodite: Two continents appear to her as two women. Asia, her homeland, appeals to her as her child. The other female, however, pulls her away with her strong arms (Europa is not unwilling) and states that she is Europe, Zeus' gift to her (14). She wakes up frightened, but she is interested in the strange woman who claimed her as her own, and hopes for the best. She then goes out to pick flowers, carrying a basket her mother had given her which has the story of Io depicted on it; as is so often the case in Hellenistic poetry, the description of a work of art is closely tied to the main narrative, and the story of Io predicts Europa's fate.

We have seen how Procne in Sophocles' *Tereus*, like Euripides' *Medea*, described the critical moment of transition from girlhood to becoming a bride: "Our lives are of all mortals the sweetest when we are young in our father's houses, for ignorance always keeps children safe and happy (Soph., *TGrF* fr. 583 = *WLGR³* 32). The same longing for the innocence of childhood is expressed in a remarkable poem dating from the fourth century, this time by a woman poet, Erinna. Although only fragments of her epyllion the *Distaff* survive, it is clear that she described her friendship with another girl, Baucis, and the games they played and that she regretted that Baucis forgot about her and their pastimes after she married: "you forgot everything that you heard from your mother . . . forgetfulness . . . Aphrodite" (*Supp.Hell.* 401. 29–30 = *WLGR³* 10).[51] Even though Baucis is now dead, Erinna seems not to be permitted to leave her home, and "blood-red shame tears . . . me" (34–35). But in Moschus' poem, Europa is curious and even eager to learn about the world outside.

In the meadow, Europa encounters a remarkably beautiful bull—it is of course Zeus in disguise, hoping both to avoid Hera's jealous anger and to fool Europa. Like Nausicaa in the *Odyssey* when she meets Odysseus, Europa does not run away. The bull is mild and gentle; there is a scent of ambrosia and the sound of music; he kneels before her and she climbs on his back. As the bull carries her off to sea, she calls to her friends, who cannot come to her (112); even then she does not despair, but speaks to the bull, asking him if he is a god, and she prays to Poseidon for help. Finally the god speaks to her and tells her what will happen. The poem ends with "and she who had been a girl became the bride of Zeus, and bore his children, and became a mother" (165–66). It is a transition as swift and painless as Zeus' metamorphosis into animal form: "he hid the god and changed his shape and became a bull" (79).

Whatever modern women might think of this ending, for Europa it is clearly happy, and almost romantic, with the music, the flowers, the scent, and the beautiful Nereids rising from the sea. Perhaps it is wishful thinking on the part of a male poet; certainly it has none of the anguish expressed by Erinna or by Procne about a past happiness that is forever lost after marriage to a mortal man. Perhaps the critical difference between these female and male descriptions of marriage is accounted for by the nature of the bridegrooms involved. Europa became the hesitant but willing bride (however temporarily) of the greatest god, and for her, as the dream indicates, her seduction marked the beginning of a new and autonomous life.

"Predatory" Goddesses

The male gods of ancient Greece are known for their interest in mortal women.[1] But goddesses also were active in seeking out mortal consorts, at least in the era before the Trojan War, when the gods were still dining with mortals ([Hes.], *Catalogue of Women*, fr. 1. 1–10 M-W; Hes., *Theogony* 585–87). Hesiod's *Theogony*, in the form in which it has come down to us, ends with a catalogue of Zeus' consorts and children and those of the other gods (886–962). To this catalogue is appended a list of "the immortal goddesses who bedded with mortal men and bore children who resembled the gods" (967–68). The couples listed are Demeter and Iasion, Harmonia and Cadmus, Callirhoe and Chrysaor, Eos and Tithonus, Eos and Cephalus, Medea[2] and Iasion, Psamathe and Aiacos, Thetis and Peleus, Aphrodite and Anchises, Circe and Odysseus,[3] and Calypso and Odysseus (969–1020). When in the *Odyssey* Calypso complains that the gods are jealous of the goddesses who sleep with mortal men, she alludes to the story of Eos and Orion, along with that of Demeter and Iasion (*Od.* 5. 118–28). Homer also mentions Eos and Clitus (*Od.* 15. 572–75), and Sappho alludes to the story of Aphrodite and Adonis (fr. 140 Voigt).[4] The Hesiodic *Catalogue of Women*, although mostly about the liaisons of gods with mortal women, appears to have included accounts of Thetis' marriage to Peleus (fr. 210–11 M-W) and of Selene's romance with Endymion (fr. 245 M-W).[5]

In view of the frequency with which these stories turn up in archaic poetry, it is not surprising that the gods' liaisons with mortals are frequently portrayed on vases by Athenian painters, or that Eos and her lovers appear in a relatively large proportion of them. In the vases catalogued by Sophia Kaempf-Dimitriadou there are more scenes depicting Eos and her lovers than scenes portraying Zeus, either with female mortals or with Ganymede.[6] Illustrations of the myth of Eos and Cephalus had special appeal for an Athenian audience, because Cephalus was a local boy, as did depictions of the abduction of the Athenian princess Oreithyia by the wind-god Boreas.[7] The Eos vases also had a wide appeal in the Italian market: 37 of 210 red-figured vases listed by Carina Weiss were found in Italy or Sicily, and 38 are Nolan amphoras.[8] Kaempf-Dimitriadou concluded that the scenes where gods abducted mortals might have served as reminders of the precariousness of human existence.[9] She also suggested that the scenes in which Eos carried off young men might in some cases have served as consolation in time of death.[10]

In recent years, however, scholars have sought to extrapolate from the scenes on the vases information about Athenian attitudes towards human male and female sexuality. Andrew Stewart, in a detailed discussion of the Eos vases, rightly makes a careful distinction between ordinary rape of mortals by mortals and the erotic interventions into human life made by gods.[11] Stewart accounts for the popularity of the Eos vases by conjecturing that they were understood as a means of defining and justifying the dominance of male sexuality: "Mythological pursuits and abductions represent nothing more or less than the projection of Athenian male desire first upon the heroic world and then upon the divine one."[12]

What role do the Eos vases play in this "projection of Athenian male desire"? Stewart suggests that the discourse about Eos and her boy victims may ultimately be intended as a warning, that these pictures not only "hint at the evils of *female* dominance (*gynaikokrateia*) and easy capitulation to desire, but nervously evoke their appalling consequences: female control of the phallus."[13] Robin Osborne agrees with Stewart that female pursuers invert the normal codes of sexual behavior.[14] In his view, the vases provide a display of what never could or should have happened in Athenian society, because of the close restrictions on female desire, at least among respectable women: "in limiting scenes of female pursuit to the case of the winged Eos, pot painters were able both to suggest that women did desire men and that female desire could not be active in the real world."[15]

I believe, however, that Kaempf-Dimitriadou's understanding of the purpose of the Eos vases is more likely to be right: the primary purpose of the vases, she concludes, was to remind viewers of the power of the gods to alter the course of human life, whether for better or worse. Painters who wished to comment on the sexuality of mortal females did not need to use depictions of goddesses to do so. In any case, there is no reason to believe that Athenian men wished to discourage female passion, even within the context of marriage. Rather, what the Eos vases portray are the various stages in the uses of persuasion and of constraint in the pursuit of the goddess's desire. None of the Eos vases depicts sexual activity, other than eye contact. Eos is no more "predatory" in her approaches to mortals than gods like Zeus and Boreas are in theirs.[16]

Why do we suppose that vases depicting abductions of mortals by gods were intended as commentaries on mortal sexual relationships? Certainly human beings project their own characteristics onto the gods, as Xenophanes observed: "Homer and Hesiod ascribed to the gods all the actions that among men cause reproach and blame, lies, adulteries, and deceptions of one another" (fr. 21 B12 I 132 D-K = 160 KRS). But it is another matter to assume that the reverse is true, that all of the actions of the gods can in turn be mirrored in the lives of human beings.[17] The Greeks never forgot about the limitations imposed on human action by the fact of mortality.[18] They made a clear distinction between human rapes and abductions by gods.[19] Abduction of a mortal woman by a god was something to boast about, even after the woman's death; but rape by a mortal was a disgrace, punishable in Athens by divorce and other social restrictions. Gods cannot serve as role models for mortal men, because a god can abduct a woman with impunity. It is essential to remember this important distinction when talking about divine abductions.[20] Gods do not (pace Eva Keuls) go on "raping expeditions"; they choose their female consorts deliberately and carefully.[21]

A similar distinction applies to goddesses who abduct mortal men; a woman cannot get away with either abduction or adultery. Phaedra (who was only *thinking* about committing adultery) hangs herself when she believes that she is going to be disgraced. In his discussion of female-initiated relationships, Osborne fails to distinguish between goddesses and women. He includes Phaedra with the goddesses Eos, Aphrodite, and Selene in a list of "females in pursuit."[22] But Phaedra is mortal; she cannot carry Hippolytus away by persuasion, let alone by force. Her passion cannot do anything positive for him, such as guaranteeing that he will have a famous son or that he can become immortal. Only a goddess could bestow some or all of these benefits on a mortal man. A god could assume the form of an animal to abduct a mortal woman. But when a mortal woman mates with an animal, her lust has dreadful consequences: Pasiphae's passion for the bull produced the Minotaur.[23]

Our present-day sensitivity to the treatment of women has made it difficult to discuss with anything like equanimity the ancient myths of divine abductions of mortals, even when we can separate them in our minds from ordinary rape, but the ancients responded to these stories in more nuanced ways.[24] When depicting divine abductions, artists avoided representing the moment of sexual union or direct manifestation of sexual arousal.[25] Like the poets, these artists concentrated on the process of seduction, and showed how the gods persuaded their mortal lovers to welcome and cooperate with their advances. As Chiron advises Apollo, when he is planning to abduct Cyrene: "hidden are the keys of wise Persuasion of holy loves; this makes gods and men alike hesitant openly to approach a sweet bed for the first time" (Pindar, *Pythian Odes* 9. 39–41).[26]

In the myths, the gods, male and female, always employ persuasion (or enchantment) to gain the cooperation of human females, even though they could easily use force. In the *Homeric Hymn to Aphrodite*, the goddess disguises herself as a mortal and tells an elaborate story about herself in order to reassure Anchises and to encourage him to make love to her; the poet states that she can persuade or outwit any god or mortal except the three virgin goddesses, Athena, Artemis, and Hestia.[27] The male gods, who could easily force mortal boys or women to give into them, prefer to draw their lovers by the power of their glance. Homosexual coupling is shown only in a few cases, where a winged young male god has frontal inter-crural intercourse with a young human male. Even in those cases, as Martin Kilmer has shown, "there is no hint of violence." The mortal seems neither to consent nor object. His passivity brings out the disparity in power between himself and the god.[28]

In general, the goddess Eos' approaches to the young men she seeks to abduct do not differ significantly from those of male gods abducting boys or women. Painters show her (1) approaching the mortal, (2) catching hold of him by his hand or arm, or (3) carrying him away. An example of the first stage is provided by a neck amphora with twisted handles by the Nausicaa Painter (Fig. 1) which shows, on the left, a winged Eos walking with arms outstretched towards a young man, whose hunting garb identifies him as Cephalus.[29] He is walking away from her, holding his right arm with his palm facing towards her, as if warding her off. His dog is jumping towards her in alarm. But at the same time Cephalus has turned his head back in order to look towards Eos, so we can see that the power of the goddess's glance has begun to keep him from getting away.[30] In a bell krater by the Christie Painter (Fig. 2), a winged Eos strides from the left towards a retreating Cephalus (again recognizable by his hunting gear), who is about a head shorter than the goddess. He is gazing back towards her, while a comrade behind the goddess is faintly visible moving off to the left.[31] Eos is the goddess of the dawn, and hunters like Cephalus are out at dawn. Schoolboys also rise early, which is why the Trojan prince Tithonus frequently is shown holding a lyre, as if on his way to his lessons, when Eos comes to carry him away. On a skyphos by the Pantoxena Painter, a winged Eos reaches out to a young man identified by an inscription as Tithonus.[32] His right arm is bent up and back, and he holds a lyre in his right hand with which he tries to strike at Eos; but again their eyes have already met, and we know that his resistance will be ineffective. When the painters depict mortal couples gazing at each other, they often show a winged Eros between or near them.[33] But the gaze of the god or goddess can be effective even without the help of the love god.

The next stage of the pursuit is pictured on a stamnos in the Walters Art Museum (Fig. 3). As Eos takes hold of Tithonus, she is shown without wings, between two young men, striding from the left towards Tithonus, who is moving away from her towards the right.[34] Her left hand rests on his right shoulder. Tithonus has dropped his lyre, which is falling to the ground. Behind Eos, on the left, a comrade is looking back toward Tithonus, but at the same time moving out of the way.[35] On a kylix by the Telephos Painter (Fig. 4), a winged Eos approaches Tithonus from the left, while he moves away from her towards the right.[36] She grasps his right wrist with her right hand, has placed her left arm around his back, and has her left hand on his left shoulder. Tithonus' left arm is bent towards her at the elbow, with his hand outstretched towards her, but not touching her. He turns round to look at her, but she is gazing upward, over his head. She does not need to attract him by her gaze, because she is holding him by the wrist (*cheir' epi karpōi*) as a bridegroom might grasp the wrist of a bride.[37]

In approaching her lovers in this way Eos follows what appears to be one of the customary rules of divine behavior. The tactics she employs are also used by male gods. Virtually the same stage of pursuit is shown on a polychrome bobbin by the Penthesilea Painter (Fig. 5).[38] Here a winged male figure, possibly Zephyr, strides from the left toward a young male (Hyacinth?) holding a lyre in his left hand. The god holds his left arm behind the young man and is reaching down towards him with his right hand. The young man is about to step off to the right, but he gazes back into the eyes of the god. The stance of the pair is similar on a hydria by the Niobid Painter in the Bowdoin College Museum of Art: a winged Boreas with winged boots approaches

FIG. 1. Neck Amphora by the Nausicaa Painter (Berlin F 2352). Eos approaching Cephalus. Courtesy of Antikensammlung, Staatliche Museen zu Berlin, Preussischer Kulturbesitz (Berlin F 2352).

FIG. 2. Bell Krater by the Christie Painter. Eos approaching Cephalus. Courtesy of The Baltimore Museum of Art, bequest of Saidie A. May (Baltimore Museum of Art 1951.486).

FIG. 3. Stamnos by the Painter of the Florentine Stamnoi. Eos approaching Tithonus. Courtesy of The Walters Art Museum, Baltimore (Walters Art Museum 48.2034).

FIG. 4. Kylix by the Telephos Painter. Eos taking hold of Tithonus. Courtesy of Museum of Fine Arts, Boston, Catharine Page Perkins Fund (Boston 95.28).

FIG. 5. Polychrome Bobbin by the Penthesilea Painter. Zephyrus taking hold of
Hyacinthus. Courtesy of The Metropolitan Museum of Art, New York, Fletcher Fund
(New York 28.167).

FIG. 6. Hydria by the Niobid Painter. Boreas taking hold of Oreithyia. Courtesy of the Bowdoin College Museum of Art, Brunswick, Maine, gift of Edward Perry Warren, Esq. (Brunswick 1908.003).

FIG. 7. Kylix by the Penthesilea Painter. Zeus taking hold of Ganymede.
Courtesy of Museo archeologico nazionale di Ferrara, Italy (Ferrara 9351).

FIG. 8. Lekythos by the Oionokles Painter. Eos carrying off Tithonus. Courtesy of Archivo fotográfico, Museo arqueológico nacional, Madrid (Madrid 11158).

FIG. 9. Bird Rhyton by the Painter of London D.15. Eos carrying off a boy.
Courtesy of The State Hermitage Museum, St. Petersburg (St. Petersburg, B 682).

FIG. 10. Etruscan Bronze and Silver Mirror. Thesan (Eos) carrying off
Cephalus. Courtesy of Archivio fotografico, Musei Vaticani (Vatican 12241).

FIG. 11. Bell Krater by the Berlin Painter. Europa running alongside Zeus. Courtesy of Soprintendenza archeologica, Ministero per i beni e le attività culturali per l'Etruria meridionale, Rome (Tarquinia RC 7456).

FIG. 12. Pelike by the Leningrad Painter. Peleus holding Thetis. Courtesy of
Musée du Louvre; photograph by H. Lewandowski (Louvre G 373).

FIG. 13. Lebes Gamikos. Peleus holding Thetis. Courtesy of the Trustees of the
British Museum, London (British Museum B 298 [XXXIX C13]).

A

FIG. 14. Kylix by Peithinos. *A*. Peleus holding Thetis. *B* and *C*. Couples courting and embracing. Courtesy of Antikensammlung, Staatliche Museen zu Berlin, Preussischer Kulturbesitz; photographs by (*A*) Jutta Tietz-Glagowand (*B* and *C*) Johannes Laurentius (Berlin F 2279).

B

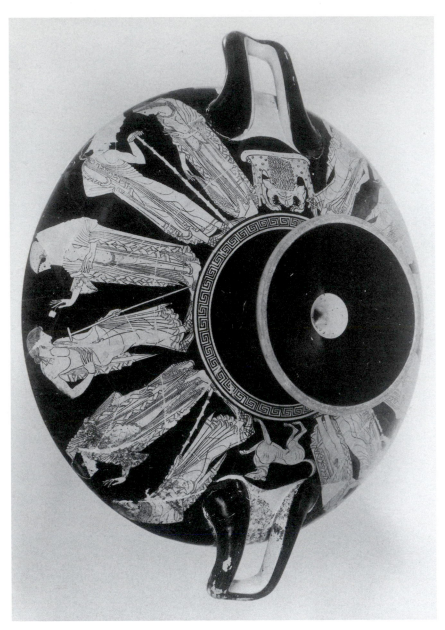

C

from the left through the air (Fig. 6).[39] The god puts his right arm around Oreithyia's waist and his left around her shoulders. Oreithyia turns toward him but does not embrace him in return. She holds both arms in the air and is still moving toward the right, away from him. The goddess Athena, holding spear and shield, stands behind Oreithyia, looking over her head towards Boreas. She does nothing to help Oreithyia or oppose Boreas; rather, she is acting as Boreas' *pompos*, or escort: according to Herodotus, Boreas made Oreithyia his wife (7. 189. 1).[40]

In the vases discussed above, the gods do not use force to compel their intended lovers to accompany them, but ancient Greek painters did not hesitate to show women protesting and suffering as they are carried off, even by a god. The exquisite wall painting in the tomb of Persephone at Vergina depicts Persephone's anguish as Hades carries her off on his chariot, while her Oceanid friend raises her arm in horror.[41] Hades may need to use both deception and violence to abduct Persephone, because she, like himself, is a divinity—powerful, immortal, and ageless. As the story is told in the *Homeric Hymn to Demeter*, Zeus tells Earth (Gaea) to produce an intoxicating narcissus, which Persephone wants to pick; Hades then takes her by surprise, by making the earth open beneath her feet, as he rushes out to carry her off on his chariot (*Hom. Hymn* 2. 8–18).[42]

But when gods approach mortals they do not need to rely on such elaborate tactics. Vase painters show male gods employing their superior strength, and the mortals whom they have chosen display surprise and initial reluctance. In a hydria in Athens, Boreas runs from the left after Oreithyia, who is fleeing to the right with her left hand raised in the air. But Boreas has caught her right hand by the wrist in his right hand and is pulling her from behind with his left hand, and she has turned her head round to look into his eyes.[43] In a kylix by the Penthesilea Painter (Fig. 7) Zeus has put down his thunderbolt and scepter and is using both his arms to pull Ganymede towards him.[44] His left foot is braced against a rock on the lower right side of the vase, and with his right hand he grasps Ganymede's right arm; Ganymede's head is turned toward him, but he is walking away from him, as if he wanted to return to his friends; in his left hand he holds the fighting cock Zeus has given him. This painting appears on the cover of Eva Keuls' *The Reign of the Phallus*, as if it were representative of the sexual violence endemic in Athenian society. But the vase does not describe sexual life in Athens. If a human male behaved that way toward a young man, he would be harshly treated, if not by the young man's relatives, then by the young man himself. Rather, the painting depicts the conflict between a god's desire and a mortal's wish to retain his independence. The onlooker knows whose power is greater, and understands that the gods always win.

The final phase of the pursuit is the abduction itself. In a lekythos by the Oionokles Painter, in Madrid (Fig. 8), a winged Eos flies while holding a young male (identified in an inscription as Cephalus) cradled in her arms.[45] The goddess's torso is turned toward the boy, but she looks upward to the left, while the boy looks downward to the right, away from her. His right arm is extended in front of her face, and his left hand still clutches his lyre. The composition brings out the tension between the goddess's desire to abduct him and his eagerness to rejoin his comrades. Another vivid contrast between Eos and the boy she is abducting appears in a bird rhyton in St. Petersburg, Russia (Fig. 9).[46] Eos again is looking away from the boy toward the left, while he looks down to the right and stretches his left arm downward as if reaching out to someone on the ground. Vermeule's caption for this vase is "Eos the dawn-goddess carries a boy to a better world."[47] But life in the palace of the Dawn would only be better for a boy if he could somehow be ageless and immortal. In the myths, only a few mortals achieve this status.[48] There are no inscriptions or literary documents that suggest that Athenians in the fifth century attached a happy ending to any of the Eos myths. They buried the dead just before dawn for practical reasons, not because they supposed the goddess would be there to carry the soul away.[49] For them, a benevolent winged Charon represented a good and easy death.[50] At best, Eos scenes on funerary *lekythoi* might have conveyed to mourners a vague hope that the deceased, like the heroes of old, might find himself in a brighter region of the lower world.[51] It is only in later antiquity that abductions by goddesses were used to suggest a mode of death and a promise of a future existence in the light, nearer to the gods.[52]

Other scenes show the boy sitting more comfortably in Eos' arms. On an Etruscan bronze and silver mirror from Vulci, now in the Vatican (Fig. 10), Cephalus looks directly into the eyes of the goddess Thesan (Eos' Etruscan counterpart) as she carries him away.[53] She is moving to the left, holding the smaller figure of Cephalus lightly in her arms. Her left arm is beneath his shoulders, and her right hand supports his knees. He has placed his right hand on her right shoulder, and his left arm hangs straight down; he is not looking back towards his friends or his hunting. In a neck amphora by the

Achilles Painter from Vulci the young man has his arm around Eos' back and looks to the left along with her.[54]

We now need to ask what the gods do to make abducted lovers compliant, or even actively cooperative. On a *kylix* by Douris in Paris, Ganymede lies back comfortably in Zeus' arms.[55] Zeus is able to hold his scepter in his left hand because he does not need to restrain the boy who, resting comfortably, faces towards him. In the terra-cotta group statue at Olympia, Ganymede calmly holds in his left hand the fighting cock that is his present from Zeus, while Zeus carries him under his right arm.[56] As we have seen (above, at note 42), when Hades wanted to put Persephone off her guard, his grandmother Earth grew a narcissus that astounded both gods and men, and its sweet scent caused heaven, earth, and sea to smile (*Hom. Hymn* 2. 8–14). When, in the Hesiodic *Catalogue of Women*, Europa was gathering flowers, Zeus changed himself into a bull and "breathed from his mouth the scent of saffron." After enticing her he picked her up, carried her over the sea to Crete, and had intercourse with her" (fr. 140 M-W). When, in a fragment of Aeschylus' *Kares* or *Europa*, Europa gives a brief account of what happened, she has no unpleasant memories: "and a friendly lush meadow was there for the bull; in that way, by waiting there, Zeus managed to take me, an effortless theft, from my aged father" (fr. 99. 1–3 *TGrF*).[57] Scenes in sixth- and early fifth-century BC vase paintings also show a contented and relaxed Europa. She is most often represented on the bull's back, riding away across the sea to Crete. In these scenes she often holds the bull's horn or neck as she sits on him, and places her other hand on the bull's back, to steady herself as the bull rushes along.[58] Some painters show her turning around to call back to her friends, as she does in the second-century BC poem of Moschus, which draws on these earlier versions (111–12).[59] She is not only completely unafraid of the bull but fascinated by him and eager to touch and embrace him.[60] She does not hesitate to climb on his back.[61]

On a bell krater by the Berlin Painter (Fig. 11), Europa is shown contentedly running alongside the bull, her feet wide apart. With her left hand she holds on to the tip of one of his horns.[62] The other side of the vase shows a girl running. Europa and the bull have not yet reached the sea, since the folds of her dress fall straight down and do not billow out in the wind; her friend is still running after her. Kilmer observes that "the 'rape' of Europa is atypical in showing contact between god and mortal; but the contact is never overtly sexual and Zeus is shown as a bull . . . what we have here is pursuit, rather than the abduction that will come from it."[63] By contrast, Keuls emphasizes the potential sexuality of this scene by stating that Europa is grasping the bull by his "phallus-horn."[64] Perhaps that is possible, but there is a simpler explanation. By having Europa hold the bull's horn and keep pace with him, the painter shows that the bull is tame and approachable.

That only a relatively few of the Eos vases show her abducted lovers in such a state of contentment, is because the vase painters were more interested in the pursuit, her first approach to the young man and his initial resistance and longing to return to his friends and previous life. It has been suggested that the painters of these vases concentrated on the negative aspects of abduction in order to send a covert message about women's sexuality: "Woman at the mercy of the male. Women available to be taken, to be raped. The proof: the inverted motif of the rape of Tithonus or Cephalus by Eos, during which, as we have seen, looking back in 'consent' is rare."[65] But why suppose that these scenes have any bearing on the behavior of mortal women? If the Eos painters concentrated on the negative, it is because the goddess's attentions bring at best mixed blessings to her lovers. Eos asked Zeus to make Tithonus immortal, but she forgot to ask Zeus to make him ageless; when he became too old to move or get up, she shut him up in a chamber and locked the doors (*Hom. Hymn* 5. 220–36). Eos allows Cephalus to return to Athens, but when he is out hunting, he accidentally kills his wife Prokris.[66] By contrast, painters allowed Europa to appear content because her fate is relatively good, given that mortals, at best, can never have a completely happy life.[67] She becomes the mother of three sons, each of them famous, Minos, Rhadamanthys, and Sarpedon (Aesch., fr. 50. 11–16 *TGrF*).

Abduction almost always causes trouble for the mortals involved, and sometimes even leads to their deaths.[68] Semele is consumed by flames as a result of her liaison with Zeus. So, in later sources, is Demeter's lover Iasion (a brother of Dardanos) because he desired Demeter (Conon 26 *FGrHist* F21). Anchises was struck by lightning because he boasted about his relations with Aphrodite (Soph., fr. 373. 2–3 *TGrF*).[69] In most cases, as it is for Anchises, the most positive aspect of an abduction by a god is the child that it produces.[70]

Only a few mortals have no regrets. Ganymede is made immortal and ageless, though his father, Tros, grieves for him until Zeus reveals to the father that he has made his son immortal and ageless and gives Tros a pair of immortal horses in compensation for his loss (*Hom. Hymn* 5. 210–17). Oreithyia (above, at note 39) becomes the consort of Boreas and lives with him in Thrace. Amymone is rescued by Poseidon from the unwelcome attentions of satyrs and given the spring of water that she was searching for, hydria in hand. Some vase painters show her looking back into the god's eyes as he approaches her, holding his trident.[71] Others show her about to let him embrace her or depict them standing together in the garden of Aphrodite, like bride and bridegroom.[72]

Like vase painters, poets are willing to represent both the negative and positive aspects of divine abduction.[73] The author of the *Homeric Hymn to Demeter* describes Persephone's anguish and Demeter's grief, but he also shows Hades treating her kindly. The sun god points out to Demeter that Hades is "not an unworthy bridegroom among the immortal gods," because he is her own brother and lord of one-third of the universe (*Hom. Hymn* 2. 82–87).[74] Cyrene, after Apollo comes to her as a "bridegroom," becomes the founder of the city of Cyrene and mother of a son, Aristaeus, who will be made immortal (Pind., *Pyth.* 9. 51–65).[75] In Euripides' *Ion*, Creusa complains that she was seduced and abandoned by Apollo and that the child she bore and abandoned was lost. Her painful narrative has struck some modern critics as emblematic of "rapes" of mortal women by the gods.[76] But at this point in the drama Creusa does not know that in fact the god has not forgotten her after all and is about to return to her the child she thought she had lost forever. Meanwhile, in her ignorance, anger, and confusion, Creusa had tried to poison her child Ion; she was jealous because she thought he was her husband Xuthus' son by another mother.[77] In the end, she is grateful to the god (Eur., *Ion* 1609–14), even though for many years he has done nothing to mitigate her suffering.[78]

As in the case of Creusa, mortals often make things worse for themselves through their lack of understanding. In the *Homeric Hymn to Aphrodite* Anchises rushes into bed with Aphrodite, stripping off the clothes and jewelry with which she had so carefully adorned herself (*Hom. Hymn* 5. 162–66, cf. 58–66).[79] The poet does not describe their copulation; rather, with great conciseness, he comments on Anchises' ignorance: "Then with the will of the gods and in accordance with fate, he, a mortal, slept with an immortal goddess, without knowing clearly what he did" (*Hom. Hymn* 5. 166–67). When he realizes what he has done, he begs the goddess not to make him "strengthless among men" (188).[80] As the author of the *Homeric Hymn to Demeter* has the goddess observe, "mortals are ignorant and without the knowledge to recognize fate beforehand, whether of coming good or of evil" (*Hom. Hymn* 2. 256–57).

The poets use the myths to remind their audiences that nothing in mortal life is an unqualified good. That is the meaning they attach to the story of Thetis and her mortal lover Peleus. Thetis, unlike Eos, did not seek to capture a mortal lover. It was the will of Zeus that she marry Peleus, and she did her best to prevent him from catching her. She changed first into fire, then took on the form of a savage lion that attacked him with tooth and claw. For Peleus, marrying a goddess was the pinnacle of human achievement, a voyage to the outer limits of the known world, the straits of Gibraltar:

> he married one of the high-throned Nereids, and he saw the circled throne, where the kings of heaven and of seas were seated, and they showed him their [wedding] gifts and revealed to him the power of his descendants; but a man cannot cross the dark boundary of Gadeira. (Pind., *Nem.* 4. 65–69)

Even though his wedding to Thetis was the high point of Peleus' life, his goddess wife Thetis was miserable in the marriage (*Il.* 18. 430–35) and soon left him. His son Achilles was the greatest Greek hero, but he died at Troy.

Marriages with goddesses are emblematic of the difficulties involved in extended relationships between immortals and mortals. Peleus wrestling with Thetis was a popular subject on Athenian vases from 520–460 BC.[81] Reeder suggests that these scenes are intended to demonstrate the need for male control of the female's animal nature, on the grounds that hunting metaphors are linked with eroticism.[82] But Thetis is a goddess, not a mortal woman. If she is shown with snakes and even with little lions (e.g., Fig. 12), it is not because her nature resembles an animal's, but rather because in the myth she turned herself into many different animals in order to avoid being caught by Peleus;[83] the vase painter has no other way of alluding to this aspect of the story, and it is also a way to identify her. No mortal woman has the power to metamorphose herself into any other form.

Whatever these scenes were intended to mean, there is little in them to suggest that the primary intention was to remind women of their subordinate role in society. For example, Rush Rehm argues that a scene with Peleus and Thetis on the pedestal of a ceremonial wedding vase or lebes gamikos (beneath a picture of a wedding procession) represents "a violent abduction" (Fig. 13).[84] Thetis is raising her arms to express her resistance, as does Persephone on the wall painting in Vergina (above, at note 41). But there is no explicit violence. Another scene, in which Peleus is holding Thetis, shows a standstill, a moment of acquisition: both figures are static (Fig. 14).[85] On the interior of this kylix, the mortal hero has caught the goddess in a waistlock.[86] Both are fully dressed, and neither is looking at the other; there is no erotic contact. The outside of the cup offers a striking contrast: it portrays fully dressed hetero- and homosexual mortal couples, negotiating and embracing. Persuasion alone is enough in the human world, as the artist's nom de plume Peithinos ("Persuasion-man") suggests.[87] But persuasion cannot help Peleus capture Thetis; he can gain his prize only by patient pertinacity and with the cooperation of gods who are even more powerful than Thetis, Zeus and Poseidon. The scene tells us little or nothing about the sexuality of Athenian women, but a great deal about the power of the gods.

Many of the vases on which the Eos scenes appear could have been used at festive occasions, such as weddings or symposia.[88] On vases given as wedding gifts, abduction scenes might even convey a sense of romantic affection; abduction by a god or goddess was an honor, despite the problems that it could introduce into a mortal's life.[89] But ultimately, vase paintings of divine abductions display recognition of the power of the gods and of mortal vulnerability. They are expressions of what Euripides says about divine intervention at the close of five of his dramas:

> Many are the forms of divinity; the gods bring many things to pass unexpectedly. And what we thought would happen did not come to pass, but the god found a means to bring about what we did not imagine. That is how this action went.

These lines celebrate the ways in which gods can change their appearance; they applaud the gods' ingenuity, and their ability always to surprise and confound mortal expectations. Their interventions can work to the advantage of the protagonists (as in *Alcestis, Andromache,* and *Helen*) or against them (as in the *Medea* and *Bacchae*).[90] Since we know that the ancient Athenians held these views about the role of gods in human life, it is a mistake not to assume that these beliefs had some bearing on the encounters between gods and mortals shown in vase paintings. If we assume that abduction scenes were primarily meant to convey the complex messages about sexuality and gender that we now attribute to them, we may prevent ourselves from seeing other meanings that were more important to the people for whom the vases were made, who still believed in the powers of their gods.

The Last Hours of
the *Parthenos*

Strange as now it may seem, in Greek myth most heroines are young women who have just reached puberty and who are on the verge of leaving that status, either to become wives or mothers and so lose their autonomy, or literally to die.[1] This was the stage, at perhaps fourteen years old, when girls (*parthenoi*) were ready for marriage.[2] When the gods wanted to punish Prometheus for bringing fire to mortals, they created a young woman with "the attractive appearance of a *parthenos*." According to the poet Hesiod, she is dangerous to men because of her beauty along with her "lies and crafty words and a thief's character" (*Works and Days*, 63, 78 = WLGR[3] 54). In his account, her name is Pandora, because each of the gods gave her a gift; she is created by Athena and Hephaestus.

The god Epimetheus takes in Pandora without realizing what he is doing. Then, as the poet Hesiod tells the story, the *parthenos* opens her jar (*pithos*) and lets cares and diseases loose in the world. When a *parthenos* has beauty combined with intelligence and persuasion, her effects can be exciting; they may instead, or in addition, be devastating, as they were for Epimetheus. He was deceived by her beautiful appearance and deceitful words and took her into his house; only then, when it was too late, did he understand that "he had something evil" (*Works and Days*, 89).

The gods know that it is at this time in their lives that women have the greatest appeal. When Aphrodite set out to seduce the mortal Anchises she assumed the form of a *parthenos* (*Homeric Hymn* 5. 82). Like Pandora, she succeeds because she is both beautiful and deceitful; she tells Anchises just what he wants to hear. It is as *parthenoi* that mortal women attract the attention of the male gods or mortal heroes, not simply because they are beautiful but because of their courage, intelligence, or physical strength. Cyrene caught the attention of Apollo because she wrestled with lions (Pindar, *Pythian Odes*

9. 26–28).[3] Atalanta participated in the hunt for the Calydonian boar and defeated the hero Peleus in wrestling. In the Hesiodic *Catalogue of Women*, the hero Melanion is only able to defeat Atalanta by resorting to trickery; he throws golden apples that she stops to pick up (fr. 76 M-W).

Since *parthenoi* were thought to be capable of competing with men, it is not surprising that they can perform acts of the greatest heroism, like volunteering to die in order to save the state or their families.[4] But it is also a time when the *parthenos* is particularly prone to error. According to the Hippocratic treatise *About Young Women* (*Peri parthenōn*), *parthenoi* at the onset of puberty are particularly liable to delusions; some become murderous, others suicidal (*WLGR³* 349).[5] So, the myths often tell of young women who make serious errors of judgment. Like Cassandra or Daphne, they reject the advances of gods, whose passion, however brief, would bring them lasting fame and give them distinguished children. Semele was too ready to believe the lies of an old woman who advised her to test her lover and see that he was really Zeus. The old woman was in fact Zeus' jealous wife Hera in disguise, and when Semele saw Zeus in his immortal form she was destroyed by one of his thunderbolts.[6]

This transitional point in women's lives, when they are ready (and able) to become wives and mothers, is of particular interest because this was considered the main role of women in ancient society. It is what Odysseus wishes for Nausicaa, when he hopes to persuade her to rescue him: "may the gods give you what your heart longs for, a husband and home" (*Odyssey* 6. 180). Even Antigone—a *parthenos* whose independence and courage have brought her into particular prominence in modern times—regrets that she must die before her wedding. She chose to defy the edict of her uncle, King Creon, that her brother not be buried. She was condemned by Creon to be sealed up in a cave. She laments that she is going to her death "unwept, friendless, unwedded" (876). Grave inscriptions bemoan the fate of *parthenoi* who died before their wedding day.[7] Perhaps, as Emily Kearns has suggested, it is this lost potential that makes the *parthenos* so desirable a sacrifice to the gods in times of crisis, because "she is giving up what is due to her in life."[8]

But there is another reason why the young women in the myths should no longer be girls, and that is that the Greeks liked the survivors (or victims) of heroic experience to be able to describe what was happening to them. Heroines express themselves as eloquently as heroes, and suffer as poignantly.[9] Even though most of the literature that has come down to us was written by men, no ancient Greek writer imagined that heroic experience was wholly enjoyable or ever easy for women, any more than it was so for men. Through both their words and actions the myths show how women were an integral part of the society, even though denied political and legal power.[10]

Homer gives us an idea of what an ideal heroic *parthenos* should be in his portrait of Nausicaa. At the moment in her life when "her marriage is near" (*Od.* 6. 27), she is beautiful, outstanding among her female companions, and comparable to Artemis (100–109). But she is also courageous and intelligent. She is willing to remain and talk to the stranger Odysseus, while her companions all run away, and she speaks with sympathy, understanding, piety, and common sense. She admires the stranger, and wishes that someone like him might be her husband (244), but as daughter of the king, she knows how important it is to protect her reputation, and so she maintains her distance. The notion that the two are well-matched is suggested by the poet with great delicacy; each is capable of making a flattering and persuasive speech, and she asks him (and he promises) not to forget her (8. 460–68).

But in other myths, the handsome stranger who appears suddenly in an isolated place turns out to be a god in disguise. Poseidon comes to rescue Amymone, who met him when she was out to find water (Apollod. 2. 1. 4). On a red-figured lekythos in the Metropolitan Museum, he has assumed the form of a handsome man, no taller than she (usually the gods are larger than mortals).[11] Gods are almost always attracted to *parthenoi* just before the time of their marriage, and never after they have taken a mortal husband. Zeus appears to Alcmene disguised as her husband before her marriage to Amphitryon has been consummated (*Shield of Heracles* 35–38). Unions with the gods always prove to bring both joy and sorrow to the mortal *parthenos* because the gods cannot be companions to these women, and so they abandon them immediately. Some women marry mortal husbands, later, and all will bear famous children, who will look after them, so that at end of their lives they can look back on the moment of their encounter with the god with pride and even with pleasure.[12]

Poets like to tell about the moments when the god finds his *parthenos* and carries her off, but what makes the woman memorable and heroic is the rest of her story. When Odysseus visits the lower world, he meets Tyro, who had fallen in love with the river god Enipeus and to whom Poseidon came disguised as the river god while she was waiting beside his streams (Homer, *Odyssey* 11. 236–54). Homer's audience would have known that the rest of the story was not so happy: Tyro's father refused to believe that a god was the father of her twin sons Neleus and Pelias. She was persecuted by her step-mother Sidero. The sufferings of her later life contrast vividly with the glorious setting in which the god made love to her. In a tragedy by Sophocles (nearly all of which is now lost) Tyro describes her misery and loneliness: her hair was cut off, and she compares herself to a young mare

> whom herdsmen have seized in the horses' stables with rough grip, and who has had the yellow mane reaped from her neck; and when she comes to the meadow to drink the water of the river, reflected in the water she sees her image, with her hair shamefully hacked off. Ah, even a pitiless person might pity her, cowering beneath the outrage, as she madly laments and bewails the luxuriant hair she had before. (Sophocles, fr. 659 *TGrF* = *WLGR*³ 32A)

In Tyro's story there is a deliberate contrast between her glorious but brief *partheneia* and the much longer period of her suffering. Comparing herself to a young horse has a special poignancy. When girls are compared to animals that need to be tamed, the poet usually speaks from the man's point of view: "now you graze in the meadows and leap lightly and play; you do not have a skilful experienced rider" (Anacreon fr. 72 = 417 *PMGF*). But Tyro (or rather, Sophocles) concentrates on what it is like to be the animal herself.

It is characteristic of the Greek view of life to call attention to the contrast between the glorious, but brief, moments of beauty or happiness and the long periods of isolation and misery that seem inevitably to follow them. As the poet Pindar puts it, apropos of a young boy's stunning victory in the Pythian Games: "in a moment delight flowers for men, and in a moment it falls to the ground, shaken by a stern decree. Humans (*anthropoi*) are creatures of a day; what is one of them, what is he not? The dream of a shadow. But when the Zeus-given glory comes, a bright radiance lies on men and life is sweet" (Pindar, *Pyth.* 8. 92–97).[13] What enables humans to survive the long intervals in their lives between these bright moments is their intelligence, and this is why heroic *parthenoi*, in addition to being beautiful, must also be wise.

The experience of one heroic *parthenos* can be held up as an example for another. The chorus of old men in Sophocles' drama *Antigone* tells the story of Danae to Antigone, after she has been condemned by her uncle Creon to be shut in a cave to die. She complains that she is being led away to die "without marriage, without bridal, having no share in wedlock or in the rearing of children." She asks why she has been deserted by her friends and the gods

(*Ant.* 916–20).[14] The chorus tells her about the fate of Danae, sealed up by her father in a bronze chamber because an oracle said he would be killed by her son. But Zeus contrives to come to her in the form of a shower of gold. The chorus does not concentrate on the glory of being a "bride" of Zeus but instead emphasizes her afflictions:

> Danae too, endured the exchange of heaven's light for a brass-fastened dwelling, and immured in the tomblike chamber, she was held prisoner. Yet she came of an honoured house, my daughter, and had the keeping of the seed of Zeus that flowed in gold. But the power of fate is strange; neither wealth nor martial valor, nor a wall, nor black ships crashing through the sea can escape it. (*Ant.* 944–54)

The chorus says nothing about what happened to Danae afterwards, because there is no hope that Antigone can escape from her imprisonment or the certain death that must follow it. Danae survived, even though her father put her and her infant son Perseus out to sea in a box. The god saw that Danae and Perseus both landed safely on the island of Seriphos. Significantly, the poet Simonides imagined that during such a voyage Danae would behave with courage and understanding. As the wind stirs up the waves, she does not become hysterical, but rather talks to her son and explains what is happening to them:

> For if the danger were danger to you, you would turn your small ear towards me. But I say that the baby must sleep, and the sea must sleep, and our troubles must sleep; let a change in our fortune come, father Zeus, from you. If there is a rash or unjust word in my prayer, pardon me. (Simonides fr. 38 = 543. 18–27 *PMGF*)

The final lines show that, even though she is very young, she understands completely the limitations of her mortality, despite having been chosen by Zeus.

Other stories illustrate by negative example why it is important for *parthenoi* to realize what was unacceptable for them to do, even if they had been loved by a god. Coronis had intercourse with a mortal while she was pregnant by Apollo.

> She spurned the god in the folly of her mind, and accepted another marriage, without her father's knowledge, even though she had been loved by Phoebus and bore the pure seed of the god. She did not wait for the bride's table, or the cry of sounding wedding songs, which her young women (*parthenoi*) friends

would sing in evening songs. But she fell in love with what was far off, as many others have also done. There are foolish people who despise what they have nearby and look beyond, hunting vanities with hopes unfulfilled. (Pindar, *Pyth.* 3. 12–23)

As a result of her poor judgment, Coronis was destroyed by fire. Creusa, another *parthenos* who was abducted by Apollo, abandoned her baby and felt that the god had deserted her. Years afterwards she remembers how she called out to her mother, as the god led her into a cave (Euripides, *Ion* 881–92). She complains bitterly to Apollo that the child she bore to him "is lost, snatched by birds for their dinner, my son and yours, poor thing; and you play your lyre, singing your paeans." (902–6). Creusa does not realize that meanwhile she has already met the son she thought she had lost, and she would have contrived to have her son murdered had the god not intervened and revealed his true identity.

These myths illustrate the power of *ate*, the delusion that affects all mortal understanding. Delusions are explained in physical terms by the writer of the medical treatise *About Young Women* (*Peri parthenōn* = WLGR³ 349): all human beings are subject to fears and destructive visions that "drive them out of their senses, so that they seem to see particular gods who are hostile to themselves, either by night, or day, or both." According to this physician, more women than men are affected by "that kind of vision" (*opsis*) because a woman's mind is less powerful and smaller than a man's. In his view, *parthenoi* around the time of their first menstrual period are particularly liable to these delusions, which he blames on retention of the menses. He prescribes marriage as a cure.

But in myth, the visions that affect human judgment are understood to be caused directly by the gods. In *Prometheus Bound*, the *parthenos* Io tells how visions in the night (*opseis ennychoi*) told her to go out to a meadow where Zeus would make love to her: "O most fortunate girl, why do you remain a *parthenos* so long, when it is possible for you to have the greatest union?" (647–54). As she tells the story, she refuses to go until Zeus makes her father drive her out of the house, after which her body and mind are "turned around"; her head is horned, and she goes to the meadow leaping, stung by a gadfly. Like the distraught *parthenoi* described by the doctor in his treatise, she wishes to die (582–84). But since the other characters in the play are gods, they can more clearly understand what has happened: they know that

Hera's jealousy is responsible for the madness (592, 704, 900) and that eventually Io will be rescued by Zeus himself, the very god she now blames for her troubles, and she will become the ancestor of a famous race.

According to the writer of the medical treatise *About Young Women*, even when a *parthenos* is not affected by visions (*phantasmata*), "a desire sets in which compels her to love death as if it were a form of good" (*WLGR*[3] 349). He blames this desire on retention of extra blood around her heart. This physician would have diagnosed Antigone's behavior as characteristic of a *parthenos* ready for marriage; she is reckless and willing to defy Creon's edict, which says that anyone who tries to bury the body of her brother Polynices will be put to death by public stoning.

> I knew that I would die, of course I knew, even if you had made no proclamation. But if I die before my time, I account that gain. For does not whoever lives among many troubles, as I do, gain by death? So it is in no way painful for me to meet with this death; if I had endured that, the son of my own mother should die and remain unburied, that would have given me pain, but this gives me none. And if you think my actions foolish, that amounts to a charge of folly by a fool! (Sophocles, *Antigone* 460–70)

Like the *parthenoi* in the treatise, she is in love with death as if it were a kind of good, and she dies by hanging herself, after she is sealed up in her tomb, even though provisions had been left for her (775).

The chorus, Theban elders, explains her conduct by her inheritance from Oedipus: "It is clear! The nature (*gennema*) of the girl is savage, like her father's, and she does not know how to bend before her troubles" (471–72). The chorus sees what has happened as the fulfillment of the family curse, the result of "folly in speech and the Erinys in the mind" (603). They tell her that she was destroyed by her "self-willed passion" (875). Her uncle, Creon, describes her behavior as willful disobedience and speaks of taming her, as one controls a spirited horse with a tight bridle (477–78). Antigone herself believes that by burying her brother she showed "reverence for reverence" (943). Each of them is right, although each sees only part of the picture. Also, Sophocles makes it clear that it is not coincidental that Antigone is a *parthenos* who is about to be married. That is the time in a woman's life when she is most capable of daring action, as he shows in the opening scene of the drama, by contrasting Antigone's reaction to Creon's edict with that of her younger sister Ismene.

These same characteristics help to account for the important roles played in the myths by *parthenoi* who volunteer to be human sacrifices.[15] Some of these myths may derive from prehistoric rituals in which a young woman was offered as a bride to a god. The epic *Cypria* (now lost) told of how Achilles' ghost demanded the sacrifice of Hecuba's daughter Polyxena. Perhaps, as Walter Burkert has suggested, the original purpose of the sacrifice was to make it possible for the hero, even in death, to have his share of the women of Troy—he had seen her when he ambushed and killed her brother Troilus.[16] Certainly the account of her sacrifice in Euripides' *Hecuba* emphasizes her physical appeal:

> when she heard the command from her [Greek] masters, she grasped her tunic from the shoulder, and tore it down to her navel; she revealed her breasts and chest—which was as beautiful as a statue's—and falling on her knees spoke most pathetically: "here is my breast, young man, strike it if you wish, or if you like, here is my throat turned towards you." And he, both willing and unwilling, in pity for the girl, cut the passages of her breath with his sword. And as she died, she nonetheless took much care to fall with modesty, hiding what should be hidden from men's eyes. (557–67)

We should note that whatever the original meaning of the myth, in this account the soldiers resist all temptations to indulge themselves. Her body is treated with respect.[17] Some gather wood to build her pyre. In a vivid departure from normal sacrificial practice, where the bystanders sprinkle the victim with grains of barley, the Greek soldiers cover her with leaves, as if she were a victor in the games.[18] They speak of her courage and nobility of heart (579–80). In his description of her decision to allow herself to be a willing sacrifice, Euripides concentrates on her courage and intelligence. Although her mother urges her to plead for mercy, she volunteers to die: she was once a princess, and does not wish to be a slave, who would be compelled to do household chores and be the bride of another slave (349–68). She will not allow her mother to die in her place, because it would subject her old body to indignities (404–8). To reveal one's breasts is not intended to arouse so much as to elicit pity from a male audience by reminding them of the mothers who nurtured them; by using the gesture in the courtroom, the courtesan Phryne managed to avoid a sentence of death.[19]

Polyxena is willing to be sacrificed in order to avoid what she believes to be an even worse fate, but other *parthenoi* have patriotic motives as well. In Eu-

ripides' *Heraclidae* one of Heracles' daughters, a *parthenos*, offered herself for
sacrifice; in later times she was identified with Macaria, who was celebrated in
cult and had a spring named after her.[20] In the drama, Heracles' children have
fled to Athens to seek protection, and their enemies are besieging the city to
capture and kill them. The oracles have called for a *parthenos* from a noble
family to be sacrificed to Persephone.[21] When no Athenian father is willing
to give up his daughter, Heracles' daughter immediately volunteers. Since all
the children of Heracles received heroic honors in Attica,[22] it may be significant that Euripides chose to portray the heroism of this *parthenos*, rather
than that of one of her brothers; even in a world where men make the decisions and fight in the wars, critical contributions can be made by women.[23]
The gods also at times request the sacrifice of males: Ares demands the sacrifice of Creon's son Menoeceus so that Thebes can be victorious over the Argives (Eur., *Phoen.*, 930–35). The tomb of the last legendary king of Athens,
Codrus, was placed on the Acropolis, in honor of his heroic self-sacrifice in
the war against the Dorians.[24]

But in Athens, the children who were ready to die for the state were
parthenoi. In his funeral oration for the Athenian dead in the battle of Chaer-
onea, Demosthenes cites the example of the daughters of Leos, who offered
to die in order to save their country from the plague (60.29). He also mentions the story of the daughters of Erechtheus (60.27), who died so that
Athens might be victorious in the war against the Eleusinians. The moral issues inevitably raised by myths of human sacrifice made them an ideal subject
for drama.[25] Euripides told the story of this heroic self-sacrifice in his drama
Erechtheus, which now survives only in fragments.[26] We do not have any of
the daughters' speeches, but we know from other sources that, while the oracle asked for only one daughter, her two sisters volunteered to die along with
her.[27] These heroic *parthenoi* were honored as the Hyacinthides in cult and in
dances by other *parthenoi*.[28] If this is the sacrifice that is depicted in the east
frieze of the Parthenon, the heroism of these *parthenoi* was evidently a myth
of central importance to all Athenians.[29]

Perhaps we can infer, from the speeches Euripides gives to Heracles'
daughter in the *Heraclidae*, the nature of the lines that would have been spoken in the *Erechtheus* by one of the king's daughters. Like Polyxena in the
Hecuba, she has personal motives. Should she refuse, no city would take in
her and her brothers, and no one would want to marry her or have children
by her. But she also is motivated by altruistic considerations. She uses the

same kind of arguments that a male hero would make when faced with the same dilemma. If the Athenians are willing to give up their lives to save hers, how can she not give up hers to save them? She wants to be worthy of her great father: "isn't it better to die than to experience insults that are unworthy of me; that might be appropriate for someone else, but not for someone as distinguished as myself" (525–28 = *WLGR*³ 27C). She must die in order to save her family and so that Athens can win the war against her enemies.

In prehistoric myth the sacrifices of *parthenoi* to the goddess Artemis in times of war probably originated as a means of atonement for the blood of the animals killed by human hunters.[30] But Athenian dramas put the emphasis on how the mortal characters react to the harsh requirements of the gods. In Aeschylus' *Agamemnon*, Iphigenia is described as a *parthenos* who "often had sung in her father's hospitable halls" and as a virgin (*ataurotos*) who had lovingly sung the paean after her father had poured the third libation to Zeus (243–46). The detail about her singing at the men's table suggests that Aeschylus in this play imagined her as being too young to be ready for marriage. It also brings out the contrast between her promise and her cruel death —gagged so that she cannot utter a curse, and subdued by force (233–37). The scene is comparable to the portrayal of the sacrifice of Polyxena on an Attic black-figure amphora of ca. 550 BC, in which Neoptolemus slits the throat of a *parthenos* wrapped tightly in a cloth.[31]

In Euripides' *Iphigenia at Aulis* she is old enough to be married, and as a result is better able to take a decisive role in the drama. At first, in an eloquent speech (1211–52), Iphigenia begs her father to spare her. She reminds him of the close relationship they had when she was a child; she asks why she should have to compensate for Helen's behavior. Employing a technique that was used to great effect in Athenian courtrooms (Plato, *Apology* 34c), she calls on her younger brother, Orestes, to weep and ask their father to spare her life. She laments in a long lyric aria the judgment of Paris that caused the war and led to the decision to sacrifice her. Then Achilles arrives and assures Iphigenia (who was to have been his bride) and her mother Clytemnestra that he will not allow Iphigenia to die and will defend her against all the other Greeks. In her earlier speech Iphigenia stated that "anyone who asks to die is insane (*mainetai*)" (1251–52). But now—without warning—she declares that she wants to be sacrificed. As we have seen, her behavior is characteristic of the *parthenoi* described by the Hippocratic writers; she actively seeks death and she displays sudden changes of mind.[32]

Iphigenia's speech is remarkably persuasive, first because she gives no one a chance to prepare any counterarguments, and then because she makes her self-sacrifice into an act of the greatest patriotic heroism, equal to that of the daughters of Erechtheus and Heracles. In her earlier speech to Agamemnon, she had spoken of the expedition primarily as a means of resolving a domestic quarrel. Now she describes it as if it were a battle for the freedom of Greece (even though Greece was not under siege by the Trojans). She explains that all Greece now depends on her, and by dying she can save the army:

> By dying I shall save you from all this, and my fame will be enviable, because I have rescued Greece. For also it is not right for me to act like a coward (*philopsychein*); for you bore me for all the Greeks, not for yourself alone. (1383–87)

In addition, by giving up her one life she can save the lives of many thousands of men—"one man's life is worth more than that of thousands of women" (1394). She sees her sacrifice as means of defending her homeland: she will give her life for Greece, so that Greeks can rule over barbarians, rather than barbarians over Greeks. She ends her speech by claiming that the essential quality of Greek civilization is its freedom: "[barbarian civilization] is a slavish thing; but [Greeks] are free" (1401).

The climax of Iphigenia's speech effectively deflects the attention of her listeners from the serious moral issues she had raised in her earlier speech about the injustice of her sacrifice. Her act now exemplifies one of the highest ideals of Greek culture, which, in the Peloponnesian War, was claimed for themselves by both Spartans and Greeks (Thuc. 2. 8. 4; 37. 2). Confident references to the superiority of Greek civilization were commonplace in contemporary poetry and in public funeral orations.[33] Her rhetoric, with its patriotic claims, makes Achilles even more eager to marry her; but she persuades him to let her "save Greece, if we can" (1420). Her sacrifice will bring "victorious salvation" (1473). Although the original ending of the play has not survived, in the text that has come down to us her conduct wins the admiration of the entire army: "everyone was amazed by the courage and nobility of the *parthenos*" (1561–62). While her father weeps and turns his head aside, she stands near him and says: "I am ready for you. I give my body for my fatherland and for all the land of Greece for you to lead as a willing sacrifice to the altar, since this is what the oracle has decreed." (1553–56).

Here, as in the cases of Heracles' daughter and Polyxena, Euripides (or whoever wrote the final section of the drama) seeks to emphasize the determination and persuasiveness of the *parthenos*. She is described as acting as bravely and boldly as Creon's son Menoeceus, when he volunteered to kill himself on behalf of Thebes: "I shall go and stand on the battlements, and slaughter myself over the dark lair of the dragon, since that is what the seer has indicated, and I shall bring freedom to the land" (*Phoenissae* 1009–12).

I do not think that there is any implication in the *Iphigenia at Aulis* that she is being sacrificed because as a female her life is less valuable than that of her brother Orestes. Her statement that "one man's life is worth more than that of thousands of women" need not be taken as representative of standard Athenian belief in the relative value of male and female lives.[34] In context it is clear that she is exaggerating for rhetorical effect: she is trying to persuade Achilles (who as a character in the play is as vain as he is courageous) to allow her to sacrifice herself. As she sees it, she is saving all of Greece—women, children, and slaves included. Certainly that is what the daughter of Heracles believes she is doing and what Erechtheus' wife, Praxithea, imagines will be achieved if she agrees to allow her daughter to be sacrificed in order to save Athens:

> We have children so that we may protect the altars of the gods and our father-land. Although the city has a single identity, we who live in it are many. How should I destroy all of them, when it is possible for me to offer one life on behalf of all the others? If I know how to count, and can distinguish greater from less, one household in its affliction does not add up to more than the whole city or have equal weight. (Eur., *Erechtheus* fr. 360. 14–21 *TGrF* = *WLGR*[3] 27B)

Praxithea points out that she would not have hesitated to send a *son* into battle: "so I shall give my daughter, who is not mine except by nature, to be sacrificed for the land. For if the city is going to be destroyed, what share have I in my children?" (fr. 360. 38–40 *TGrF*). Her comments make it clear that she regards her daughter's death as equivalent to that of a son in war.

Perhaps it is because modern scholars have been so eager to discover the original purpose of these human sacrifices that they have assumed that they retained some of their original significance in historical times.[35] But whatever their meaning in the past, in Euripides' drama the sacrifice of a maiden is hardly the equivalent of a marriage; rather it has become a heroic service to family and state. As we have seen, there is in the surviving texts no special emphasis on sexuality, but rather a concentration on the full potential of women's heroism. It is significant that the plays containing these examples of self-sacrifice were acted during the long and demanding course of the Peloponnesian War. It is also characteristic of the genius of these writers that they chose to endow these heroic *parthenoi* with the characteristics of real-life young women: passionate temperament, sudden decisiveness, and courageous determination.

Women in the Panathenaic
and Other Festivals

Scholars who write about women in ancient Athens have tended to emphasize the restrictions and limitations of their lives, their confinement within the sphere of the *oikos*, and their exclusion from political life. They point out how these limitations were defined and even celebrated in Athenian myths.[1] But in such assessments of the status of Athenian women, curiously little has been said about the one area of Athenian life in which women played a prominent role in both public and private matters, which is, of course, religion.[2] Yet, it is a feature of women's lives that ancient women themselves were well aware of, at least to judge from a speech by one of Euripides' women characters which was quoted by later writers as evidence that Euripides could and did speak in defense of women.[3] The context is lost, but we know that the speaker of these lines is Melanippe, the daughter of Aeolus:

> Women run households and protect within their homes what has been carried across the sea, and without a woman no home is clean or prosperous. Consider their role in religion, for that, in my opinion, comes first. We women play the most important part, because women prophesy the will of Loxias in the oracles of Phoebus. And at the holy site of Dodona near the Sacred Oak, females convey the will of Zeus to inquirers from Greece. As for the sacred rituals for the Fates and the Nameless goddesses [i.e., the Furies], all these would not be holy if performed by men, but prosper in women's hands. In this way women have a rightful share (*dike*) in the service of the gods. (Fr. 494. 9–22 *TGrF* = *WLGR*[3] 34)

Melanippe can claim that religion "comes first" because in antiquity religion—after survival—was the central aspect of human life. As Peleus says in Euripides' lost drama, "no mortal can prosper without a god's [assistance]" (*Peleus* fr. 617a *TGrF*),[4] and there was virtually no ceremony nor public or private occasion at which the gods' presence was not invoked. What John Graham has observed about women in Greek colonies is also true of that most autochthonous of cities, Athens: "Greek women were essential to a well-ordered Greek community," and therefore, "if we wish to find out the truth about [Greek] women, we only need to think about the gods."[5]

In no civic festival do women play a more prominent role than in the Panathenaia. Young women's ritual cries (ololygmata)[6] and choral dances were an established feature of the pannychis the night before the great procession (Eur., Heraclid. 781–83).[7] Women were responsible for the creation and presentation to Athena of the peplos (cloak) with a tapestry portraying her victory over the Giants (e.g., Plato, Euthyphro 6bc).[8] The peplos, which was offered as a birthday gift to the goddess was the goal and principal feature of the ceremony.[9] The warp for the peplos was set on the loom by the priestesses of Athena, along with the arrhephoroi (schol. Eur. Hec. 467), the young girls selected for special service to the goddess (IG II[2] 1034).[10] The arrhephoroi were considered sufficiently important to be housed, during the term of their service, near the temple of Athena Polias on the Acropolis (Paus. 1. 27. 3).[11] Once the warp was set on the loom, the peplos tapestry itself was woven by a specially chosen group of maidens from aristocratic families, the Ergastinai.[12] Some of the Ergastinai, along with other aristocratic women, might also serve as kanephoroi, bearers of the baskets of barley in which the knives used for sacrifice were hidden, both in the pannychis held the night before the procession (IG II[2] 334.15) and in the procession itself. It is almost certainly the kanephoroi who are portrayed on the right half of the east frieze of the Parthenon.[13]

In the fifth century, serving as a kanephoros was an important indication of a woman's status; the chorus of old women in Aristophanes' Lysistrata boast that after they had served as arrephoroi and performed as "bears" in the festival of Artemis at Brauron, they "were basket-carriers (kanephoroi)—a lovely girl with a basket of figs" (640–45 = WLGR[3] 399).[14] That the kanephoroi were not in any way peripheral—at least in the fourth century—is clear from an inscription that designates the portions of sacrificial meat accorded to various officials: kanephoroi receive the same share as male participants in the procession (LSCG 33 = IG II[2] 334. 11–16).[15] In 305–304 BC, providing golden ornaments for the kanephoroi was a noteworthy liturgy or public service required of wealthy Athenian citizens.[16] By the middle of the century, the wives and daughters of metics (noncitizens resident in Athens) also participated in the procession, not as kanephoroi, since that role was reserved for

Athenian women, but as carriers of water jars (*hydriai*) and sun-shades (*skiadia*) for the *kanephoroi*.[17]

From a modern point of view it is easy to dismiss woolworking as a routine chore that limits women's freedom of movement, but to the ancient Athenians to be selected to work on the *peplos* was a significant civic honor. Even as late as the first century BC, maidens who worked the wool, took part in the procession, and dedicated (at their own expense) a silver cup to the goddess were honored, at their fathers' request, by a public decree (*IG II²* 1034). The purpose of offering a precious woven garment to the goddess is explained in *Iliad* 6, where Theano, a priestess of Athena, selects a *peplos* and places it on the knees of the statue of the goddess and asks her to save the city from harm and to "take pity on the city of Troy and the wives of the Trojans and their innocent children" (6. 302–10). It is an indication of the honor conferred by participating in the Athenian version of this *peplos* ritual that votive statues were set up for *arrhephoroi* on the Acropolis and at least one *arrhephoros* was named for the Trojan priestess (*IG II²* 3634 = *WLGR³* 434).[18] A third-century inscription (*IG II²* 3477) indicates that service as a *kanephoros* was noteworthy. We also know this from a famous incident: in 514 BC, Hippias and his brother Hipparchus refused to allow Harmodius' sister to serve as a *kanephoros* in the Panathenaic procession, and the refusal was sufficient motivation for Harmodius to assassinate Hipparchus (Thuc. 6. 56. 1).

Why were these honors taken so seriously? I do not think it is sufficient to assume that the weaving of the *peplos* and service as an *arrhephoros* were rites of passage that helped young girls mark the transition from girlhood to womanhood.[19] Even if the Panathenaic rites marked a significant development in the lives of some women, they are not particularly female in character. In practical terms, women may have been chosen to make the *peplos* because females ordinarily did the weaving in the household, but there must have been a particular reason why the ritual *peplos* was woven by the aristocratic *ergastinai* themselves, rather than by slaves.[20] The reason is surely that these women were by definition citizens with known ancestry; as the orator Apollodorus points out in his speech *Against Neaera*, to allow a noncitizen to perform secret rites is an act of impiety ([Demosthenes] 69. 77 = *WLGR³* 90).[21]

Also if coming of age, that is, personal development, had been the primary reason for celebrating the Panathenaia and Arrhephoria, why were *public* honors consistently conferred on the participants? The very route chosen for the Panathenaic procession shows that the presentation of the *peplos* was the most public and civic of rituals. The procession started from the Ceramicus district, both the site of the city cemetery and a thriving center of trade; and then proceeded through the Agora, the political and religious center of the city; past the shrine of the twelve gods and the courtroom to the Eleusinion, the starting point of another great civic event, the procession to Eleusis; before continuing to the sacred *temenos* of Athena, the Acropolis.[22] Whatever personal significance there may have been for female participants in other rituals, such as the Brauronia, in the Panathenaia the priestesses are concerned not for themselves but for the city. It is the ritual that distinguishes the women of Athens from the women of other states, such as Delos (Eur., *Hec.* 466–74). And it is significant that it is a ritual in which women and men both play important roles.

As is so often the case, no evidence survives that has told us what the *ergastinai* and *arrhephoroi* themselves would have said about what they were doing, but it is possible to get a sense of the larger significance of these rituals from what was written about and for these women, even if by men. For example, in a second-century AD epigram the *arrhephoros* named after the Trojan priestess Theano is represented as saying that her five brothers and sisters have dedicated her to the goddess, and she prays, "grant that they may reach maturity, and that my parents reach old age" (*IG* II^2 3634 = *WLGR*^{3} 434). In other words, such priestly service is a form of insurance or protection; the original Theano offered the *peplos* to Athena for the protection of the city of Troy as a whole; the wife of the Athenian archon Basileus performs a secret sacrifice on behalf of the city ([Dem.] 69. 73). In religion, even if in no other aspect of civic life, women could and did act on behalf of the state.

To understand the reason why women could assume in the religion of the *polis* a role equal in importance to that played by men, we need only look at Athenian foundation myths. In these, as in cult practice, women are concerned with the welfare of the state. Athena entrusted the care of the baby Erichthonius, who was to become king of Athens, to Pandrosus, a daughter of Cecrops, who had judged the contest with Poseidon in Athena's favor. Pandrosus was instructed not to open the chest in which the baby was kept. But her sisters Aglaurus and Herse opened the chest, saw the baby surrounded by snakes, or even saw that Erichthonius himself was part snake, and threw themselves off the side of the Acropolis. Athena then raised Erichthonius, and he became king of Athens and set up the wooden image of Athena on the Acropolis and instituted the festival of the Panathenaia (Apollod., *Bib.* 3.

14.6).[23] The custom that women of distinction played an important role at the Panathenaia and other festivals as bearers of sacrifical baskets *was* also believed to go back to the time of Erichthonius' reign (Philochorus 328 *FGrHist* F 8).

The sisters were afterwards worshipped as heroines—Aglaurus (and Herse?) in a sanctuary in a cave at the east end of the Acropolis, Pandrosus near the Erechtheion (ibid., 192)—and the celebration of the Arrhephoria was connected with this story, though Pausanias is reluctant to say precisely how (i. 27. 3). In his day (second century AD) neither the priestess of Athena nor the *arrephoroi* knew what it was they were carrying, but they brought something down to the precinct of the gardens of Aphrodite and took something else back up, after which they were replaced by new *arrhephoroi*.[24] Noel Robertson, in his careful study of all the evidence about this strange ritual, has suggested that the *arrhephoroi* carried dough cakes to the sacred snakes in the Ilissus region and brought back a stone wrapped in swaddling clothes, which they placed in the Parthenon.[25] The ritual reenacts in outline the story of the myth and thus demonstrates to the goddess that the community has not forgotten Athena's gift to the city. It thereby secures her protection for another year.[26]

The two young *arrhephoroi* who perform the service must carry out the frightening task of offering food to the snakes; they therefore experience (at least in ritual terms) some degree of danger in the course of caring for the goddess's foster child, or the stone that represents him. It is clear from other myths that there is a significant risk involved for mortals who are required to look after the children of gods, or the mortals that gods favor.[27] Another such incident is celebrated in the myth and ritual associated with the other great Athenian festival, the Eleusinian mysteries. The *Homeric Hymn to Demeter* describes how the goddess Demeter, while searching for her daughter Persephone, disguised herself as an old woman and came to Eleusis, where she was taken into the household of Celeus as a nurse for their infant son Demophoōn (235–91). Initiating a process that would make the child immortal, the goddess anointed him with ambrosia, breathed on him, and at night would hide him "like a log in the fire, without his parents' knowledge" (239–40). She would have succeeded in making him immortal, if the child's mother had not discovered this unusual behavior and, thinking that the nurse was destroying her precious child, stopped it, with the result that he lost his opportunity to become immortal and ageless. The goddess, enraged at being thwarted, took the child from the fire and threw him on the ground, leaving him to his sisters to look after.

The incident makes a dramatic statement about the difference between gods and mortals: mortals are ignorant of their fate and concern themselves with the immediate moment rather than the long-range future.[28] Because of this ignorance, the infant is suddenly cast out from the goddess's care into a harsh and cold environment, and he immediately recognizes the difference: "his heart was not consoled, for inferior nurses held him now" (290–91). As Robert Parker observes in his article on myths of early Athens, Apollodorus in his account of the Erichthonius myth says that Athena had also hoped to make the baby immortal, but, presumably as a result of the intervention of Cecrops' daughters, like Demophoōn he lost his chance.[29] Even if this version of the story does not go back to earliest times and was only later assimilated into the story of Demeter and Demophoōn, the story of the goddess's anger and the death of the interfering sisters warns of the dangers involved in incurring the wrath of the goddess. It also suggests the means by which that anger might be avoided, that is, by retelling the myth and reenacting it in ritual. Parker calls attention to a vase that portrays the daughters of Cecrops, Athena, and Erichthonius in the company of Soteria, the goddess of safety or salvation.[30]

I would add that this association of the birth and nursing of infants, with potential danger and even death for the nurses *and* infants, helps to explain why the *arrhephoroi* and other women are honored for their service to the goddess. According to Euripides, it was the custom for Athenian mothers to protect their babies with golden amulets in the form of snakes (*Ion* 25–26).[31] The practice was started by Creusa, the youngest daughter of Erechtheus. When Creusa abandoned Ion, her infant son by Apollo, to die, she put around his neck two golden chains that bore the form of snakes (20–21). Creusa had inherited the golden snakes from her father Erechtheus, who had in turn received them from Erichthonius. Each contained a drop of the Gorgon's blood, one causing death and the other offering protection from disease (1002–7).

The myths of Erichthonius and of Demophoōn testify to the risk involved in bearing and nursing young children, for both mother and child. They demonstrate the human capacity for harming, through curiosity, jealousy, or ignorance, even the best intentions of the gods: Herse and Aglaurus want to see what is in the casket; Metaneira stops Demeter from putting her child in the fire. The stories also show that even well-intentioned human behavior cannot restore the damage done: despite the kindly care of his sisters Demophoön will never be immortal. But at the same time, the *Homeric Hymn to Demeter* testifies to the positive side of human capacity: the sisters and their mother display great kindness to the old lady who comes to look after their brother, as well as to one another; and despite Metaneira's failure to understand what the goddess was doing, Demeter entrusts to her husband Celeus and his descendants the performance of her secret rites and ceremonies at Eleusis (473–79). By having given birth to Demophoön, even though he must remain mortal, Metaneira has ensured that Demeter's cult will be perpetuated; and his sisters, by caring for him, have assisted in that important process.

As one might expect, women's potential for doing good and evil was never forgotten by the society at large. The *Homeric Hymn to Demeter* offers a moving account of women's best potential for caring for and serving the gods; the narrative also suggests ways in which females have the potential for causing serious damage. In addition to the inadvertent wrong done by Metaneira, in the hymn the goddess herself demonstrates a terrifying capacity for destruction. She holds the seed within the earth so that no crops can grow and men starve and have no sacrifices to offer the gods. Mortal women's capacity for damage is proportionately smaller, but nonetheless present. A mother has the power deliberately to destroy the life of a child, as in the myths of Medea or Ion. The myths tell of abandoned babies, like Ion, and there are the many foundlings whose names were not recorded in myth.

Medea, in famous lines given to her by Euripides, describes the dangers involved in mothering, for both parent and child: "they say that we [women] lead a life without danger inside our homes, while the men fight in war; but they are wrong. I would rather serve three times in battle than give birth once" (*Med.* 248–51 = *WLGR*[3] 28). We are not meant to infer from her lines that ordinary Athenian men thought that women had a safe and easy life, because, as fourth-century gravestones attest, they frequently witnessed and commemorated deaths in childbirth.[32] That women did not die fighting in battles does not mean that their service to family and state was not commemorated or appreciated.[33] In Athens, as in Sparta, the principal service that free-born women performed for the state was producing and raising children.[34] In effect, the cult at Eleusis, with its great emphasis on the nurturing of the young, celebrates women's positive potential: the birth of Demophoön brings great joy both to Celeus and his family and to the goddess, whose cult will thus be continued. Presumably this event was reflected also in the aspect of the Eleusinian ritual that celebrated the birth of the divine male child who represents the wealth of the Earth.[35]

Because they were guardians of the young, aristocratic Athenian women regarded themselves as public servants, since it was only by their efforts as parents that the cults of the gods could be continued and the safety of the state ensured. The first offering of the Panathenaia was given to the goddess Gē (Earth) in her role as *kourotrophos*, "nurse of children."[36] The importance of motherhood is celebrated in Athenian literature, particularly in writing that is both public and patriotic in character. Euripides' *Erechtheus* told the story of how Erechtheus,[37] king of Athens, asked the oracle at Delphi how he might win the war against the Eleusinians and was told that he must sacrifice one of his daughters. Although the oracle placed Erechtheus in essentially the same situation as Agamemnon, who was told that he must sacrifice Iphigenia if the Greek fleet was to be able to sail to Troy, Erechtheus' family responds to the god's command in a way different from Agamemnon's, perhaps because in their case it was their homeland and not an international expedition that was involved.

Only fragments of the *Erechtheus* survive, but fortunately a long excerpt from his wife's speech is among them (fr. 360 *TGrF* = *WLGR*[3] 27B). In this case, unlike that of Clytemnestra in the *Agamemnon*, Praxithea speaks not as an autocrat but as a citizen concerned primarily for the welfare and honor of the *polis*.[38] She regards her children as the property of the state and sees herself, almost as a Spartan mother might, as having made a contribution to the state by bearing them.[39] She agrees without hesitation to give up her child for him to kill and gives her reasoning (fr. 360. 4–5): (1) She is proud to be an autochthonous citizen of Athens (5–13). (2) " . . . it was because of this that I gave birth to children, to protect the altars of the gods and my fatherland" (14–15) (note that in this statement she makes no distinction between male and female children). (3) It would be selfish to refuse to give one life if many others could be saved thereby (16–21).[40] (4) If she had had a son instead of daughters, she would not have hesitated to send him into battle out of fear that he would be killed (22–25). (5) Women should encourage their children to be brave and should not hesitate to send them off to battle, since if they die they will win lasting fame and glory (25–34).

The action of the play allows Praxithea opportunity to show that she can live up to her ideals, since at the end of the play she has lost all but one of her daughters, the others having taken an oath to die with the sister who was sacrificed (Apollod. 3. 15. 4), and her husband has been killed in the battle. The daughter who is sacrificed (we do not know her name)[41] is buried where she died (fr. 370. 67),[42] like Tellus the Athenian in Herodotus' story of Solon and Croesus (i. 30. 5) and like the Athenians who died at Marathon (Paus. i. 32. 4).[43] As Praxithea had predicted, like a male, the sacrificed daughter won, all by herself, the crown of victory (fr. 360. 34–35). The goddess Athena explains *ex machina* at the end of the play that she and her sisters, who committed suicide so as not to abandon their oath to die with her, shall all be honored along with her in cult, because of their nobility (fr. 370. 68–74). Athena also sees to it that their mother is rewarded for her service to the state, by making her priestess of her own cult in Athens (96–97), a significant honor, as we can judge from the long career of Lysimache (Plin., *NH* 34. 76), who was honored by a commemorative statue[44] and who probably served as the model for Aristophanes' *Lysistrata*.[45] The goddess's speech makes it clear that in this case the city has been saved not only by the heroism of men but by the noble self-sacrifice and civic-mindedness of women. There is no suggestion, at least in the surviving text, that the lives of women are in any way less valuable or helpful to the city than those of men;[46] in fact, Praxithea's speech is used by the orator Lycurgus as a paradigm for patriotic behavior: "if women have the courage to do this, then *men* ought to have an incomparable devotion to their country" (*Leocr.* 101).[47]

On the basis of what survives of the *Erechtheus* it is not possible to learn what the daughters of Erechtheus and Praxithea thought about the sacrifice, but we can supply the kind of arguments they might have made from the lines Euripides gives to Heracles' daughter in his drama the *Heraclidae*. In this patriotic and idealistic play,[48] in response to an oracle this young woman offers her own life without hesitation so that the Athenians can win the victory (*Heracl.* 381–499).

The daughter, in a long speech, explains why she should die to save the city of Athens. If the Athenians were ready to fight on her behalf, how could she refuse to die on theirs? To fear death would not be worthy of a child of Heracles. If she were to refuse and then go into exile again, no other city would be willing to receive her on account of her cowardice. Her final and most telling point is that if she did survive, no one would want to marry her and have children by her, and that would not be an appropriate fate for a distinguished person like herself. At that point she asks to be led off to where she must die, to be wreathed in the sacrificial crown and for the ritual to begin. Her message to her siblings is that she is dying on their behalf and that she has made the most glorious discovery of a heroic death (500–534). When her guardian, Iolaus, objects and instead proposes that at least she and her sisters should draw lots to see who is to die, she replies that it is better to have a willing victim like herself than one who is compelled; in a sacrifice the victim must always seem to be willing, so that no pollution results from the sacrifice (547–51).[49] In her final speech to Iolaus, she claims that she will have her heroic death as a possession beneath the ground instead of children and maidenhood (591–92).

For our purposes—that is, for the understanding of the significance for women of Athenian foundation myths—it is interesting that the daughter in this speech twice speaks of dying on behalf of the state and of bearing children as if they were alternatives: first, if she refused to die for Athens, no one would marry her (523–24), and then that her death would be a substitute for children and marriageable maidenhood (591–92). Like Praxithea, she does not hesitate to serve the state because she is female, nor for that reason does she face death any less bravely than a man would in similar circumstances.[50] A clear indication that female heroism "counts" as much as male is provided by Demosthenes in his *Funeral Oration*, which was delivered in honor of the Athenians who died in the battle of Chaironeia in 338 BC. The orator claims that the courageous behavior of Erechtheus and his daughters sets an example for the young men of the Athenian tribe *Erechtheidai* (Dem. 60. 27), that the tribe *Pandionidai* had wished to show the same spirit as the daughters of Pandion, Procne and Philomela, who avenged the outrage done to them (60. 28). Similarly, Demosthenes claims that the tribe *Leontidai* was inspired by the example of the daughters of Leos (60. 29), who offered themselves as a sacrifice to save their country from a plague (Suda, L 261–62 Adler) and whose heroon seems to have been in the northwest corner of the Agora, where it would have been on the route of the Panathenaic procession.[51] As we have seen (ch. 7), the willingness of maidens like the daughter of Heracles and the daughters of Erechtheus to sacrifice themselves is no less heroic than self-sacrifice by males, such as Menoeceus, the son of Creon, who killed himself so that Thebes could defeat the Argives, or Codrus, the Athenian king, who contrived to be killed by the enemy even though they knew that if he died their expedition would be defeated (Lycurgus, *Leocr.* 83–86).[52]

Of course, we have no direct way of knowing what precisely the *arrhephoroi*, the *kanephoroi*, and the other participants had in mind as they enacted their roles in the Panathenaic procession. Since rituals are commemorative as well as practical, and if, as Joan Connelly has recently argued, it is the sacrifice of the Erechtheids that is the subject of the Parthenon frieze, it is clear that all the women in the Panathenaic procession were aware of the heroism of the Erechtheids and of the other services performed by women on behalf of the city, particularly by Praxithea, the first priestess of Athena Polias.[53] Perhaps they, like their fathers, regarded their participation in the procession as a significant public and religious service, without which the state could not enjoy the full protection of the goddess.[54] Undoubtedly also, some share of their attention was turned to practical considerations, such as how they looked and who saw them. In Aristophanes' *Frogs* the participants in the procession of Eleusis intend to have fun in the process of the ritual (407). But participation in the great procession to Eleusis was open to everyone, while to be chosen for the Panathenaic procession was an honor.

There is another significant respect in which participation in the Panathenaia differed from participation in Eleusinian ritual. The rites at Eleusis were directed toward the individual, as the concluding "beatitudes" (*makarismoi*) of the *Homeric Hymn* indicate: watching the rites, even if only from the sidelines, guarantees the individual a better life after death;[55] in addition, initiation was also thought to offer individual protection from hunger and want.[56] The personal nature of these *makarismoi* can be seen by contrast with the prayers offered by women celebrating the Thesmophoria (at least to the extent that we can get a sense of what their prayers were like from Aristophanes' *Thesmophoriazousai*).[57] Women celebrating the Thesmophoria pray for the city of Athens and for themselves (304–5)[58] and for the city's people (*demos*, 352–53).[59] The purpose of participation in the Panathenaia likewise is to seek protection of the deity for the city as a whole. In these two important rituals, each of which serves deities without whose support the city would cease to exist, women play a critical role, and in the Thesmophoria the only role. Melanippe's claim stands up in Athens, as in every other part of Greece: "in the service of the gods we women play a most important part" (fr. 494. 12–13 *TGrF* = *WLGR*[3] 34).[60]

Women without Men

Myths describe women at only particular stages in the ordinary female span of life. Other stages, including some we now consider particularly significant in the course of human development, seldom or never appear in even the most extended narrations. We meet the women in the Hesiodic *Catalogue* at the moment when the god sees them, or at the time of their marriage to a mortal man; or in the case of Alcmena in the *Shield*, both of those at once:

> She came to Thebes with warlike Amphitryon, daughter of Electryon protector of the people; she surpassed all other women in appearance and height; and no one could contend with her in intelligence of all the women whom mortal women bore after intercourse with mortal men. (*Shield* 2–6)

Of her girlhood we hear nothing except that she was the only child left "as a joy to her parents" after her brothers were killed (*Catalogue* fr. 193. 19). But the poet does not describe the effect of this tragedy on her adolescent mind. We learn how she feels only by her actions as a bride: she loves and honors Amphitryon more than any wife ever honored her husband (*Shield* 9–10), but she refuses to sleep with him until he has avenged the death of her brothers (*Shield* 14–18).

"Exceptional" women like the warrior Atalanta or the huntress Cyrene are not exceptions; we learn about them only when they are old enough to be married. Atalanta stops to pick up the apples that Hippomenes drops for her and so loses the race and becomes his bride (fr. 76); Apollo is drawn to Cyrene because of her courage, when he sees her wrestling alone with a lion (fr. 215, quoted by the scholiast to Pindar, *Pythian Odes* 9. 6, II. 221 Dr.). Before she lost the race to Hippomenes, Atalanta killed two Centaurs who tried to attack her; she was one of the participants in the hunt for the Calydonian boar, and there she met the hero Peleus, who wrestled with her and was defeated by her at the funeral games of Pelias (Apollodorus 2. 9. 2). Vase painters liked to portray their match, no doubt because wrestling in antiquity, as now, had obvious sexual connotations.[1] In other myths, heterosexual wrestling serves as a prelude to intercourse. Peleus had to wrestle with and defeat the goddess Thetis before he could marry her and beget Achilles (Pindar, *Nemean* 4. 61–64; Apollodorus 3. 3. 5).[2] Apollo fell in love with Cassandra, who, according to Homer, was the most beautiful of Priam's daughters (*eidos aristēn, Iliad* 13. 365); and as Aeschylus has her describe it in the *Agamemnon*, "he was a wrestler (*palaistes*) who mightily breathed his grace on me" (1206). In other words, he attempted to make love to her (by "grace," *charis*, she means what we might call sex appeal); but her account continues, "I gave my consent and then I played him false" (1208). As his part of the bargain, Apollo had given her the gift of prophecy (1210). When she broke her promise, his revenge was to keep her from ever being believed (1211).[3]

Of course, these women had childhoods, and occasionally a poet in the course of a narrative will describe young girls. When in the *Homeric Hymn to Demeter*, the goddess, grieving for her lost daughter, sits down in mortal form beside the Maiden Well at Eleusis, she is discovered by the four daughters of the king of Eleusis, Celeus: "They came after the water that was good-to-draw, to bring it in bronze jugs to the dear home of their father, four of them, like goddesses in the bloom of youth, Callidice and Cleisidice and lovely Demo and Callithoe, who was the oldest" (*Homeric Hymn* 2. 106–10). They ask the old lady who she is, and when she says she would be willing to work as a nurse in their household, Callidice, who is the most beautiful (*eidos aristē*), answers her (146). Then they run home, after filling their jugs, get their mother's permission, and return to the goddess: "they leapt like deer or calves in the springtime in meadow, satisfying their appetites with food, so they ran, holding the folds of their lovely clothes along the hollow wagon-road, and their hair streamed about their shoulders like the crocus flower" (174–78). The contrast between the lively young girls and the sedentary mourning goddess is most effective. But even this delightful description suggests some of the limitations of the lives of young girls: for safety, they went out in groups, and only to public places, though even at wells girls might be accosted. They use their intelligence, but of course must ask for permission before taking action. By contrast, the old woman "who is excluded from childbearing and the gifts of Aphrodite who loves garlands" (101–2) is safe although sitting alone. Sexuality, or perhaps more accurately, sexual vulnerability, determines the degree of freedom or mobility a mortal woman can have.[4]

For this reason, when a god wishes to abduct a mortal woman, he has to devise a way to remove her from her home or from the group of girls with whom she would ordinarily travel.[5] The myth of the "rape" of Persephone provides a model. At the beginning of the *Homeric Hymn to Demeter*, Aidoneus (Hades) snatches Persephone

> ... when she was playing apart from her mother Demeter of the gold sword, of the shining harvest, with the deep-bosomed daughters of Ocean, gathering flowers, meadow and iris and hyacinth and the narcissus, which Earth made to grow as a snare for the maiden with eyes like buds, in accordance with the will of Zeus, marvelous, and bright, a thing of wonder to all who saw it, immortal gods or mortal men ... it sent forth such a sweet scent that the broad heaven above and all the earth laughed and the salt swell of the sea. And she then in wonder reached out with both hands to take the beautiful plaything. And the earth with its wide ways opened in the Nysian plain and the lord, Receiver of Many, rose up to meet her with his immortal horses, the son of Cronus who has many names. (4–18)

Later in the poem, when Aidoneus sends her back to her mother, Persephone tells Demeter "all of us were in the lovely meadow, Leucippe and Phaeno and Electre and Ianthe, and Melite and Iache and Rhodeia and Callithoe"—she lists twenty-three names in all, including at the end "Pallas, rouser of battles, and Artemis delighting in arrows" (417–24). The catalogue seems intended to assure her mother that in such a large and formidable company she could ordinarily have expected to be safe. Indeed, in another version of the myth, so well-known in Euripides' time that it needed no elaboration, the others came to her aid: "swift as the whirlwind they rushed after her, Artemis with her arrows, and, in her armor with the Gorgon's face, Athena with her spear" (*Helen* 1314a–16).[6]

The techniques employed by the gods in the abduction of Persephone recur in stories about Zeus and mortal women. To seduce Europa, who like Persephone was gathering flowers with her friends, Zeus changed himself into a bull and, as an outline of the *Catalogue* puts it, "exhaled the scent of saffron from his mouth" (fr. 140). Hellenistic accounts add details that make the bull sound if not attractive, at least magical, intriguing, and deceptively harmless, like the narcissus flower.[7] As Io tells her story in the *Prometheus Bound*, Zeus resorts to dreams that urge her to leave her maiden chamber and go alone to the wide meadow of Lerna to meet him (647–54).[8]

The author of the *Homeric Hymn to Demeter* emphasizes that when Hades carried her off, Persephone was unwilling and miserable:

> She cried out loud and called on her father. (21) . . . As long as Persephone saw the earth and the flowing sea with its fish and the rays of the sun, she still hoped to see her dear mother and the family of the immortal gods . . . the tops of the mountains and the depths of the sea resounded with her immortal voice, and her goddess mother heard her, and sharp pain seized her heart. (33–40)

The poet makes it clear that Persephone is frightened not so much by Aidoneus as by the thought of being separated from what was familiar to her—a fear particularly real in her case because she literally will be taken away from the world of light and life to dwell beneath the earth with the dead. Europa, on the other hand, was taken only across the sea, from Phoenicia to Crete, and sent to live with the king, Asterion (fr. 140). Nonetheless, other poets realized that a young girl's reaction to such sudden change might equally well be terror. In the *Prometheus Bound*, Io recalls how Zeus tried to get her to come outside alone so that he could seduce her:

> Visions at night kept coming to my maiden chamber and saying with entreating speeches, "O greatly fortunate girl, why are you remaining a maiden so long, when it is possible for you to have the greatest marriage? Zeus is inflamed for you by the arrow of passion . . . My child, don't despise the bed of Zeus but come out to the wide meadow of Lerna, to your father's sheepfolds, so Zeus' eye may be relieved of longing." (647–54)

The dreams neglect to explain precisely how *she* will profit from the experience, and she does not respond until an oracle comes directing her father to drive her out of his house, "against his will and hers" (663–72).

Homer indicates that Nausicaa has extraordinary presence of mind when she alone remains to confront the naked Odysseus, "who seemed terrifying to them [Nausicaa's companions] because he was fouled with salt, and they fled trembling one after the other to the wagons" (*Odyssey* 6. 137–38). Odysseus knows what to say to reassure Nausicaa, making "a gentle and crafty speech" (148). But Electra in Euripides' play is immediately suspicious when she sees strange armed men before her house. She tells the women of the chorus, "You flee down the road and I will avoid these evil men by running into the house" (218–19).

The myths give the impression that while a young woman can freely associate with other young women and their fathers and brothers, any encounter with an extraneous male is potentially dangerous. Clytemnestra in Sophocles' *Electra* complains that her daughter "is running around loose as usual outside the house" because her stepfather Aegisthus is not at home to restrain her from "disgracing her family" (516–18). Creon decrees that both Antigone and Ismene "be women and not range about outside" (*Antigone* 578–79). Since fifth-century BC dramatists portray young girls' seclusion as normal, at least in the heroic age that their plays describe, it is tempting to think that Athenian girls—at least of the upper classes—also led such protected lives. Menander seems able to assume that his audience too will take it for granted that no respectable girl ought to go out alone. When, in the *Dyscolus*, Cnemon's daughter meets a young man on her way back from the well and he offers to draw water for her, Cnemon's old slave, who sees them talking, naturally assumes that the young man is planning to seduce her and blames Cnemon for failing to provide her with an attendant:

> I don't like this at all. A young man looking after a girl! It's no good. Cnemon, I hope the gods almighty destroy you. You let your innocent daughter go alone into the countryside without anyone to guard her. Probably the boy found out about it and sneaked up, thinking it a rare stroke of luck. (218–26)

The slave then goes off to get the girl's brother. The situation is the same in rural modern Greece. Whenever a girl

> goes out on some errand to gather firewood or carry water, she has a companion go with her. In the popular mind wells and illicit sexual intercourse are linked together. If a man for any reason wants to see the local girls he has only to sit by the well and by and by he will see them all.[9]

In fact, the young man in the *Dyscolus* has fallen in love with Cnemon's daughter, and his intentions are honorable. Although love at first sight may be primarily a convention of romantic comedy and of novels, its existence in so many plots suggests that young men and women of marriageable age were kept segregated as much as possible, and that myth accurately reflects the importance of virginity, or to put it the other way around, of being able to certify paternity.

By concentrating on the moment when a girl catches a man's eye, the myths seem to be implying that motherhood is a woman's most important destiny, and her first encounters with men are more significant in emotional terms than any experience of her childhood. In these stories, the outdoors seems to mark the first stage of separation of the child from her family, as well as the first involvement with the unfamiliar, in all senses of that word. Thus it appears that aside from this first and irreversible break, ancient girls were not perceived to have the developmental problems that even the smallest infants are believed to experience in our society, from the trauma of birth to the first awareness of sexuality, in the period of latency, preteen anxiety, and the stress of menarche. For ancient women, the only one of these problems that counted was menarche, and that in large measure because it coincided with betrothal and marriage. The writer of the Hippocratic treatise *On the Diseases of Young Women* (*Peri Parthenon* L viii 468 = *WLGR*[3] 349) observes that if young women become hysterical it is because the blood in the womb has no place to flow out and so backs up and adversely affects the other organs; the cure, naturally, is to widen the egress from the womb by intercourse with a man and pregnancy.[10] If there were other problems peculiar to young girls, neither the myths nor the medical treatises focus on them.

Of course, the myths as they have come down to us were written by men, who did not necessarily have either the inclination or the opportunity to observe what women felt or thought when they were away from them. The author of the *Homeric Hymn to Demeter* describes women (and goddesses) talking to each other, though only in response to the rather extraordinary situation of the story. Still, we can glean from their conversations a sense of women's strong affections and sympathy for one another and their concern for the relationship between mother and child. The goddess Hecate, herself a virgin, hears Persephone's cries and comes to tell Demeter about them, and then goes with her to ask Helios, who sees all, for more information. Celeus' daughters and later their mother Metaneira comfort the old woman they meet at the well, much as Achilles comforts Priam or Nausicaa reassures the wretched Odysseus, by reminding her that mortals must endure what the gods give.[11] An old woman, Iambe, "with kind intentions," gives Demeter a seat and cheers her up by telling her jokes (194–205). When Demeter in anger abandons the baby Demophoön, his sisters come to the rescue: "one took the child in her arms and held it on her lap, another re-lit the fire, a third rushed on gentle feet to revive her mother" (285–87). When Persephone and Demeter are reunited, Hecate stays beside them and embraces Persephone, and Rhea, Demeter's mother, comes to persuade her daughter to rejoin the company of the gods.

The devotion of Demophoōn's sisters to their mother and their brother, and their kindness to the old lady they find at the well, along with Metaneira's anguish over the treatment of her only son, help to express in terms of mortal experience what the goddesses Demeter and Persephone feel when they believe they are to be separated permanently from each other. Of course, by definition, goddesses cannot die, but Demeter's reaction, when she hears Persephone's cries, resembles closely the responses of Hecuba and Andromache when they see that Achilles has killed Hector and has begun to mistreat his corpse.[12] When Hermes brings Persephone back from the lower world, "as soon as she saw her Demeter rushed towards her like a maenad along the mountainside shadowed by forest, and Persephone opposite jumped down and ran . . ." (385–89). The simile of the maenad, which in the *Iliad* is used to describe Andromache when she is afraid that Hector has been killed in battle (6. 389, 22. 460), here may signify fear as well as joy, since Demeter immediately asks Persephone the question that will determine whether or not they can be permanently reunited, whether she has eaten anything when she was in the world below.

It is this reunion of mother and child, with the promise of its renewal each year, that marks the climax of the poem and that is meant to offer hope to mortals by its celebration in the Eleusinian mysteries. Demeter gets Persephone back, though she is not quite the same Persephone, and only for a portion of the year. Yet they accept this compromise gladly: "for the whole day with one spirit (*homophrona thymon*) they soothed their hearts and spirits with embraces and their spirits ceased from lamentation; they received joy from one another and gave it back in return" (434–36). There is a striking contrast between the goddesses' rejoicing and the description of human existence at the end of the *Iliad* where, as Achilles says, men must live in grief while the gods are without care, and the best a man can get from the two jars on Zeus' threshold is a *mixture* of evil and good (24. 525–30). Did the Mysteries (the rites of initiation into the cult of Eleusis) symbolize that in reunions of parent with child, Persephone with Demeter, Demeter with Rhea and the other gods, lies the secret of the continuation of life, not so much the life of the individual, but of the race? Demeter, when deprived of her own child, immediately seeks to nurse another, and it is this act, and the kindness the young girls show her, that eventually leads to her partial recovery of her own child. It leads also, though the hymn (perhaps deliberately) does not say how, to the birth of a new child, here called Plutus, "Wealth," who according to Hesiod is the son of Demeter and a mortal man, Iasion, with whom she had intercourse in a ploughed field (*Theogony* 971).[13] Thus, mothers' love for their children and women's role in sustaining life are, in various mutually reinforcing ways fundamental to one of the most important and long-lived cults in the ancient world.

Grave inscriptions suggest that women in real life also were remembered primarily for their role in the family. Scenes with women and children are frequently depicted in funeral sculpture and on vases (e.g., Amphareté),[14] but perhaps the clearest expression of the importance of the roles of wife and mother may be found in the memorials left explicitly to those who were denied them. In the sixth and fifth centuries BC, there are many fewer memorials to young women than to young men. Since it was the custom to avoid personal details and to stick to essentials when crafting inscriptions, it is the more striking that parents chose to add that their young daughters had never been married: Phrasicleia (ca. 540 BC) is represented on her tomb as saying, "I shall be called a maiden always. This is the name the gods gave me instead of wife."[15] In tragedy, of young girls who are about to die it is said that they marry Hades, or, less vividly, that a funeral is to be substituted for their wedding—a convention that indicates why an ancient audience would have been moved by the portrayal of Demeter's grief in the *Homeric Hymn*.[16] The same notion is occasionally applied to boys,[17] but in the poems collected in the Hellenistic anthology, which preserve conventional thoughts in their most polished form, only girls are said to marry death.[18] It could be argued that these sentiments represent primarily a man's view of the value of a woman's life, as in the case of the husband who complains that Hades is less discriminating than himself in his choice of wives:

> Nico was the lawful wife of Archon; but Hades has carried her off, who does not take any account of evil or of good. But she was clever and blameless; her husband placed her here with his own hands when she died, the Cretan daughter of Aristocles, a double sorrow, before the pious woman could bear fine children. Let someone else marry a wife like her with a happier fate, a wife who knows how to manage a sound household. (Peek 866, third century BC, Alexandria)

But since several of the epigrams in the *Palatine Anthology* were written by professional *women* poets, like Anyte and Erinna, it may be that women regarded a girl's untimely death with much the same regrets as men:

I weep for Antibia, a virgin. Many suitors wanted her and came to her father's house, where she was known for her beauty and cleverness. But fate sent all their hopes rolling away. (648 G-P)[19]

The only women who are seen to express different notions about their primary role in life, or are seen to complain of it, are the women of epic and tragedy who bring destruction on their families and on themselves, like Clytemnestra, Deianeira, and Medea.

But perhaps it can be argued that if women, rather than men, had written these works, we might have found more support for other, or at least more varied, roles that women could play. It is certainly true that male poets, so far as we know, did not describe intense emotional (and physical) attachments between girls in the same age group (*hēlikia*), such as the ones Sappho describes in her poems:

"The truth is, I wish I were dead." She left me, whispering often, and she said this, "Oh what a cruel fate is ours, Sappho, yes, I leave you against my will." And I answered her, "Farewell, go and remember me, for you know how we cared for you. If you do forget, I want to remind you of violets you set beside me and with woven garlands made of flowers around your soft neck . . . and with perfume . . . royal, rich . . . you anointed yourself and on soft beds you would get rid of your desire . . ." (94 Voigt = WLGR³ 4)

In another poem, another girl has left Lesbos and now

is unique among Lydian women, as the moon once the sun has set stands out among the stars, and her light grasps both the salt sea and the flowering meadows and fair dew flows forth, and soft roses and chervil and melilot bloom. Often as she goes out, she remembers gentle Atthis, and her tender heart is eaten by grief. (96 Voigt = WLGR³ 5)

Has the girl gone off to be married? Or has she simply gone back home after being trained by Sappho to dance in the chorus? Whatever the context of the original poems, their language and situations were adapted by later poets to express the most extreme manifestations of *heterosexual* passion. The poet Erinna speaks with eloquence of a childhood shared with a girl friend and of the sorrow the death of this friend—just after her marriage—has brought her (*Supp.Hell.* 401 = WLGR³ 10). It is impossible to say whether these isolated voices represent what ordinary girls felt about one another or whether they simply demonstrate how (especially in Sappho's case) a great poet can endow the transient experience of adolescent friendships with lasting significance.

When "good" women in Greek epic and tragedy are seen in conversation with one another, they do not speak of their lost childhood or friendships with other girls but of the family. Even though their behavior represents what men (rather than the women themselves) would desire, the male poets should be given credit for allowing the women to play important roles and to make the final, and perhaps most sensible, judgments about the value of the male world.

Starting with Homer, Greek poets portray women as the survivors of the wars men fought for and around them, and in this role the poets allow women to speak the final judgments on human achievement, judgments that, in most cases, would surely be different from men's.[20] Not that Homer meant Andromache's view of war to override or negate Hector's; in the text the two views coexist, although in an irresolvable tension. It would seem that the Greeks *did* care to represent what women thought; even in works about war, the poets sought to give women's views recognition.

Women attain heroic stature in epic and drama by managing, through suffering, to understand and to endure; Hecuba and Andromache attain prominence as characters this way. But it would be wrong to infer that the characteristics of women's heroism—suffering, endurance—are exclusively feminine or that women could not achieve heroic stature by taking aggressive action. As Winnington-Ingram has pointed out, Sophoclean women, especially Electra and Antigone, are ready to assume the initiative and to express to men and women alike a degree of hostility and anger worthy of an Achilles.[21] But women in the myths are for the most part placed in positions where they are powerless to effect any change, and for that reason the poets often chose them to represent the condition of mankind in general.[22]

Euripides uses the same character, Hecuba, to describe both the active and passive forms of "heroism." In the *Hecuba*, she endures the loss of two of her children and then deceives her son's murderer and avenges his death by having her women slaves blind him and kill the murderer's two sons. In the *Trojan Women*, Hecuba simply endures one sorrow after another. She comments in the course of the drama on a series of actions taken by others, but because she is mortal she cannot see that her advice and observations will prove to be correct. At the end of the play, she wishes that she could die in Troy, in contradiction to the advice she gave earlier to Andromache, that living, even in slavery, was better than dying: "Death is not the same as being alive; for death is nothing, but in life there are hopes" (631–32). When she gave that advice, she had only seen her daughter Cassandra led away to be Agamemnon's concubine and learned that her daughter Polyxena had been sacrificed on Achilles' tomb. By the end of the play she has seen Andromache carried off, Menelaus unable to kill Helen, and her grandson Astyanax thrown from the walls. But the audience knows that she will die near Troy and that she will soon be avenged, because they have heard Poseidon promise to "stir up the Aegean sea" so that the Greek fleet will be scattered, and they have heard Cassandra prophesy that Agamemnon will be murdered on his return.

For this reason, the *Trojan Women* cannot really be considered a "peace play," though it has long been fashionable to think of it as a countercultural statement, expressing the horror of a pacifist playwright[23] at the war crimes committed by the Athenians in Melos, and his sympathy for the Melian women and children who were sold as slaves after the Athenians had killed their men.[24] Certainly Poseidon's warning at the end of the prologue is meant to have a general application: "Any mortal is a fool who destroys cities and temples and tombs, the shrines of the dead; when he gives them over to destruction he himself perishes afterwards" (95–97). In the context of the drama it is a warning to soldiers who commit impiety, like Ajax son of Oileus, who raped Cassandra in Athena's temple, not to soldiers who carry out the cruel but necessary work of subduing a potentially dangerous enemy.

Hecuba and all the women in the play are helpless, but by no means complacent. Cassandra reminds Hecuba of the past achievements of the Trojans who have died honorably in war, and she claims that by serving as Agamemnon's concubine she will destroy those whom she and her mother most hate, a boast that the herald Talthybius permits only because he believes her to be insane. Andromache accuses the Greeks of having invented evil barbarian practices because they wish to kill her innocent son; she suggests that they wish to dine on his flesh, as if he were a human sacrifice. Hecuba later adds a mock epitaph that the Greeks killed him because they were afraid of him, "a disgraceful inscription for the Greeks" (1190–91). The killing of Astyanax was a crime far more serious than anything the Athenians are known to have committed in the action against Melos, where the children were not murdered but enslaved (Thucydides 5. 116. 4); the Greek legal formula "children and women" emphasizes the higher priority given to children.[25] Hecuba says to Andromache, before she knows that Astyanax is to be killed,

> Honor your new master, and give him a good indication of your character, and if you do this, you will make friends for the common good, and you could raise this child to be a great hope for Troy, since children born from you might resettle Ilium again, and there might he another city. (699–705)

This possibility of regeneration is one of the "hopes in life" that Hecuba tells Andromache about. Once again we see women advising each other and, indirectly, all of us, about their crucial role in the survival of the race.

Because men and women both regarded mothering as woman's most important role, anyone who wished to make fun of women would portray them as being preoccupied with adultery and abortion. Semonides, in his satire on women, says that only the bee-woman, the one good kind of woman out of a total of ten types, "takes no pleasure in sitting among women in places where they tell stories about love" (fr. 7W, 90–91).[26] Hippolytus, hardly a sympathetic observer, insists that women should have dumb beasts instead of slaves to live with them, "so that they could neither speak to anyone or get a reply from them in turn" (Euripides, *Hippolytus* 645–48); presumably every slave would behave as a go-between, like Phaedra's old nurse. But when poets allow us to eavesdrop on women's conversations, especially in the elegant little hexameter poems that were meant to offer to literate Hellenistic audiences impressions of ordinary life, women are seen chatting about a variety of subjects, mainly practical ones. Some of these concern men, like Herodas' mime about the old procuress who wants a *hetaira* to take a new lover (Herodas 1 = *WLGR*[3] 230), or are substitutes for men, like the woman who wants to find out where to buy the best dildo (Herodas 6 = *WLGR*[3] 228). Some women complain about their husbands' insensitivity and inefficiency:

> He brings me here to the ends of the earth, and gets me a hovel, not a house, so that we can't be neighbors, out of spite, envious brute, he never changes . . . Just the other day I said to him, Daddy, go and buy some soap and rouge at the booth, and he came back with salt, the big ox. (Theocritus, *Idylls* 15. 8–10, 15–17 = *WLGR*[3] 229)

Women paying a visit to the temple of Asclepius admire the sculptures for their verisimilitude:[27] "Look at this naked boy; if I scratch him, he'll bleed, won't he, Cynna?" (Herodas 4. 59–60). Most of these women complain about the laziness and stupidity of their slaves, of everyone's greed but their own, and all go back home again at the end to their husbands: "Dioclidas hasn't had his dinner; he's all vinegar, don't go near him when he's hungry" (Theocritus 15. 147–48). Their conversation can be banal, selfish, and trivial, but then, so can a man's, even when he is talking about love; the Cyclops, pining for Galatea, remarks that he seems to himself to be good-looking, when he looked into the sea, "but to avoid the evil eye, I spit into my lap three times" (Theocritus *Idyll* 6. 35–40).

According to the comic poet Aristophanes, when women gather at the festival of Demeter Thesmophoros,[28] they hold a formal meeting to indict Euripides for making men think that they behave like Stheneboea and other disreputable females in his dramas. The most outrageous "revelations" about adulteresses in action are made (as we might expect) by a man dressed as a woman, who concludes: "And don't we all do these evil things? By Artemis we do. So then why are we angry at Euripides, when we are getting only the punishment that we deserve?" (*Thesmophoriazousae* 517–19). But it would be foolish to mistake this entertaining parody for a serious description of what actually happened at any actual festival of the Thesmophoria, when women met without men present. No one, apparently, thought it worth recording what the women said to each other, just as they did not record what anyone, male or female, said during the actual procession to Eleusis or in any other ritual celebration. What mattered was the eternal, the continuation of the ritual itself. And if we trust a particularly astute observer of the purpose of ancient cult, the third-century BC poet Callimachus of Cyrene, the point of the Thesmophoria was to ensure Demeter's continued protection of human beings and of crops. Callimachus of course only saw and explained what women did in the public part of the festival:

> As we walk through the city without sandals and with our hair unbound, so we shall have our feet and hands unharmed forever. And as the basket-bearers bring baskets full of gold, so may we acquire boundless gold. The uninitiated women may proceed as far as the city hall; the initiated right to the goddess' temple, all who are younger than sixty ... (*Hymn* 6. 124–30 = WLGR[3] 394)

What did the initiated women do and say inside the temple? Aristophanes tells us that the women prayed to divinities, like Demeter and Persphone, who would help them in their present lives as wives and mothers, to Plutus the god of wealth, to Calligeneia the goddess of fair progeny, to the goddess Kourotrophos the Sustainer of the Young, to Hermes, and to the Graces (*Thesmophoriazousae* 295–300). In the rites at Eleusis at least, there was some celebration of the birth of Plutus, as the *Homeric Hymn to Demeter* suggests:

"Blessed is the mortal whom the two goddesses eagerly love; they will then send Plutus to dwell with him in his great house, Plutus who gives wealth to mortal men" (486–89).[29] We know that at Eleusis at least Demeter was encouraged to eat, and thus to renew her care for human life, by Iambe's telling her jokes (203), an event that was commemorated in the ritual jesting of the Eleusis festival. Since it is very likely that these jokes were indecent,[30] once again the evidence seems to suggest that women were in private, as in public, primarily concerned with the process of becoming wives and mothers.

Nor does the information we have about other rituals celebrated by women suggest that any of these occasions were used to protest about women's role or the way the men were running the world. When in Aristophanes' *Lysistrata* the herald complains that the orator Demostratus' requests to the Assembly for ships for Sicily and men for Zacynthus were interrupted by his wife's lamentations for Adonis, he is merely complaining that women are notoriously self-indulgent (*exelampen hē truphē gynaikōn*) and can't abandon their amusements to pay attention to the serious business of the men (387–96). At this festival, as Sappho describes it, the women lamented not their own fate, but Adonis' short life and the brief span of his romance with Aphrodite: "Gentle Adonis is dying, Cytherea, what should we do? Beat your breasts, maidens, and rend your chitons" (fr. 140 Voigt).[31] Part of the appeal of the story lay in Adonis' age; he was young enough to be a son but old enough to be a man: "His beard is still downy, so his kiss doesn't scratch" (Theocritus 15. 130). The celebration itself provided opportunity for flirtation. In Menander's *Samia*, a young man explains how he was able to observe the Adonia:

> Since the festival provided much opportunity for fun, as usual, I was present, alas, as a spectator. The noise inspired in me a certain wakefulness; I carried some gardens up to the roof; the women were dancing, and went off separately to celebrate all night. I hesitate to say what follows. I guess I'm ashamed. It's no use. But I'm still ashamed. The girl is pregnant. (41–49)

The gardens he mentions consisted of seeds planted in pots that grew quickly and died, like Adonis himself.[32] So it seems that the Adonia, like the Thesmophoria, were concerned primarily with the continuation of life:

> Dear Adonis, the story is that you alone of the gods come here and go to Acheron . . . be favorable, dear Adonis, and come again next year. You have made us happy by coming this year, and when you come again, you will be welcome. (Theocritus 15. 136–44)

The lamentations for lost girlhood in women's poetry may have a function analogous to the ritual for Adonis in that they help place particular experience into a general pattern and enable women to prepare for a major transition in their lives. Homosexual experience is in one sense a preparation for heterosexual experience; the same goddess, Aphrodite, offers satisfaction in both, and in Sappho's poem (fr. 2 Voigt = WLGR³ 1) we cannot tell whether the sleep that comes down from the rustling leaves in the temple grove of Aphrodite follows fulfillment from hetero- or homosexual relationships. In Alcman's *partheneion* (fr. 1 PMGF = WLGR³ 401), the singers state that it is the leader of their chorus who arouses them (*teirei*, 77), but at the same time they describe her in ways that would appeal no less to men: Hagesichora is like a horse among the herds, strong, prize-winning, with thundering hooves, a horse of the world of dreams (45–49).[33] Cyrene catches Apollo's eye when she is wrestling with a lion; Atalanta had defeated Peleus and was able to run faster than any man when she was caught by Hippomenes' trick with the apples (Hesiodic *Catalogue* fr. 43A).[34] It is (as we have seen) at the moment when a woman seems most singular even to other women that she most appeals to men. Sappho relates in her poem about the girl who went away, "now she is unique among Lydian women, as the moon once the sun has set stands out among the stars," whose light makes the meadows bloom (fr. 96. 6–14 Voigt = WLGR³ 5).

If one of these outstanding women managed to avoid the god's eye, or persuaded her father not to marry her to a mortal man, what could she expect to do for the rest of her life? For goddesses, virginity guaranteed independence, but goddesses had the power of Zeus to defend their immunity from the works of Aphrodite. Two of the virgin goddesses are concerned with what was ordinarily man's work. Athena deals with wars and the work of Ares, conflicts and battles and glorious works; she first taught mortal carpenters to make war chariots and chariots worked with bronze (*Homeric Hymn* 5. 8–13). Artemis enjoys bows and arrows and slaughtering wild beasts (16–20). Both Athena and Artemis also share in women's activities, like weaving (14–15) and dancing (19–20), and other virgin goddesses have existences that more closely resemble mortal women's. Hestia is allowed by Zeus, in exchange for marriage, to sit in the midst of the household as well as in all the temples of the gods, and to take the fat from the hearth (29–32). Hecate, according to Hesiod, like Demeter, has control over the fertility both of humans and of the earth and also over the success of men's livelihoods

(*Theogony* 416–49). But human virgins, because they are mortal, have no supernatural protector and will grow old and have none of these powers or privileges. Artemis can stand "head and forehead" above all the nymphs of the field, so that her mother can rejoice in her heart and she herself can be easily recognized; but if Nausicaa, whom Homer likens to Artemis, had encountered a god or even a man less honorable than Odysseus, what would she have been able to do to defend herself (*Odyssey* 6. 105–8)?

For a mortal woman, maintaining celibacy required keeping a low profile, staying in the crowd of other women, doing women's work, like the several unattached females who took refuge from the war in the house of their relative Aristarchus, who could not afford to feed them, until Socrates advised him to put them to work, as one would female slaves (Xenophon, *Memorabilia* 2. 7 = WLGR[3] 236). An old woman, as we have seen in the story of Demeter, can go about by herself. The priestess of Apollo at Delphi, an old peasant woman, can go outside alone, as we see her at the beginning of Aeschylus' *Eumenides*. But she too is helpless in an emergency: "an old woman afraid is nothing, no better than a child" (38). Presumably a virgin or old woman was chosen to be Apollo's priestess[35] because it was necessary for her to be completely subject to him, like a wife, in order to be able to prophesy. Cassandra, who would not submit, was doomed not to be believed. For the Vestal Virgins also, virginity was a form of service as well as of reward (Plutarch, *Numa* 9–10 = WLGR[3] 408), as for the goddess Hestia/Vesta herself, in exchange for marriage. As the Lemnian women discovered, when they murdered their sons and husbands and sent the king off their island, they could run the country for a while, but literally and figuratively could not manage long without men: they needed an army in case of invasion, they needed children once the young women began to grow up, they needed someone with the strength to plough the fields (Apollonius of Rhodes, 1. 675–76). No ancient author, male or female, fails to attribute to women their share of intelligence, but none suggests that it is possible or desirable for women to adopt any pattern of existence other than those traditionally assigned to them, or, to put it another way, to live in a world without men.

Wives

Before the civil rights movement of the 1960s, assessments of women's lives in the ancient world tended to single out the accomplishments of certain exceptional women.[1] But it does not follow from the existence of extraordinary lives that most women found such roles attainable or desirable. Virtually all the ancient women who accomplished something notable were aristocrats, and almost always related to an important man. Artemisia of Halicarnassus, a sea captain (Herodotus 8. 87–88 = $WLGR^3$ 164), and Cynna, an Illyrian strategist (Athenaeus 13. 560f.), had "professions" because their fathers were kings. Cynisca of Sparta in the early fourth century BC claimed to have been the first woman to have won the four-horse chariot race (*AP* 13. 16 = $WLGR^3$ 202), but she too was daughter of a king; another female chariot race winner was Bilistiche, the *hetaera* (or mistress) of Ptolemy Philadelphus, king of Egypt (*POxy* 2082 = $WLGR^3$ 203).[2] If women like Sappho and Corinna were able to be poets, it was in large measure because women could compose verse at home without moving outside the ordinary routine of women's existence.[3] Aristocratic women in all periods composed poetry: the Argive poet Telesilla was said to have studied music because she was sickly (Plutarch, *Moralia* 245c = $WLGR^3$ 160); we have a papyrus fragment of Erinna's epic poem "The Distaff" (*Supp.Hell.* 401 = $WLGR^3$ 10), and epigrams by several Hellenistic women are preserved in the Greek anthology.

But I doubt that there is any justification for assuming that the majority of ancient women would have wanted to emulate these accomplishments, even if they had had the opportunity. Many documents indicate that many women were content to lead a conventional existence, and to win praise from men for doing so. The definition of a good woman is clearly set forth in Semonides' celebrated satire (fr. 7W = $WLGR^3$ 57). In this poem, as so often, the right is defined primarily by means of the wrong. One laudable type of female, the woman supposedly descended from a bee, is described after a list of eight despicable women; and since the bee woman herself is followed by reflections on women's deceptiveness, the poet leaves the impression that a good woman is (to say the least) exceptional, because she occupies only 11 of the surviving 118 lines of his poem:

> Another is from a bee; the man who gets her is fortunate, for on her alone blame does not settle. She causes his property to grow and increase, and she grows old with a husband whom she loves and who loves her, the mother of a handsome and reputable family. She stands out among all women, and a godlike beauty plays about her. She takes no pleasure in sitting among women in places where they tell stories about love. Women like her are the best and most sensible whom Zeus bestows on men. (83–93, tr. Lloyd-Jones 1975)

Some of this positive description is expressed in negative terms: "On her alone blame does not settle" (84) and "she takes no pleasure in sitting among women in places where they tell stories about love" (*aphrodisious logous*). Also, except for the phrase "She grows old with a husband whom she loves," nothing is said about how she feels; the rest is stated from her husband's point of view: she causes his property to increase; he loves her; she has fine children; she stands out among all women (the phrase implies heroic stature). If such women are judged best and "most sensible," it is because their lives are dedicated to serving their husbands and maintaining their households. It is significant that the bee woman is praised for not talking with other women about sex, first because that would encourage infidelity, and secondly because it would take her away from work or even send her outside the home in order to meet with other women.

It is easy enough to understand from Semonides' poem why her husband loves her, but why does *she* love her husband? Since Sappho, the only woman poet we know about who was roughly contemporary with Semonides, did not write poetry about women's affection for men, we must turn to poetry by men for information. I suggest that we begin with characterizations of Penelope[4] and Alcestis; they are the archetypes of good women, at least according to a husband in a fourth-century BC comedy, who can only come up with those two names to set against a long list of bad women (Eubulus, frs. 77, 115 PCG = WLGR[3] 63). Penelope conforms to Semonides' positive criteria: she remains faithful to her husband for twenty years, despite constant temptation; she stays in her rooms in the palace, except for brief public appearances when she is accompanied by maids or her son Telemachus. She does not associate with other women (except for the female slaves who attend her). Her suitors acknowledge that she is superior to all other women, particularly in her intelligence:

> She keeps in mind the gifts that Athena lavished upon her, an understanding of fine workmanship, good sense, and guile, such as we have never heard of in a woman in the past, the Achaean women of old with their lovely tresses, Tyro, Alcmene, and Mycene with her beautiful crown, none of these is like Penelope in intelligence. (*Odyssey* 2. 116–22)

This description, which is offered by the suitor Antinous, suggests that hers is a special kind of intelligence, involving plotting and planning that seems to men devious because they cannot immediately understand it. As Semonides said, "In the beginning the god [i.e., Zeus] made the female mind separately." But Penelope uses her particular intelligence to remain faithful to her husband, first by tricking the suitors for three years by unraveling at night the shroud she was weaving (in Antinous' words, "this she plotted unfairly," 2. 122) and then by testing Odysseus to see if he really is her husband, by pretending not to know the secret of the construction of their marriage bed (23. 177–80). Certainly by the end of the *Odyssey* we understand why Odysseus was willing to give up Calypso and a promise of immortality to return to Penelope, even though, as he says to Calypso, "I myself know very well that wise Penelope is inferior to you in appearance and stature, for she is mortal, and you are immortal and ageless" (5. 217). But why does Penelope wait for Odysseus?

In part, it is because Odysseus, as Penelope herself says, was "such a great man . . . who is famous throughout Greece and in the center of Argos" (1. 343–44). In part also, it is his house, which he himself helped to build, "so beautiful, filled with wealth, which I think I shall remember even in my dreams" (21. 77–79). But there is also the matter of reputation: she wonders if she "should stay here with my son, and keep everything as it is, my property, my slaves, and my big home with its lofty roof, respecting my husband's bed and the opinion of his people" (19. 524–26). As she says after she has recognized Odysseus, "Even Argive Helen, daughter of Zeus, would not have slept with a foreign man, if she had known that the warlike Achaeans would bring her home again to her fatherland" (23. 218–21). Helen's action was wrong because it caused suffering and death for so many; Penelope also calls it "folly" (*atē*, 222) because it seems clear to her that Helen would not have left Menelaus had she been free to remain; as Homer shows in Book 4, Helen has no complaint about her life with Menelaus after the Trojan War in his fine house in Sparta. It is possible to infer from Penelope's remarks that a woman has reason to be faithful if her husband is a person entitled to respect and if she herself is well treated; certainly both she and Helen, because of their husbands' wealth and position, live in security and comfort.

What else does Penelope expect (and get) from Odysseus? First of all, proof that she in her way is as important to him as he is to her. She does not demand strict fidelity; she and Helen do not object to their husbands' liaisons with other women, so long as they are temporary; Odysseus tells Penelope about Circe and Calypso; Menelaus is able jointly to celebrate the marriage of Hermione, his daughter by Helen, and of Megapenthes, his son by a slave woman (4. 4). But, as Penelope's questions about their bed indicate, it is important that they sleep together, also that he tell her immediately what he knows about his plan for the future, since that will affect both of them. Odysseus listens to her describing her experiences with the suitors before he tells her about his journey. But Penelope does not question his right to tell her what to do or seek to persuade him not to set out again for new battles and journeys, since it is success in these endeavors that defines his importance in the world, and to her, and she counts on him (in a society without police and law courts) to protect her against their many enemies.

Alcestis, at least as Euripides portrays her, lives in a world that is not presently threatened by human violence; yet her attitude toward her husband, Admetus, is much the same as Penelope's to Odysseus. She is classified as "good" because she offered to die in her husband's stead, when no one else, not even his aged parents, would volunteer. Euripides' drama takes place on the day of her death. Like John of Gaunt in *Richard II*, she speaks portentous last words on stage, but Euripides also conveys to us her more private thoughts, by having one of her female slaves report to the chorus what Alcestis has said in her own quarters before coming out of the palace for the last time to be seen by the community at large. These private words and actions conform to the pattern of behavior that society (to judge from Semonides) would approve. She washes and dresses in special clothing (like Socrates before he drinks the hemlock, in consideration for the women who must prepare her corpse for burial). Then she prays that her children both make good marriages and live full lives; she sees that the appropriate myrtle boughs are placed on the altars. She does all this calmly, without shedding a tear. But even when she does break down and cry, her thoughts are for her husband, her children, and her household. First she addresses her marriage bed: "Here I lost my maidenhood to this man, on whose behalf I die; farewell, I don't hate you; you have destroyed only me, for since I was reluctant to betray you and my husband I am dying. Another woman will possess you; not more chaste, but perhaps more fortunate" (177–82). Then she throws herself on the bed, weeping, then walks about the room only to throw herself on the bed again; her children cling to her, and she embraces them; all the slaves are weeping, but she gives her hand to each and speaks to every one of them, even the most lowly. In all this time she does not confide specially in another woman, not even a sister or a nurse; her sorrow, like Penelope's, is private, and we learn of it only at second hand.

Alcestis' public appearances, like Penelope's, are conducted with dignity and control. After she is carried outside, she addresses Admetus and reminds him of the reasons she decided to die for him, but again without complaint. She could have lived and married another king, but she did not want to live without him, with orphaned children, since she had had "all she needed to be happy" (289). Nor did she want to deprive his parents, who were too old to have children, of their only son. She asks Admetus only one favor, not to marry again, because she does not want her children to have a stepmother, who would wish to put her own children ahead of them (305–7). She is not asking him to be celibate or not to take a concubine but specifically not to acquire another legitimate wife, and Admetus himself readily agrees "even in death you will be called my wife" (329–30). It is testimony of his remarkable devotion to her that at the end of the play he is reluctant even to accept a concubine, when Heracles appears to be offering him one.

In a society like ours, where the lives of male and female have, under the law at least, an equal value, Admetus might seem unduly selfish in allowing Alcestis to die for him. Some[5] have even sensed hypocrisy in his request to her, "Do not betray us" (202, 250, 275), even though that is what survivors might say to the dead person on grave inscriptions (e.g., "You rush off to the gods, Domnina, and forget your husband," Pleket 26 = WLGR³ 171). But it is important to note that Alcestis, even behind the scenes, is never represented as having hesitated over her decision or as having complained about it. Admetus himself does not question her choice until after his father has accused him of murder and cowardice and Alcestis herself has been placed in her tomb; then Admetus admits that he now understands (*arti manthanō*, 940) that he will be unhappy without her wherever he goes, that he can't bear the thought of another woman or the criticism that he was a coward. Some scholars have interpreted this speech as a confession of guilt, but Admetus never says that he thought he should have died instead of she, just that with Alcestis dead he does not want to go on living, which is quite a different matter.

Aside from the practical reason (in terms of Athenian inheritance laws) that as the only surviving son Admetus was the person who could serve as guardian of the family position and property, why does Alcestis readily agree to die for him? Euripides could have chosen to portray her as a morbid, impulsive psychotic, but instead he makes it clear that her decision was undertaken deliberately and rationally. Like Penelope, she would have been able to marry again: "I could have the man I wanted from among the Thessalians and live with a ruler in his prosperous home" (286). When she says she had from Admetus everything she needed to make her happy, we can assume that Admetus at least fulfilled the basic roles of protector and provider, and Euripides also shows us in the drama that he was justly renowned for his hospitality and generosity. Whether these qualities were in themselves responsible for Alcestis' devotion to him, Alcestis herself does not say; but her dialogue with him indicates that she trusts him to do as he promises, and her actions when she is alone inside the house show that she is reluctant to leave the marriage bed that (in her words) "has destroyed" her (179). It is possible that she is afraid that a second time she might be less fortunate—as Medea puts it, "everything depends upon whether you get a bad man or a good one" (235–36); but Alcestis, even in her soliloquy, says nothing like that, nor does she speak (as a Puritan woman might) of doing her duty.

Euripides apparently could count on his audience's being able to believe that married couples could be as devoted to one another as Admetus and Alcestis. Inscriptions from gravestones indicate that such sentiments were at least conventionally expressed, if not actually felt. There is, for instance, the inscription on a fourth-century BC *stele* that shows a woman holding out her hand to her husband, with verses that awkwardly represent a dialogue between them:

> Farewell, tomb of Melite, a good (*chrēstē*) woman lies here. Your husband Onesimus loved you and you loved him in return (*philount' antiphilousa*). You were the best (*kratistē*), and so he laments your death, for you were a good woman.

And to you farewell, dearest (*philtate*) of men; love (*philei*) my children. (Kaibel 79 = WLGR³ 237)

Alcestis' last request is virtually the same. Admetus implores her: "Lift up your head, don't leave your children." Alcestis replies: "I wouldn't if I could help it; children, farewell" (388–89, cf. 302–3).

It is understandable that children would provide the principal reason for a married couple's devotion to each other, but even when there are no offspring or their presence seems to be unimportant, strong ties of affection seem to have existed between spouses, and even sexual attraction (though some contemporary scholars imply that ancient Greek men had little physical interest in their wives).[6] In the *Suppliants* Euripides describes Evadne and Capaneus virtually as lovers. She refuses to abandon him in death (*prodousa*, 1024, the same word Admetus used of Alcestis), and throws herself on Capaneus' funeral pyre: "I will join my body to my husband in the burning flame, placing my beloved flesh next to his" (1020–21); "hallowed is the bridegroom who is softened by the guileless attraction of his noble wife"[7] (1029–30).

There are indications that similar devotion existed outside the context of the ideal marriages of myth, even in the ordinary marriages arranged by Athenian fathers for their children. In a fragment of a lost comedy, a young husband who thinks his wife has betrayed him explains that "since the night I was married . . . I haven't been away from bed a single night, away from my wife . . . I wanted (*erōn*) her, honestly . . . I was tied to her by her noble character and her unaffected ways; she loved me (*philousan*) and I cared for her (*ēgapōn*)" (fr. PCG VIII 1084 = WLGR³ 238). Three of the Greek words for love occur in this passage, *eraō*, denoting sexual passion, *phileō*, love for family and friends, and *agapaō*, affection. In his commentary on this fragment, Hugh Lloyd-Jones observes that this appears to be the only instance in extant Greek literature where the three words "recur at such short intervals, in each case referring to love between a man and a woman, and indeed between a husband and a wife"; but it is possible that if more literature about ordinary life had survived, this concurrence, even in the context of marriage, of all forms of love would no longer appear unique.[8]

Another papyrus fragment indicates that wives sometimes displayed extraordinary affection for a husband who seems to lack the trait one might deduce from myth was the single most important male virtue—wealth. The fragment preserves part of a speech by a wife to her father; she is begging him not to take her away from her husband, who is bankrupt, in order to marry her to a richer man:

> Explain to me how, by whatever he has done, he has done me wrong. There is a covenant between man and wife; he must feel affection for her (*stergein*) always, till the end, and she must never cease to do what gives her husband pleasure. He was all that I wished with regard to me, and my pleasure is his pleasure, Father. But suppose he is satisfactory as far as I am concerned but is bankrupt, and you, as you say, now want to give me to a rich man to save me from living out my life in distress. Where does so much money exist, Father, that having it can give me more pleasure than my husband can? How can it be just or honorable that I should take a share in any good things he has, but take no share in his poverty? (fr. 1000 *PCG* VIII 13–26 = *WLGR*³ 38)[9]

Since the rest of the play is lost, we do not know anything about this wife's circumstances other than what she tells us in this speech; here she is deferential to her father, disparaging her own intelligence and suggesting that perhaps only in the case of her own affairs may a woman know what is right. To judge from her words, much of the "pleasure" she derives from marriage comes from obedience and an opportunity to serve; also she makes it clear that her husband has been good to her in respects other than financial.

This wife's attitude reflects a new emphasis—at least in drama—on human relationships. Among families with property, marriages had been arranged primarily to ensure the safe transmission of property: a man in his will could leave his wife to a freedman or a daughter to a close friend; if a man died without male issue, his daughter was required to marry his closest male relative, even if that man had to leave his wife for her to do so.[10] Euripides in his *Andromache* demonstrated that marriages arranged for political or financial purposes could be less than successful: "A sensible man will arrange to marry children from a noble house to noble people, and not have any desire for base marriages, not even if they bring vastly rich dowries to his house" (1279–82). The devoted wife in the papyrus fragment, instead of discussing inheritance laws, speaks of "a covenant (*nomos keimenos*) between man and wife; he must feel affection for her always, till the end, and she must never cease to do what gives her husband pleasure." The Greek word *nomos*, here translated as "covenant," is usually translated "law" but *nomos* does not so much denote a law in our sense of the word, that is, a statute or the carefully documented precedent of court decision. *Nomos* is better understood as "practice" and must be translated differently in different contexts.

The *nomos keimenos*, or the enduring practice that the wife here describes positively, is expressed in tragedy in negative terms, and we can understand what she means in saying that a husband must always feel affection for his wife by comparing how Hermione and Deianeira complain that their husbands have ignored them and given a wife's status to a concubine: "Husbands who want to live in a happy home show affection (*stergousin*) by keeping their eyes on one Cypris [i.e., sexual relationship] in their marriage" (Euripides, *Andromache* 179–80). In reply to Hermione, Andromache describes the second half of the covenant, how "a woman must, even if she has been given in marriage to a bad husband, feel affection (*stergein*) for him, and not hold a contest of wills" (213–14); "It is not beauty, but excellence that makes a husband happy" (*terpousi* 207–8). Andromache claims that she "shared" (*synerōn*) Hector's sexual misadventures with him, and often nursed his bastards herself, so as not to show him any bitterness, "and by so doing I won my husband over by my excellence" (222–27).

Euripides' Andromache is perhaps exaggerating in order to emphasize the justice of her cause against Hermione—in the *Iliad* it is the priestess Theano, not Andromache, who brings up her husband's bastard son "in order to please him" (5. 70). But still, a wife had no choice under the law (or *nomos*) other than to be tolerant of her husband's sexual relations with other women, so long as her status as wife was recognized. As for deference to her husband's will, the wife in the papyrus fragment illustrates that this is the *nomos* by her insistence that her father knows best and must make the decision, even though she does not agree with him. That she is able to express her point of view within the context of that *nomos* suggests that the heroines of tragedy, like Andromache or Alcestis, are not stepping out of line when they politely, but eloquently, speak to the men in their families. The male speaker of Lysias' oration *Against Diogeiton* recounts how a widow not only knew the terms of her husband's will but was able effectively to argue before her male kinsman how her own father had failed in his duties as guardian (32. 13–18 = WLGR³ 82).

These passages from drama and comedy suggest that more women, from the upper classes at least, managed to express themselves and influence their male relatives under Athenian "law" or *nomoi* than the simple restatement of the laws in trials or treatises would lead us to believe.[11] Law by nature emphasizes prohibition and so fails to stress the positive; the arguments for chastity, for example, are always stated negatively:

> if she breaks the law (by committing adultery) she wrongs the gods of her family and provides her family and home not with its own offspring but with bastards. She wrongs the true gods, etc. . . . she wrongs her own fatherland because she does not abide by its established rules . . . She should also consider this, that there is no means of atoning for this sin; no way she can approach the shrines or the altars of a pure woman, beloved of god. (WLGR³ 208)[12]

Between the lines one can discern the practical reason why adultery could cause a serious problem in a society without sure contraception and where citizenship (especially in Athens) was determined by the citizenship of one's parents. The "law" about adultery implies that a wife by her chastity performed a valuable service to the state; in Athens a woman caught in adultery must not only be repudiated by her husband but is forbidden to offer public sacrifice; a foreign woman and a prostitute is similarly excluded (we learn this from the case of the notorious Neaera's daughter Phano, who was both: [Demosthenes] 59. 38 = WLGR³ 90).[13] Fifth- and fourth-century BC law forbids a woman to make a will or to own (at least in Athens) property other than her own clothes and jewelry, but the system also guarantees her financial protection and guardianship by her male relatives (Isaeus 10. 100).[14]

That I have had to rely primarily on tragedy and comedy in the preceding discussion suggests yet another reason why we have so little detailed information about what nonmythical fifth- and fourth-century BC husbands and wives felt about each other. The only other sources of evidence, grave inscriptions, offer only very limited information. Fifth century epitaphs tend to emphasize the general archetypal forms of excellence: "of a worthy wife this is the tomb here, by the road that throngs with people—of Aspasia, who is dead; in response to her noble disposition Euopides set up this monument for her; she was his consort" (139 Friedländer-Hoffleit = WLGR³ 37). In epitaphs from the fourth and third centuries, there is more emphasis on the relationship of individuals to their family (a pattern that is also represented in the arrangement of their tombs).[15] The cause of death is mentioned, or some distinguishing feature; Melite was "the best"; Dionysia "did not admire clothes or gold when she was alive but her husband," who in return for her youth adorns her tomb (IG II² 11162 = WLGR³ 38);[16] Nicephorus left four children, "and died in the arms of his good wife" (Kaibel 327 = *IG* II² 1094). But even these epitaphs are brief and general, and the sculptures that accompany them represent stereotypical scenes, with no attempt at realistic portraiture. We may learn more about the intensity of family affection from the consistency with which family members desired to be entombed together: Aristotle's will ends with a request that the bones of his wife be exhumed and buried with his, "in accordance with her own instructions" (Diogenes *Laertius* 5. 16 = *WLGR*³ 79).

We may have more specific information about "real" people in the Hellenistic Age and after, because there is an increasing emphasis on individuality in literature as well as in art. In a world greatly expanded by Alexander's conquests, it was less possible to define oneself as a member of a particular small community; a fifth- or fourth-century epitaph might speak of a woman's *hēlikia*, the group of contemporaries with whom she was educated in dance and song (e.g., Kaibel 73, 78). Fourth-century epitaphs and inscriptions mention a woman's occupation, but particularly from the point of view of the bereaved: "Thanostrate, a midwife and physician, lies here; she caused pain to none and all lamented her death" (Kaibel 45 = Pleket 1). "Hippostrate still misses you: 'I loved you while you were alive, nurse, I love you still now even beneath the earth'" (Kaibel 481 = *IG* II² 7873 = *WLGR*³ 379). But in Greco-Roman Egypt and in Rome itself, information on inscriptions clearly distinguishes one person from another; a mother describes how she went from Athens to Alexandria when her daughter, one of Cleopatra's attendants, was sick, but arrived too late and brought her remains back to Athens (Kaibel 118 = *WLGR*³ 333).

As for women's relations with their husbands, one gets the impression that women in Hellenistic Egypt were freer to move about than Athenian women and were no longer closely restricted to the house by custom. In Theocritus' *Idyll* 15, set in suburban Alexandria, a woman calls on a woman friend and they go together to the festival of Adonis, but their conversation tells us that their husbands still do the shopping and make the decisions about where they are to live; the wife can complain, but she cannot change the decision. A woman was able to make a will in her own name and could decide how to dispose of the property she inherited from her father, but as in fifth- and fourth-century BC Athens, the document had to be approved by a male guardian (*SB* X. 10756 = *WLGR*³ 152).[17] Legal documents protected the status of both wives and concubines, in the case of divorce or transfer, and rate of payment of a dowry;[18] perhaps such contracts had always existed, at least verbally, but we know about them only from Egypt, because the climate was able to preserve them. Roman law, particularly from the Empire, spells out the rights of women in detail, drawing many subtle distinctions and allowing for exceptions with a precision and flexibility that was not possible in Classical Athens, where individual cases were subsumed into the general *nomos*. Roman law thus gives the impression that there was a considerable improvement (from our point of view) in women's status. In practice, however, notions of the proper role of wives do not seem to have undergone any radical change.

In the Roman Empire, epitaphs in Greek, perhaps because of the conventions established in Classical models, continue to emphasize the standard wifely qualities: chastity, care for husband and children, and management of household (*oikos*). This second-century AD inscription from Pergamum is an example:

> Farewell, lady Panthia from your husband. After your departure, I keep up my lasting grief for your cruel death. Hera, goddess of marriage, never saw such a wife: your beauty, your wisdom, your chastity. You bore me children completely like myself; you cared for your bridegroom and your children; you guided straight the rudder of life in our home and raised high our common fame in healing—though you were a woman you were not behind me in skill. In recognition of this your bridegroom Glycon built this tomb for you. I also buried here the body of (my father) immortal Philadelphus, and I myself will lie here when I die, since with you alone I shared my bed when I was alive, so may I cover myself in ground that we share. (Pleket 20 = WLGR³ 373)

Again, as in fourth-century BC Athens, though now it is stated explicitly, the pattern of burial represents the unity of the family in life. Custom now permits a fuller description of the *oikos*; it is sustained not by farming, like most *oikoi* in Attica, but by the practice of healing, in which both husband and wife share. The statement "though you were a woman you were not behind me in skill" sounds condescending but (like many such remarks) was meant as a compliment; like Admetus, Glycon assumes his own priority, both as the head of the household and as a man.

Latin inscriptions, especially from the Empire, provide even more detail; some record whole eulogies which, like Roman portraits, lead us to believe that we might be able literally to recognize the people they describe: specific incidents from the past are mentioned, appearances are described, conversations remembered. We learn why a person has claim to the standard virtues ascribed to him or her. One of the most famous of these long inscriptions is the eulogy by a husband for a woman who is not named but has been traditionally identified with the heroic Turia (*ILS* 8393 = *WLGR*³ 168).¹⁹ The husband records how his wife helped avenge her parents' deaths after they were murdered during the civil war (1.3 ff.) and how she raised some young female relatives and gave them dowries from her own inheritance (2.2a ff.). He also describes how she helped bring him back safely from exile during the proscriptions in 42 BC, when the triumvir Marcus Lepidus objected to her husband's return:

> When you prostrated yourself at [Lepidus'] feet, he not only did not raise you up, but dragged you along and abused you as though a common slave; your body was all covered with bruises, yet with unflinching steadfastness of purpose, you recalled to him Caesar's [i.e., Octavian's] edict of pardon and the letter of felicitation on my return that accompanied it. Braving his taunts and suffering the most brutal treatment, you denounced these cruelties publicly so that Lepidus was branded as the author of all my perils and misfortunes. (2. 14–18)

The husband even claims that her protest was instrumental in bringing about Lepidus' downfall (2.19 ff.). This wife's performance was not unique: the historian Appian recalls other cases of wives interceding for their husbands, or choosing, despite great hardship, to go into exile with them. Wartime conditions demanded that women go to extremes to preserve the unity of their families (Appian 4. 39–40 = *WLGR*³ 167).

But "Turia's" sacrifices for her husband were not limited to wartime. Her husband in his funeral elegy explains that when they found that they were unable to have children,

> You did not believe you could be fertile and were disconsolate to see me without children; you did not wish me by continuing my marriage to you to give up hope of having children, and to be on that account unhappy, so you proposed divorce, that you would vacate the house and turn it over to a woman more fertile; your only intention was that because of our mutual affection (*concordia*) you yourself would search for and provide me with a worthy spouse, and that you would affirm that you would have treated the children as your own; and you said that you would make no division between inheritances which we had heretofore held in common, but that it would continue to be left in my control, or if I wished in your management; nothing would be sequestered, and you would have nothing separate, and that you would henceforth render to me the services and devotion of a sister or mother-in-law. (2. 31–39)

Most interesting for us is that the husband records his response to this extraordinary offer, and it is not at all what one would expect him to say—from a Marxist or a feminist point of view:

> I will admit that I was so irritated and shocked by such a proposition that I had difficulty in restraining my anger and in remaining master of myself. You spoke of divorce before the decree of fate had forced us to separate, and I could not comprehend how you could conceive of any reason why you, while I was still alive, should not be my wife, you who while I was in exile virtually from life had always remained most faithful . . . How could my desire to or need for having children have been so great, that for that reason I would have broken my promise to you, and exchanged what I could count on for uncertainties? There is nothing more to say. You remained in my house; I could not have agreed to your request without disgracing myself or causing us both unhappiness. (2. 40–43, 44–47)

The husband concludes the oration by stating: "You deserved all, and I must remain without having been able to give you all; your wishes have been my law, and I will continue to provide whatever still has been permitted for me to do" (2. 67–68). This wife's self-sacrifice and deference to her husband apparently not only set an example for Octavian but for the husband himself, even though Octavian once he became emperor offered prizes for the begetting of children (Dio Cassius 54. 10). The husband refused to accept his wife's offer of divorce and remained childless rather than lose her. So Andromache may not have been overstating her case when she claimed that by extraordinary service (in her case nursing her husband's bastards) she "won her husband over" by her excellence (Euripides, *Andromache* 207–8).

The "Turia" inscription indicates that, in certain upper-class Roman marriages, wives could and did participate in all important decisions; one would expect them to do so, because the law allowed them to own property, did not deny them access to the outside world, and specified their rights.[20] However, women may have been freer to determine the course of their own lives than most chose to be in practice. A woman like the notorious Clodia, who entertained a sequence of boyfriends, including perhaps Catullus, in her house after her husband's death, was fair game for a lawyer like Cicero, who could effectively destroy her credibility simply by contrasting her life-style with approved patterns of behavior.[21] The highest compliment on epitaphs remained service to home and husband;[22] in another eulogy, composed about the same time, a son praises his mother, Murdia, for being "on an equal level with other good women in modesty, propriety, chastity, obedience, woolworking, and industry" (*ILS* 8394 = *WLGR*³ 43),[23] as well as for her sound financial judgment and generosity to her children by two marriages.

Turia's husband relates that he "had difficulty in restraining" his anger and "remaining master" of himself, but that was only in response to his wife's extraordinary generosity. There is a consistent emphasis even in shorter grave inscriptions from this period and after on domestic harmony: for example, "For Lollia Victoriana his sweetest wife Lollianus Porresimus the Procurator bought this monument, because she deserved it. With her he lived twenty years without any fault-finding on either side. That is having loved" (*CIL* 10. 1951). In an inscription from Carthage, a wife says she "set up this monument to her blessed husband, who was most generous and dutiful; while I lived with him, he never said a cruel word to me, never gave offense to me or any one else."[24] It would be naïve to take these or any eulogies or epitaphs as precise representations of the reality of the time, but at least they offer valid testimony to an ideal. These wives, like the fourth-century BC Athenian woman who wants to remain with her bankrupt husband, appreciated their husband's constant "affection."

One expects to find lower-class wives involved in their husbands' occupation; for example, we find pairs of grocers in both Greek and Latin inscriptions. In first-century BC Rome a butcher in praising his wife includes financial honesty among her traditional virtues. "She lived as a faithful wife to a faithful husband with affection equal to my own, since she never let avarice keep her from her duty" (*ILS* 7472 = *WLGR*³ 239). His wife, on the same inscription, boasts that her husband "flourished at all times through her diligent performance of duty." But the "Turia" inscription and many of the anecdotes about wives' heroism in times of persecution suggest that political circumstances also encouraged close companionship among upper-class couples. As a final example, I would like to consider a long inscription about a husband and wife who lived in the late fourth century AD. Their account of their lives is of particular interest because the husband, Praetextatus, was one of the last important pagans, and he held office not only under Julian the Apostate but under several Christian emperors.[25] What he and his wife, Paulina, are represented as saying about each other is virtually the last evidence we have of pagan ideals.

The grave monument (*ILS* 4154 = *WLGR*[3] 439) of Praetextatus and Paulina is inscribed on all four sides; the front lists their names, their religious offices, and some of Praetextatus' public offices.[26] On the sides of the monument are eulogies in verse to Paulina: on the right side she is said to be "conscious of truth and chastity, devoted to temples and friend of the divinities: she put her husband before herself, and Rome before her husband, proper, faithful, pure in mind and body, kindly to all, helpful to her family gods." In earlier inscriptions, a wife's or husband's piety might be routinely mentioned (Alcestis before her death prayed to Hestia and decorated all the altars), but here it is explicitly detailed, and there is a striking emphasis on her patriotism. The inscription speaks of Paulina's devotion to husband and family, but also of "the experience of our life together, the alliance of our marriage, our pure, faithful, simple concord; you helped your husband, loved him, honored him, cared for him."

On the back of the monument, Paulina gives (again in verse) an even more detailed eulogy of Praetextatus. She claims that her greatest honor is having been his wife. She praises him for his civic achievement and for his scholarship, but she places even more importance on his religious piety: "You as pious initiate conceal in the secrecy of your mind what was revealed in the sacred mysteries, and you with knowledge worship the manifold divinity of the gods; you kindly include as colleague in the rites your wife, who is respectful of men and gods and is faithful to you . . . My husband, by the gift of your learning you keep me from the fate of death pure and chaste; you take me into the temples and devote me as the servant of the gods. With you as my witness I am introduced to all the mysteries; you, my pious consort, honor me as priestess of Dindymene and Attis with the sacrificial rites of the *taurobolium*; you instruct me as minister of Hecate in the triple secret and you make me worthy of the rites of the Greek Ceres . . . Now men, now women approve the insignia that you as teacher have given me." From this inscription and other evidence we have about Praetextatus, it seems that for him religion was closely bound up with his service to the state; apparently when he was governor of the Greek province of Achaea in AD 362 under Julian he restored some of the cults that he and his wife were initiated into. Her eulogy of him indicates that he served as both mentor and teacher to her; but it is significant that he wanted her to share in the rituals he himself took so seriously. I am inclined to think that she meant what she said about her gratitude for having been included in this important aspect of his life, first because the monument was put up after his death (whoever composed the elegant verse), and secondly because other aristocratic women are eager to record their participation in some of the same rituals. It seems that members of family groups would be initiated together, especially in rituals like the *taurobolium*;[27] so perhaps a pagan husband's taking a close interest in his wife's religious education is not as unusual as evidence gleaned from the Christian Fathers might suggest.[28]

In this chapter I have sought to show that certain attitudes persisted throughout Classical antiquity, despite significant changes in women's legal status and over a great range of time and geography, but I am not trying to argue that all ancient marriages were happy or that in contemporary society we should accept ancient values. After all, so far as we know, every document we have considered was written or at least inscribed (since only men were stonecutters) by a man, and some men may have been able to hear only part of what the women were saying to them. In his treatise *Advice on Marriage*, Plutarch urges the bridegroom to be understanding and faithful, but it is clear from what he says that he expected most of the adjustments to be made by the wife. He advocates the kind of marriage described in the inscription about Praetextatus and Paulina: the woman should worship the husband's gods; marriage should be a partnership; a wife ought to be able to say, "Dear husband, to me you are guide, philosopher and teacher in all that is beautiful and most divine"; women should study geometry and philosophy to put their mind on higher things (*Moralia* 145c–d). He believes that woman can and should be educated, though as tradition would dictate within the context of their husbands' homes. Clearly he means his advice for the best; can we really blame him for not being able to imagine a system in which women could be completely independent? He was an antiquarian and historian and he had studied and read enough to know that the concept of a married woman's role had not changed very much over seven hundred years.

11

Influential Women

When Greek colonists set up new cities in the then unknown frontier of Italy, they soon discovered myths that connected them with their ancestors and that gave their customs and their shrines legitimacy. It seems that all people who initiate new styles of government or patterns of living—political colonists, we might call them—also tend to seek precedents in the prestigious civilizations of the past. Proponents of slavery in the United States discovered support for their views in Greek and Roman writings; so, of course, did the Abolitionists.[1] Karl Marx found that the notion of free, rather than enforced, sale of labor first occurred in the Roman army.[2] Feminists have sought evidence of matriarchal societies and have called attention to the extraordinary achievements of a few women, as if searching for a pattern that twentieth-century women might emulate and revive, and finally bring into full realization.

When I observe that in the ancient world women neither had nor sought political power for themselves but worked through their husbands or fathers or sons, people often object, asking, "What about Antigone, Clytemnestra, Artemisia, Agrippina?" But I believe that it is possible to show in all these cases, as well as in many others, that women in ancient Greece and Rome took political action only under certain closely defined conditions and that, unless they did so at least ostensibly on behalf of a male relative, they and others around them came to a bad end. I will begin by talking about women in myth, that is, in specific works of literature, because myths illustrate common attitudes more clearly and simply than does history; but history too can be shown to follow the patterns of myth, in part because those patterns provided a means of making sense of human experience, and in part because ancient societies, for practical reasons, offered women little opportunity to act as individuals outside the context of their families.

Ancient women could certainly be courageous, but they could not be truly independent. Antigone herself is an example. In Sophocles' drama, she contrives to bury her brother in defiance of an order by her uncle, Creon, the king of Thebes, that her brother Polynices, who had attacked their homeland, remain unburied. Denial of burial was a traditional penalty for treason. Antigone had the moral sensibility to see that Creon's order ran counter to another established custom, the obligation of the family, or *genos*, to bury and then worship the remains of their deceased members.[3]

Some critics have suggested that Antigone, in acting against her sister's advice and Creon's edict, assumed an essentially masculine role;[4] that in defending her blood relationship to Polynices she "must undercut the form and potential of the family";[5] that Antigone adopted the aggressive stance of an Orestes, "a younger son revenging or redeeming the death of an unburied brother."[6] In the process of interpretation these critics assume that Creon, or the city elders in the chorus, represent not themselves but the State, a government supported and accepted by the majority of Theban citizens, whose laws and customs Antigone is threatening,[7] and that therefore, the drama *Antigone* calls into question the traditional structure of society.[8]

But I do not believe that Sophocles or his audience would have seen Antigone's action as unconventional or have recognized in the play an attempt to define or promote new family structures or modes of behavior. In the first place, it is not established custom that Antigone opposes but the orders of one particular individual, Creon; Creon may equate his own opinions with the city's (e.g., 736), but the outcome of the drama makes it clear that he is mistaken. The analogy of Antigone to Orestes is misleading, because Antigone is not trying to avenge or redeem her brother's death; she is seeking only to bury him with appropriate rites for the dead.[9] The difference may seem trivial to us, but to the Greeks it was (and in some remote villages still is) essential; men avenge murders of kin, and women prepare bodies for burial and sing laments over the body.[10]

If Sophocles from time to time in the play states explicitly that Antigone and her sister, Ismene, are women, it is to emphasize to his audience that Creon's edict violates established custom and that by demanding obedience to it he is misusing his power as a ruler, that is, he is behaving like a tyrant. "Consider," says Ismene to Antigone at the beginning of the drama, "that we two are left alone [i.e., without father or brothers to protect them], and how cruelly we will perish, if we oppose the edict of the king (*tyrannon*) or his power. You must remember that the two of us are born women and as such do not fight with men; since we are in the power of those who are stronger, we must obey these orders, and orders even more painful than these" (61–64). When Sophocles has Creon complain that he would be weaker than a woman if he allowed her to get away with disobeying his order (525), or insist that "she and her sister must now be women and not allowed outside the house" (579), he is not describing normal male-female relations; he is portraying a man desperately trying to justify a decision that only he in the whole city (690 ff.) considers to be correct.[11]

In fact, far from being unconventional, Antigone is only doing what her family might have expected of her, as she herself says: "But I have great hope that when I come [to the lower world] I shall come welcome to my father, and welcome to you, mother, and welcome to you, dear brother, since when each of you died I washed and dressed you and poured libations on your tombs" (897–902). In the fifth and fourth centuries BC (i.e., in Sophocles' lifetime and for a century afterwards), it was common belief that families were reunited in death.[12] Special care was taken to bury family members in the same plot, even if bones had to be exhumed from other localities and reburied. I do not think an ancient audience would have considered it unusual or excessive when Sophocles' Electra laments over what she supposes to be the urn that holds her brother's ashes: "So now you receive me into this house of yours, I who am nothing to your nothing, so that for the rest of time I can live with you below; for when we were above ground I shared the same things with you, and now I wish to die and not be left outside your tomb" (*Electra* 1165–69). When Antigone is captured, even Ismene asks to die with her and to give the rites to their dead brother (544–45). The guard who catches Antigone says that when she saw the corpse of Polynices unburied, "she wailed out the sharp cry of an anguished bird, as when in its empty nest it sees its bed stripped of its nestlings" (424–25). To us, Antigone's or Electra's failure to distinguish between living and dead may seem strange; but to Antigone the important link was not life but blood kinship:[13] "My life died long ago, so that I might serve my dead [family]" (559–60). Antigone says explicitly that she would not have risked her life for a husband, or if she had had children of her own; but without any other family, her first duty was to her brother—whether dead or alive does not seem to matter. Nor does Ismene count as a reason for her to stay alive, because she is female and so not able to inherit or continue the family line. When Antigone replies to Creon's accusations that she could disobey his edict but not the "unwritten customs" (*agrapta nomima*) of the gods, she is simply claiming that family loyalty must take precedence over rulings that have not existed since time immemorial. She is questioning not Creon's right to power or the structure of government but his own intelligence and judgment: "If I had put up with my mother's son having died an unburied corpse, that would have caused me pain; but I am not pained by what I have done. If I seem to you to have acted foolishly, then I have been accused of folly by a fool" (466–70).

To put it another way, Antigone must be female for the dramatic action to occur in the first place, because only a mother or sister would have felt so strongly the obligation to bury the dead.[14] As Ismene suggests, if she had failed to bury her brother, it would have been possible for her to ask the gods of the lower world for forgiveness on the ground that she was forcibly prevented by the (male) rulers of Thebes (66–67). It would also have been possible for her to have tried first to work through a man, like Haemon, as Aethra did when she persuaded her son Theseus to allow the mothers of the Argive heroes who fell at Thebes to bury their sons. "It's natural for women, if they are clever, to do everything through men" (Euripides, *Suppliant Women* 40–41). We might choose to call Antigone courageous or generous, but the chorus states that she is foolish: "Unhappy child of an unhappy father Oedipus; what has happened? It isn't true that they have caught you in folly and bring you in disobedient to the king's laws?" (379–82). They regard her, as she does herself, as a victim of the family curse that destroyed her parents and her brother: "Your respect [for your brother] is one kind of right respect, but one also ought not to transgress in any way the power of him to whom power belongs. Your self-willed anger has destroyed you" (872–75). This anger and folly (*aphrosyne*, "un-thinking") are aspects of the family curse, and the action of the curse, far from being disapproved of by the gods, is part of their system: "Evil seems good to the person whose mind the god is leading toward delusion" (622–23).

Sophocles' audience would have seen Antigone's action as courageous and laudable but risky (she does end up dead on account of it, after all) and certainly within the bounds of acceptable female behavior.[15] Antigone's conduct does not set a new revolutionary standard any more than it can be said to serve as a prototype of female Christian martyrdom—an interpretation that profoundly impressed the composer Mendelssohn, even though he knew no Greek.[16] Winning praise for acting on behalf of her family is something Antigone shares with other women in epic and drama: Penelope deceives the suitors (and so holds out for her husband Odysseus) for three years before she is discovered unraveling her weaving at night; Andromache defies Hermione and Menelaus in order to protect her young son; Iphigenia tricks the wicked king in order to save her brother Orestes; Helen tells lies to rescue Menelaus. It is important to note that in all these cases the women offer only passive resistance to authority. Apparently, acts of treachery were acceptable in a woman only if they were nonviolent and undertaken on behalf of a male relative.

But a woman was not permitted, even with justification, to take the law into her own hands. After the fall of Troy, when all the Trojan men are dead, Hecuba herself avenges the murder of her youngest son Polydorus. He had been sent to Polymestor in Thrace for safekeeping, but Hecuba discovers that Polymestor has murdered him, and when Polymestor arrives in Troy with his young sons in the hope of collecting more money, Hecuba and her servant women use their brooches to put out Polymestor's eyes and to stab his sons to death. Polymestor asks Agamemnon to punish Hecuba, but Agamemnon lets her get away with her revenge. "Alas," Polymestor complains, "it seems that I have been defeated by a woman and a slave, and suffer vengeance from my inferiors" (Euripides, *Hecuba* 1252–53). But Hecuba's triumph is short-lived: Polymestor predicts that Hecuba will throw herself from the ship that takes her from Troy, that she will be turned into a dog, and that her grave will be known as the "poor dog's tomb," a landmark for sailors (1273). Her death, in other words, will be sordid (the Greeks did not like dogs) and, more significantly, anonymous. On the other hand, for Penelope, who could leave the execution of the suitors to her husband and son, "for her the fame of her virtue (*aretē*) will never perish; the immortals will fashion a lovely song for mortal men about good Penelope; she did not devise evil deeds, like Tyndareus' daughter [Clytemnestra], killing her wedded husband; but for Clytemnestra there will be a hateful song among men, and she will give women a bad reputation, even to the woman who does good deeds" (*Odyssey* 24. 196–202).

It may seem unfair that the speaker of these lines, the dead Agamemnon, believes that no woman can be trusted after what Clytemnestra did. Polymestor, too, after he has described to Agamemnon how the Trojan women stabbed his children and put his own eyes out, concludes by condemning women in general: "Neither sea nor land sustains a race like them" (1181–82); they are monsters.[17] Semonides of Amorgos, in his satire on women (fr. 7W = WLGR³ 57), identifies, as we have seen, nine types of bad women, but only one good type. Perhaps the low proportion of good women could be taken as evidence of enduring misogyny on the part of (male) Greek poets; but it is important to remember that these statements about bad women all occur in the context of invective and so are likely to be exaggerated. Compare the way in which an angry woman who feels she has been wronged, like Medea in Euripides' drama, contrasts the unfortunate lot of (all) women with the enviable life led—without exception—by men (230 ff.).

It is also possible to argue that the limitations that apply to women in epic and in drama apply as well to the "political" women in Aristophanes' comedies. Lysistrata in particular is often cited as the first liberated woman; but consider what she actually accomplishes. In order to bring about peace, she summons all Greek women to a meeting (to which they of course arrive late) and gets them to swear not to have sexual intercourse with their husbands until the men agree to end the war between Athens and Sparta. Her plan works, and then her organization of women disbands and the women go back to their husbands. So, even in the fantasy world of comedy, women take action only to preserve and to return to their families. Women have intelligence and understanding, but they speak out only in emergencies, and even then their models are men. As she concludes the peace, Lysistrata begins her statement by quoting Euripides, "Although I am a woman, I have intelligence;[18] for my own part, I do not have bad judgment. I have listened to many speeches by my father and older men and so am not badly educated" (*Lysistrata* 1124–27). When in the *Thesmophoriazusae* the women meet to attack Euripides, their proceedings are a burlesque of the Athenian men's assembly. Aristophanes realizes that his audience would find the very notion of women meeting together, making speeches and voting, hilariously funny.

In the comedy *Ecclesiazusae* (or "Women Meeting in the Assembly"), women in male disguise manage to infiltrate the assembly and vote to let women run the city, on the grounds that "we [the assembly] ought to turn the city over to women, for we use them also as guardians and stewards in our households" (210–12). The infiltrated assembly passes two new laws: (1) that all possessions (including wives and children) shall be held in common, and (2) that the ugliest and oldest women will have first chance at getting men. The first law is a parody of what Athenians understood to be the constitution of Sparta; after Athens lost the war to Sparta, the Spartan system of government appeared to have special merit. In 392 BC, when the *Ecclesiazusae* was performed, Aristophanes still could make fun of the notion that women might have equal rights with men. A generation later, Plato realized that people might still ridicule the idea that women should be educated (*Republic* 452b), but nonetheless he incorporated into the model government of his Republic equal education for men and women and common marriages and children, so that women might be able to be companions of men and co-guardians of his ideal state (456b). But even in his utopia Plato included the proviso that women, because their natures were weaker, should be assigned lighter duties in wartime (he does not specify what they would be).

Of course such socialistic theories, however much they were debated in intellectual circles, were never practiced, at least in Athens.[19] In fact, Aristotle claimed that the liberty permitted to Spartan women[20] in the days of Sparta's great military successes had by the middle of the fourth century BC led directly to Sparta's defeat by the Thebans. Women, observed Aristotle, had not been subject to the same restrictions as men under the Spartan constitution, and so had lived intemperate and luxurious lives, while the men remained in military training. As a result, the Spartan women at the time of the Theban invasion of 369 were "utterly useless and caused more confusion than the enemy" (*Politics* 1269b 5)."The disorder of women," he observed, "not only of itself gives an air of indecorum to the state, but tends to foster avarice" (1207a 9). In his view, one particularly unfortunate consequence was that two-fifths of Sparta was owned by women (1270a 10–11), who, unlike their Athenian counterparts, could inherit and bequeath property.[21]

Here, as in his theories of human physiology, Aristotle appears to regard as normative what was acceptable in Athenian life and to consider all other practices deviations. But he, not Plato, had the last word. If Greek women, whether in history or in literature, ever had an opportunity to govern, it was only for a brief period, in order to cope with a particular problem or emergency, or in the case of monarchies and tyrannies if they happened to be related to the man in charge, like Artemisia or Cynna.[22]

I will now consider briefly the role played by ancient Greek women in history, as opposed to in literature, to the extent that the two can be separated. References to women by biographers and historians tend to be anecdotal and so not necessarily pinned down to particular times or events; rather, they are illustrative of character in general and timeless ways. For example, Cornelia[23] is praised by several ancient writers for having educated her sons, the Gracchi, but how and when and what she taught them is not specified. Whatever the source of the information, the same rules seem to apply in history as in myth: women can affect the course of political events only if they act through or on behalf of the men in their families. They can take independent action, like Lysistrata, in an emergency, but then must retire when the problem is solved. The earliest instance of such an event in history is recorded by Plutarch in his treatise on the bravery of women. When the Argive army had suffered a severe setback, early in the fifth century BC, Telesilla of Argos,[24] an aristocrat known to be of weak constitution, organized the women of Argos to arm themselves and led them in a successful defense of their city's fortifications against the Spartans (*Moralia* 245c–f = *WLGR*[3] 160). But as soon as the crisis was over, the women resumed their conventional roles; and because so many Argive men had been killed, the Argive women were married to the aristocratic citizens of the neighboring cities.

Plutarch preserves another dramatic instance of a woman's political effectiveness in a crisis, this time, as he says, from a period much closer to his own time, the first century BC.[25] Aretaphila of Cyrene was compelled to marry the tyrant who had murdered her husband. First she tried to poison him. She survived the torture inflicted on her when her plot failed, but she succeeded in getting rid of her tyrant husband by marrying her daughter to his brother and persuading her son-in-law to murder his brother. Then, she contrived to have the ruler of a neighboring state capture her son-in-law and turn him and his mother over to the citizens of Cyrene to be murdered. The people of Cyrene treated her like a hero and asked her to share in the government and management of the city with the aristocrats, but she "as if she had played in a sort of drama or competed in a contest up to the point of winning the prize," returned home to the women's quarters and spent the rest of her life working at her loom in the company of her family (*Moralia* 257d–e).

Even if the original story of Aretaphila was embellished by Plutarch or his sources until it conformed to the standard pattern of women's behavior in myth, it does indicate how implausible it seemed, even in the Hellenistic Age, that women should share in the actual process of government (*synarchein, syndioikein,* 257d). It seems clear from papyri and inscriptions—the most authentic contemporary evidence preserved about the role of women in public life—that even when women were legally entitled to own property and to make wills, they might be welcomed as benefactors of cities and given honorific titles but they were never accorded a real place on the town council or an actual vote in the assembly. The traditional female virtues were listed along with their benefactions, and even though their own names are now conspicuously mentioned (unlike proper aristocratic women in the fifth and fourth centuries BC, who remained incognito),[26] due credit was always given to the men in their families: "Phile, daughter of Apollonius, wife of Thessalus son of Polydeuces; as the first woman *stephanephorus*, she dedicated[27] at her own expense a receptacle for water and the water pipes in the city [Priene]" (Pleket 5 = *WLGR*[3] 194, first century BC); "The council and the people, to Flavia Publicia Nicomachis, daughter of Dinomachus and Procle . . . their benefactor, and benefactor through her ancestors, founder of our city, president for life, in recognition of her complete virtue" (Pleket 19 = *WLGR*[3] 198, Asia Minor, second century AD); Aurelia Leite, "daughter of Theodotus, wife of the foremost man in the city, Marcus Aurelius Faustus . . . she was gymnasiarch of the gymnasium which she repaired and renewed when it had been dilapidated for many years . . . She loved wisdom, her husband, her children, her native city [Paros]" (Pleket 31 = *WLGR*[3] 200 [AD 300]).

Ancient philosophical theory, as so often is still the case, was based on and reinforced social practice. Aristotle believed that women were capable of virtue and of understanding, though he could not accept what Plato proposed, that self-control, courage, and justice were the same for women and for men. Aristotle stated that "men's courage is shown in commanding (or ruling, *archein*) and women's in obeying" (*Politics* 1260a 8). A treatise on women written in the third or second century BC by Neopythagorean philosophers in Italy, in the form of a letter from one woman to another, also assumes that a woman's capacity to govern was considerably less than a man's:

> Some people think that it is not appropriate for a woman to be a philosopher, just as a woman should not be a cavalry officer or a politician . . . I agree that men should be generals and city officials and politicians, and women should keep house and stay inside and receive and take care of their husbands. But I believe that courage, justice and intelligence are qualities that men and women have in common . . . Courage and intelligence are more appropriately male qualities because of the strength of men's bodies and the power of their minds. Chastity is more appropriately female.[28]

The apparent exceptions only prove the rule that women could not be accepted as governors unless they acted in conjunction with a man. Hellenistic queens have been regarded as the first examples of truly independent women.[29] They organized court intrigues (including murders), they directed strategy of naval and land battles, and they made decisions affecting governmental policy. But it is important to remember that even the most capable of these women worked through, or at least with the titular presence of, a male consort.[30] Arsinoe, queen of Egypt from 274 to 270 BC, enjoyed power as the consort of her brother; Berenice,[31] wife and cousin of Arsinoe's adopted son Ptolemy III Euergetes, was praised by Callimachus for the courage she showed as a young girl, which won her her husband.[32] The unwritten law appears to be that the co-ruling (*synarchein*) and co-management (*syndioikein*) unthinkable for Aretaphila in conjunction with unrelated males,[33] is available to women with husbands, fathers, or brothers. Cleopatra VII (69–30 BC) came to the throne with her brother. Then she enlisted the aid first of Julius Caesar, who became at least for a short time her consort, to remain on the throne by defeating her brother and installing a younger brother as co-ruler. After that she used Mark Antony to stay in power, though even when she sat with Antony on twin thrones she was addressed as "co-ruler with Caesarion," her son (allegedly) by Caesar (Plutarch, *Antony* 54).[34] For ordinary women also, civil law ensured that men had at least nominal control. Greek women in the Hellenistic Age could draw up contracts and make wills, but only with the consent of a male guardian, or *kyrios*, usually a close relative.[35]

Upper-class Romans in Cicero's day could claim that their wives enjoyed greater social freedom than women in Greek cities (Nepos, praef. 6); the aristocratic Aretaphila of Greek Cyrene returned to the women's quarters and saw only other women and members of her family. But, as we have seen (in chapter 10), inscriptions and letters explain how Roman women assisted the men in their families in their political careers. "Turia's" husband records how his wife managed to have him brought back from exile and indicates how her accusations helped contribute to the downfall of the triumvir Lepidus (*WLGR*[3] 168).[36] The proscriptions of the triumvirs apparently elicited similarly heroic behavior on the part of other aristocrats' wives:[37] Acilius' wife (as suits a proper Athenian woman, her own name is not given) bribed soldiers with her jewelry not to turn her husband over to be executed; Lentulus' wife[38] donned male disguise in order to join her husband in exile; Rheginus' wife hid her husband in a sewer; Coponius' wife slept with Antony in order to purchase her husband's safety, "thus curing one evil with another," as the historian Appian remarks (*Civil Wars* 4. 39–40 = *WLGR*[3] 167). Brutus, the murderer of Caesar, appears to have been aided at every step in his career by his mother Servilia.[39] Certainly one reason why Caesar pardoned Brutus after he had fought against him in 48 BC was that Servilia had been Caesar's mistress. After the conspiracy that led to Caesar's death, she received and transmitted messages for her son (*ad Att.* 416. 4). Cicero, in a letter, describes how she took charge of a family conference at Antium at which she contrived to silence even Cicero with the comment that she had "never heard anything like" what he was proposing; she herself proposed to have legislation changed on her son's behalf, and she was apparently successful (389. 2). But for all Servilia's initiative, Cicero himself clearly thinks of her as her son's agent, rather than as an independent operator. He remarks to his friend Atticus (whom he teased about having Servilia as a "pal," *familiaris,* 389. 2): "It's just like you not to fault Servilia, which is to say, Brutus" (394).

Women in Pompeii joined with men in supporting candidates for local political offices, as graffiti on painted walls reveal: "Amandio along with his wife asks you to vote for Gnaeus Sabinus for aedile" (*CIL* iv. 913 = *WLGR*[3] 179). Some of the men and women appear to have been co-workers in shops: "Appuleia and Narcissus along with their neighbor Mustius, ask you to vote for Pupius" (*ILS* 6408a). One woman, Statia, asks on her own for support of her candidate (*CIL* iv. 3684)—of course, she could not vote for him herself.

But generally women who spoke out on their own behalf, rather than on behalf of a close male relative, were criticized for being selfish, licentious, and avaricious. The speech attributed by Livy to the formidable moralist Cato the Elder provides an example of the kind of thing that was said about ambitious women. The issue under discussion is whether to repeal the Oppian law limiting women's right to own property (195 BC).

> Our ancestors did not want women to conduct any—not even private—business without a guardian; they wanted them to be under the authority of parents, brothers, or husbands; we (the gods help us!) even now let them snatch at the government and meddle in the Forum and our assemblies . . . Give rein to their unbridled nature and this unmastered creature, and hope that they will put limits on their own freedom! They want freedom, nay license (if we are to speak the truth) in all things . . . If they are victorious now, what will they not attempt? As soon as they begin to be your equals, they will have become your superiors. (34. 2. 11–3. 2 = *WLGR*[3] 173)[40]

Of Sempronia, who supported the conspiracy of Catiline (who was not a relative of hers), it was said, "there was nothing she set a smaller value on than seemliness and chastity, and she was as careless of her reputation as she was of her money" (Sallust, *Catiline* 24–25 = *WLGR*[3] 174).[41] We are told that the name of Gaia Afrania, a contemporary of Caesar's who brought lawsuits herself without using (male) lawyers, was used to designate any woman of low morals (Valerius Maximus 8. 3 = WLGR³ 178).

In popular belief, not only was self-assertion on a woman's part regarded as self-indulgence and licentiousness, but a crowd of women was considered a public menace. Livy has Cato complain of the women seeking repeal of the Oppian law "running around in public, blocking streets and speaking to other women's husbands" (WLGR³ 173). In practice women were permitted to organize themselves into formal groups only for some social or religious purpose, rather on the lines of a modern ladies' auxiliary. For example, in the third century BC the matrons "purely and chastely" dedicated a golden bowl to Juno out of contributions from their dowries (Livy 27. 37. 8–9 = WLGR³ 187). Inscriptions from the Roman Empire record grants of money donated to women's organizations for public services, and women apparently could meet to set rules of social conduct and to discipline one another (Suetonius, *Galba* 5. 1; *Historia Augusta* [*Elagabalus*] 4. 3–4 = WLGR³ 188, 189).

On the other hand, Hortensia, daughter of a famous orator, was praised for her plea to the triumvirs in 42 BC that rich women be relieved of a special tax: "Quintus Hortensius lived again in the female line and breathed in his daughter's words" (Valerius Maximus 8. 3 = WLGR³ 178). Her speech—unlike that of any other woman—was said to have been preserved verbatim, probably because what she said would have won male approval. In the one version of the speech that has come down to us, she claims that women had never supported despotic governments in the past; she recalls to the triumvirs what women would have done to serve the state, and also reminds them that in the present crisis the women have lost fathers, husbands, and sons. Significantly, she does not dwell on issues like taxation without representation or women's rights, or the pleasures and luxuries that their money might buy (Appian, *Civil Wars* 4. 32–33 = WLGR³ 176). If such arguments had had any appeal, Livy would have put them into the mouth of Lucius Valerius Flaccus, the opponent of Cato the Elder in the senatorial debate about the repeal of the Oppian law. Instead, Livy makes Valerius concentrate on the services that Roman women in the past performed on behalf of their country. He allows Valerius only one "equal opportunity" argument, and this with great condescension: men can wear the purple in civil magistracies not available to women; depriving men of such honors "could wound the spirits of men; what do you think it could do to the spirits of our little women (*mulierculae*), whom even small problems disturb?" Livy's Valerius concludes by arguing that women prefer that their adornment be subject to their husband's or father's judgment rather than to a law: "A woman's slavery is never put off while her male relatives are safe and sound, and they hate the liberty that widowhood or orphanage allows them . . . It is for the weaker sex to submit to whatever you advise. The more power you possess, all the more moderately should you exercise your authority" (34. 6–7 = WLGR³ 173).

Given this background, I do not find it at all surprising that during the Empire, when the principal liberty guaranteed to male citizens was the right to petition, women's initiative was restricted to helping male relatives.[42] Arria killed herself before her husband (who was about to be taken away to be executed), while uttering the famous words, "Look, it doesn't hurt" (Pliny, *Letters* 3. 16 = WLGR³ 170). Agrippina, Nero's mother, was even more aggressive than Servilia, Brutus' mother, in promoting her son's career. She married her uncle, the emperor Claudius, and got him to appoint her son as his heir.

Wives and mothers of emperors appeared on coins for propaganda purposes, for example, Antony with Cleopatra.[43] Clearly the rulers of these vast and constantly threatened realms needed the participation of wives and mothers for political as well as for personal reasons.[44] Again, mythology (i.e., literature) gives us the best indication of the response the emperors were seeking to elicit from their subjects. A man who had the support of a wife or mother was more easily approachable and more capable of clemency. In Euripides' drama *The Suppliants*, the mothers of the Argive captains who help Polynices attack Thebes first ask Aethra, Theseus' mother, not Theseus himself, to help them get military protection so that they can bury their sons (Polynices' burial was not the only problem created by that war): "You have borne a son yourself, queen" (55–56). When the king of Argos, Adrastus, fails to persuade Theseus to help, Aethra intercedes. Theseus listens to her, because "even women can provide much intelligent advice" (294). Aethra is successful where Antigone fails, because she is able to persuade Theseus to help; of course, he is a much more reasonable man than Creon: "For what will my detractors say, when you, my mother, who are anxious on my behalf, are the first to tell me to undertake this task [of allowing the Argive women to bury their dead]" (342–45).

In Rome, emperors' wives and even mistresses could save the lives (or fortunes) of individuals who were able to approach them directly and so get the emperor's ear.[45] That, as we have seen, was only a traditional pattern of behavior. The pattern survived through the Middle Ages and strongly affected

Christianity. By the fifth century AD the characterization of Christian divinities had undergone subtle but important changes; in iconography, Jesus, previously depicted as kindly and approachable, had become more closely identified with and sometimes even indistinguishable from his father. To receive his mercy, appeal must be made to his mother, who in the synoptic gospels is not at all an important or influential figure.[46] Thus the model of the "power behind the throne" was incorporated into religion from the world of politics. It survived not only in modern Christianity but in notions of approved behavior for women in the first half of the twentieth century.

12

Martyrs

Of all the roles played by women in Greek myth, certainly the most active, and therefore the most deserving of the praise ordinarily accorded to men, is self-sacrifice. Usually the occasion is presented by a battle: an oracle is given that in order to win, a young person must be sacrificed to a god. The most famous incident is, of course, Agamemnon's sacrifice of his daughter Iphigenia, in a story told by Aeschylus in his drama *Agamemnon*. According to earlier accounts, the goddess allowed a deer to be substituted for the human child; these stories provided (among other things) an explanation of why the goddess accepted animal sacrifices before the battle.[1] But by returning to what would have been considered a more primitive form of the myth, Aeschylus was able to emphasize the consequences of the taking of a human life, even when according to other ethical standards the killing might seem justified. Euripides also included myths of human sacrifice in several of his plays, and it is noteworthy that with one exception the victims are female. The preference in myth for the females for sacrifice is intriguing. It does not indicate that the Greeks considered female life less valuable. If that were the case, why would the gods care to demand the sacrifice? Rather, as the connection with the cult of the Mistress of Animals suggests, it shows that women, in religious terms, were the most appropriate victims.[2] But whatever the original significance in cult, female sacrifice in drama seems intended to demonstrate women's ability to be as courageous as men and as responsible for maintaining the values of society.

In the *Agamemnon* the sacrifice of Iphigenia is one (though not the only) justification offered by Clytemnestra for taking her husband's life; she blames the citizens of Argos for not having protested against his act:

Then you raised no opposition to this man who, holding it of no special account, as though it were the death of a beast, where sheep in their fleecy flocks abound, sacrificed his own child, a travail most dear to me, to charm the winds of Thrace. Was it not he whom you should have driven from this land, as penalty for his polluting act? (1413–20)³

The old men of Argos, though they took no action at the time, are not indifferent. In the account they give of the sacrifice in their opening song, they do not underestimate the difficulty of the decision, but they make it clear that Agamemnon did wrong in choosing to sacrifice his daughter:

> And when he had put on the yoke-strap of compulsion, his spirit's wind veering to an impious blast, impure, unholy, from that moment his mind changed to a temper of utter ruthlessness. For mortals are made reckless by the evil counsels of merciless Infatuation (*parakopa*), beginner of disaster. And so he steeled himself to become the sacrificer of his daughter, to aid a war fought to avenge a woman's loss and to pay beforehand for his ships. (218–27)

After all, it would have been possible for him not to pay the price, but instead to turn back and abandon the expedition, thus saving his child's life. The chorus's description of the sacrifice makes it clear that his action is unnatural, violating the normal pattern of family life:

> And her prayers and cries of "Father," and her maiden years they go for nothing ... she shot each of the sacrificers with a piteous dart from her eye, standing out as in a picture, wishing to address each by name, since often in her father's hospitable halls she had sung, and virginal with pure voice had lovingly honored the paean of felicity at the third libation of her loving father. (228–29, 240–47)

If the chorus emphasize that she was young and female, it is to stress that she was defenseless and vulnerable, an unwilling victim who was denied the one retaliation left to the powerless, the curse that even her mother was able to release upon her son and murderer, Orestes.

That Agamemnon's attitude would have seemed unnecessarily cruel is apparent from the story of the eighth-century BC Messenian king Aristodemus, who offers his daughter as a sacrifice against the Spartans in response to an oracle but murders her first, in anger, to show that she is not pregnant;⁴ she is then accepted as a substitute for the sacrificial victim (Pausanias 4. 9. 4–9). Later, in despair, the king dreams of her and kills himself: "He reckoned ... that he had become the murderer of his daughter to no purpose, and seeing that there was no hope of salvation for his country, he killed himself on his daughter's tomb" (4. 14. 4). In Apuleius' *Metamorphoses*, when an oracle demanded that the king place his beautiful daughter Psyche on a high cliff to become the bride of a monster, "he moaned, wept, lamented for many days;" even though Psyche does not blame him, because she knows the blame should fall on the goddess Venus, her parents shut themselves up in their house and "devote themselves to eternal night" (4. 33–34).

Euripides, in contrast to Aeschylus, allows both Iphigenia and Clytemnestra to confront Agamemnon directly before the sacrifice. In the *Iphigenia at Aulis*, Agamemnon, on the pretext that he wishes Iphigenia to marry Achilles, summons her and his wife to Aulis, where the Greek ships are beached in preparation for their departure to Troy. But Clytemnestra and Iphigenia discover what Agamemnon's real plans are, and Iphigenia herself tries to persuade her father not to kill her. Unlike the *Agamemnon*, where the chorus reflect not only on the breach of normal family ties but also on the delusion and arrogance inherent in Agamemnon's action, in Euripides' drama Iphigenia concentrates on his role as father and hers as his first-born. She clasps his knees with her body, reminding him that he begot her and that by killing her he will separate her not only from life but from her family: "Do not force me to see what lies below the earth. I was first to call you father and you first to call me your child. I was first to entrust my body to your lap and to give and receive sweet embraces" (1220–21). She reminds him of what they used to say to each other about the future, his hopes for her marriage and her plans to look after him in his old age, "offering a nurse's care in return for your pains" (1230). What, she asks, has she got to do with the marriage of Helen and Paris (1236–37)? "Look at me, give me your face to kiss, so that I will have this as memory when I die, in case I can't persuade you" (1238–40). She asks her brother Orestes to plead for her, and while the two children stand before him, she concludes, not inappropriately to the parent who gave her life, that life is what matters, and living badly is better than dying well. This final statement echoes what Achilles says about the importance of being alive, even as a poor man's slave, when Odysseus speaks to him in the world of the dead (*Odyssey* 11. 488 ff.), in marked contrast to the value he attached to honor when he made his decision to die young and gloriously in the *Iliad* (18. 98–99).[5]

But later in the play, after hearing her mother and Achilles discuss what they might do to rescue her, Iphigenia changes her mind and tells her mother that she wishes to die. This time, she sees that she can save Achilles' life, since he would certainly have been killed if he had tried to rescue her, and that she can prevent her mother from being slandered by the army. Whereas in her first speech she described the world of childhood, now she is concerned primarily with the world outside herself. She will save Greece, and prevent Greek women from being carried away from their homes by barbarians, as Helen was by Paris (1377–82); she has now seen how Helen and Paris's marriage does matter to her.[6] Iphigenia has, in fact, now adopted all the values of the heroic world, in which honor and shame count more than family ties or even survival: "I shall save all these things by dying, and my reputation, because I have brought freedom to Hellas, will be blessed. You bore me for all the Greeks, not for yourself alone" (1383–86).

Why, she asks, should her one life hold back an army of tens of thousands of men? Her second major concern is for Achilles: why should he die for the sake of a woman? "It is better for one man to live than ten thousand women" (1393–94). As we have seen, these lines have been taken as evidence of Greek misogyny, but it is important to remember that Iphigenia is using all possible arguments to persuade her mother not to try to fight the inevitable.[7] She concludes by reminding her mother that Artemis demanded the sacrifice and that one cannot successfully oppose a god.[8] In the end, not only does she win the "undying fame" (*doxan aphthiton*, 1606) that she and the great Homeric heroes hoped for, but she escapes with her life, because at the last moment the goddess sends a deer to take her place at the sacrificial altar.

It is interesting that in the *Iphigenia at Aulis*, one of Euripides' last plays (ca. 406 BC),[9] the girl who accepts the values of the male world wins the greatest reward, victory for her country, glory (and survival) for herself. Rather than criticize the standard ethic of Athenian behavior towards the end of his life, as scholars continue to suppose he was doing, Euripides appeals to the basic patriotism of his earlier plays. In one of these, the *Children of Heracles* (430 BC),[10] Demophoön, the king of Athens, can win the war against the attacking Argives and save not only his city but Heracles' nephew Iolaus and the children of Heracles who are suppliant at the altars in Athens, but only if a young girl is sacrificed to Persephone. Demophoön refuses to offer one of his own children or to demand that any other citizen do so against his will, but the eldest of Heracles' daughters volunteers. She reasons that if the Athenians are willing to die on her behalf, she should be ready to die on theirs, especially since she is a daughter of the hero Heracles. In any case, death is preferable to the dishonor that she would suffer should Athens be taken or if she should be forced to go into exile, where people would accuse her of cowardice and drive her away because she betrayed her friends. She reasons: "Who would want to have me as a destitute maiden or as a wife or to get children on me? It would be better to die than to end up disgraced for this, despite my noble birth" (523–36 = $WLGR^3$ 27C). Pausanias records the similar legend of how, when an oracle demanded of the Thebans the sacrifice of the citizen of the most noble descent, "Antipoenus, who had the most distinguished ancestry, did not care to die on behalf of the city, but his daughters were willing. So they took their own lives, and have [ritual] honors on that account" (9. 17. 1).

As we have seen, similar arguments are put forward, after the fall of Troy in the *Hecuba*, by Hecuba's daughter Polyxena, who goes willingly to be sacrificed to the ghost of Achilles.[11] Polyxena does not want to be thought a coward, and she asks what use there is for her to live now that her father is dead and her kingdom lost? Like Heracles' daughter, she stresses her noble birth: before, she had been like a goddess, except for having to die; now, she is a slave. Suppose that she was acquired by a harsh master and made to be a cook or a housecleaner or to spend all day weaving, or still worse, forced to share her master's bed? (342–72). Later in the play the Greek herald Talthybius reports that, as Polyxena was about to be sacrificed, she reminded her captors that she was dying willingly and as a free woman; she asked them not to hold her down, since she would be ashamed to be called a slave princess among the dead (547–52). She undoes her *peplos*, so that her breast is revealed, and she offers Achilles' son Neoptolemus the choice of her chest or her throat, in order to emphasize that she is going to her death voluntarily and that he can kill her as he might an enemy, rather than slit her throat as if she were an animal.[12] Neoptolemus follows sacrificial ritual and cuts her throat, but the herald Talthybius observes that "although she was dying, she took care to fall in a seemly way, hiding what ought to be hidden from the eyes of men" (569–70). This behavior, provocative as it might seem to us, arouses only respect and pity in the Greek army who observed it; they bring leaves and branches to throw on her, and they demand that their fellows offer something to this girl, who excelled in courage and nobility (557–58). If anything, the references to her sexuality provide a grim reminder that if Troy had not fallen when it did she would have been ready for marriage. Her mother requests that no one in the army be allowed to touch her corpse, fearing that in the confusion someone might do it harm. She asks that water be brought for her to wash her daughter for the last time, not as would have been normal, before her wedding, but to prepare her body for burial—"bride that is no bride and young girl who is young girl no longer" (612)—reflecting, as so often in grave inscriptions, on the contrast between a parent's hopes and the present grim reality.[13]

The notion that death was preferable to slavery would not have seemed surprising to a Greek audience. In the *Trojan Women* (415 BC), Andromache is prepared to kill herself before allowing herself to be possessed by a new master, and she is restrained only by the hope, which soon proves to be false, that she will live to keep her son Astyanax safe in captivity. But an epitaph by the third-century BC poet Anyte records that in real life also maidens committed suicide rather than face rape or enslavement: "We leave you, Miletus, dear homeland, because we rejected the lawless insolence of impious Gauls [277 BC]. We were three maidens, your citizens. The violent aggression of the Celts brought us to this fate. We did not wait for unholy union or marriage, but found ourselves a protector in death" (*AP* 7. 492 = xxiii G-P = *WLGR*³ 12).

Another epigram, probably by the second-century poet Antipater of Sidon, describes how a mother killed herself and her two daughters during the sack of Corinth in 146 BC: "We chose a brave death . . . for us the fate of freedom was better than slavery" (*AP* 7. 493 = lxvii G-P). Pausanias records how, at the same time, the Greek general Diaeus of Megalopolis killed his wife, so that she would not become a captive of the Romans, and then killed himself by drinking poison (7. 16. 6). A pagan inscription from Paphlagonia describes how Domitilla, a fourteen-year-old girl who had been married only seven months, killed herself during the invasion of the Goths in AD 262–63: "She won the crown of chastity. She was the only one of the young girls whom the [Goths] were about to violate . . . who was not afraid to choose death instead of harsh violence (*hybris*)."[14]

Euripides, by having his characters emphasize the importance to them of the value that society throughout the Greek world placed on women's honor, makes the idea of willing death seem believable, even in a time when human sacrifice was unthinkable and animal sacrifices were regularly offered before battles.[15] In another play of Euripides where invaders can be repelled only by the sacrifice of the king's daughter, the *Erechtheus* (ca. 423 BC), the king's wife, Praxithea, is moved by patriotism to offer her child willingly (fr. 360 *TGrF* = *WLGR*³ 27B). Athens, she claims, with its indigenous population and its real right of citizenship, is the best possible city; her children were born in order to defend their city. She would not have kept a son from the fighting: "I hate mothers who instead of honor choose that their children should live, and advise cowardice" (30–31). Instead, her daughter's one life will save many: "O fatherland, would that all who dwell in you loved you as much as I" (50–54). In the *Erechtheus*, as in the *Children of Heracles*, the women are shown to be capable of the greatest heroism in male terms, willing, as men must be in war, to sacrifice their families and their own comfort and their very lives to fight for their country. In Euripides' *Phoenician Women* (ca. 409 BC), even though his father, Creon, tries to get him to escape, Menoeceus, the oldest son, willingly offers himself as a human sacrifice for his country because of patriotism and honor both: "I shall go and save my city and give my life to die on behalf of this land; for not to do so is disgraceful. The hoplites who stand in battle are not compelled by oracles or the gods and do not hesitate to die . . . and if I betrayed my father, brother, and my city, I would go as a coward outside my land, and wherever I would live would seem a coward" (998–1005).

In Sophocles' dramas, family honor compels Electra, when she thinks her brother Orestes is dead, to consider killing Aegisthus herself, and Antigone is willing to risk death in order to bury her brother Polynices in defiance of her uncle Creon's edict.[16] "I knew that I would die, how should I not, even if you had not proclaimed the death penalty? But if I die before my time, I count that as a benefit, for whoever lives as I do, surrounded by evils, how can he not benefit by dying?" (460–64). Antigone claims that she has carried out the wishes of the god of the dead: "It is Hades who desires these rites" (*nomoi*, 519), and the "rites" or "laws" (*nomoi*) she is observing, although unwritten, were established by the gods (450–57). Creon insists that the laws laid down by men (*nomoi prokeimenoi*) must also be observed and that she is doing violence to them (*hybrizein*, 480–81) by disobeying, and further violence by disobeying them openly and boasting of it (482–83). He suspects that Antigone and her sister Ismene are plotting his overthrow (533), and he refuses to let a woman rule over him (*arxei*, 525). Both sisters "must now be women and not unrestrained" (579), that is, they must be like wives instead of the unmarried maidens that they are—they must be restricted to the palace. Clearly, Creon feels that giving in to a woman's wishes would be dishonorable; but his primary motive in seeing that the death sentence is carried out, even against his niece, is that a law designed for the benefit of his city has been broken. But by the end of the play the gods show that it is the law of the gods that must first be obeyed, even at the expense of human values.

Antigone says that she knows that she must die, but she does not go to her death gladly, even though she knows that she will be reunited with the family that she has kept together by ensuring that Polynices is given due rites of burial (896–902). Instead, she laments that she has died "without a marriage bed, without a bridal song, without a share of marriage or the raising of children" (917–18), that is, what women, according to their own words, most desire in life.[17] "Cursed and unwed" she goes to share a home with her family in the lower world (869), an existence that no Greek could imagine to be superior to a happy life on earth.

Because the Greeks did not believe in a rewarding afterlife, these mythical martyrs show a moral courage that may surpass that of the more celebrated historical martyrs of the early Church. It is interesting that, during the first centuries of the Church, women continued to be prominent among those who were willing to sacrifice themselves on behalf of a higher cause. We must ask, as we have for the pagan martyrs, to what extent sex was a factor in their deaths, either in their decision to die or in the motives of those who executed them.

One of the earliest martyrologies, the *Acts of Perpetua and Felicity* of Carthage, about two women who were sentenced to death in AD 203, includes what is said to be the memoirs of the martyr Perpetua herself.[18] Also, unlike other martyrologies, Perpetua's tells not only about herself but about the other members of her family.[19] Perpetua was a young mother with a nursing baby when she was taken into custody; she brings her baby with her to prison, then gives it to her mother to look after, then gets the baby back again, to her delight: "At once I recovered my health, relieved as I was of my worry and anxiety over the child. My prison had suddenly become a palace, so that I wanted to be there rather than anywhere else" (3. 4–5 = $WLGR^3$ 445).[20] Then Perpetua's father takes the baby away from her and begs her to give up her faith in order to return to her family, but she refuses to take the oath of loyalty to the emperor and make the required sacrifice for his safety. Her father keeps trying to plead with her, and he is beaten with rods by soldiers. She reports then that the baby suddenly and miraculously no longer needs her milk, and she adds, "Nor did I suffer any inflammation; and so I was relieved of any anxiety for my child and of any discomfort in my breasts" (6. 8). This narrative of a mother's concern for her infant is unique in ancient literature, and the details about her family make it seem the more remarkable (and painful) that she was able to give up her child, her husband, and her parents.

The usual explanation is, of course, that one's faith should dictate the rules of one's conduct; but in most cases, as we have seen, extenuating circumstances also contribute. Her conflict with her father is so marked in the narrative that she appears to some extent to be rebelling against her family (women were married young, at about 14), and it seems that part of the appeal of her new faith was that it offered a new, more egalitarian existence, in which women and men worked together and lived as sisters and brothers, rather than in the structure of traditional families, in which husbands and fathers dictated where and how women lived. It seems significant that in the last vision she records before she is led off to her death, she dreams that, in order to fight against the Devil, she becomes a man, and defeats him in a wrestling match (10. 13–14). Did her Christianity offer her a means of breaking out of the limiting patterns that life in the male-dominated world had defined for her as a woman?

In a previous discussion of this martyrology, I suggested that Perpetua did believe that her religion offered her an opportunity to break away from the traditional patriarchal values of pagan society.[21] I should have noted that these patriarchal values were also present in the early Church, and that the father whom she seeks to abandon had treated her with greater kindness than prevailing custom dictated. Perpetua is shown arguing with her father primarily because he, as the male head of the household, was the one with legal authority over her. Far from having treated her badly, he did, as he points out, actually take care of her till she was an adult, and "put her before all her brothers" (5.2), behavior that would not be remarkable in a twentieth-century Western father but was particularly enlightened conduct for a citizen of Carthage at the beginning of the third century AD. Most pagan societies had a high rate of infanticide, and we have for Carthage[22] extensive archaeological evidence of human sacrifice until the second century BC, when the city was destroyed by Rome.[23] If a man raised a daughter and gave her preferential treatment, he was rich, and certainly humane. Nor, in his plea to her, does he express any attempt to order her about; rather, he appeals to her ties and responsibilities not only to himself but to all of her family: "Do not abandon me to be the reproach of men. Think of your brothers, think of your mother and your aunt, think of your child, who will not be able to live once you are gone. Give up your pride! You will destroy all of us! None of us will ever be able to speak freely again if anything happens to you" (5. 2–4).

Thus, Perpetua goes to her death not so much because she is a woman but in order not to be a woman, with all the usual responsibilities to her family. The narrative reveals a desire on Perpetua's part for general rebellion against her family and her old way of life, with all that it involved. The new existence that she hoped to obtain through Christianity offered her a new family, in which she still sought the approval and protection of males, but without conventional demands of sexuality and reproduction. The early Church offered recognition and opportunities for service to women, but only if they denied their sexual and reproductive functions. Hence, for her moment of final triumph over the devil, St. Augustine praises her in his sermons for behaving with manly courage (*Serm.* 280. 1, 281. 1, 282. 3; *PL* v. 38). She found a form of liberation, perhaps, but one that was even more restrictive than the traditional roles assigned to women by the pagans.

Another interesting martyrology describes the trials and martyrdom of eight women living in Thessalonica, in northern Greece, in AD 304, a century after Perpetua's death (*WLGR*³ 446).[24] The story of their persecution and suffering was the basis of a little drama, *Dulcitius,* by a tenth-century nun, Hroswitha of Gandersheim,[25] in Saxony, who turns it into the triumph of purity and virginity over lascivious and clownish Roman persecutors. But the original martyrs were not all virgins (one was pregnant), and they were persecuted not merely for being Christians but for what apparently struck the Romans as threatening behavior: they had gone together to the mountains to read Holy Scripture. At the time, it would have been unusual for women to be living together by themselves away from their families and without the company or supervision of men (in other martyrologies devoted Christians lived together as "brothers and sisters," like the chaste couples Paul knew in Corinth (1 Cor. 7. 29, 36–38).[26] The Romans would also have been worried by the books the women had with them, not because they considered it unsuitable for women to read, since upper-class women, at least, were often literate. The documents in these women's possession, however, because they were not traditional, could have seemed to the Romans seditious, or possibly even magical.[27] The women were arrested and the books confiscated.

In the trial, the Roman prefect Dulcitius is reported to have said:

> You have deliberately kept even till now so many tablets, books, parchments, codices and pages of the writings of the former Christians of unholy name . . . Who was it that advised you to retain those parchments and writings up to the present time? . . . Was anyone else aware that the documents were in the house

where you lived? . . . Now after you returned from the mountain where you
had been, as you say, were any persons present at the reading of these books?
(5. 1–7)

Dulcitius could hardly have found reassuring the reply of the most prominent of the women, Irene:

> As for our own relatives, we considered them worse than our enemies, in fear
> that they would denounce us. Hence we told no one [where the documents
> were] . . . It caused us much distress that we could not devote ourselves to them
> night and day as we had done from the beginning until that day last year when
> we hid them. (5. 3–8)

The prefect sentences Irene to be placed naked in the public brothel; the writings and the chests that contained them were publicly burned. It is reported
as a miracle that no one touched her or even insulted her when she was in the
brothel, but it is also possible that the men of the city avoided her because
they thought of her as a dangerous sorceress, on account of her strange behavior in the mountains and with the books.[28] At first, he sentences only two
of Irene's comrades to death; "because of their youth," (4. 4) he puts the others
in jail. Irene and her companions were martyred in AD 304.

How much of the persecution directed against these martyrs was because
they were *women*? In the nun Hroswitha's version of this story, all traces of
discrimination on Dulcitius' part vanish; he is simply lustful and sadistic, and
there is no reference to the problem of the books and papers that the women
tried to hide. Consigning Irene to a public brothel certainly sounds like sexual
persecution; but it is interesting to note that in the original transcript of the
trial she is not, like many male martyrs, tortured or beaten. By placing her in
the brothel, the real Dulcitius, a Roman magistrate, may have hoped to get
her to abandon her faith and confess any seditious crimes she may have committed, since, for a woman of noble family, losing her virginity in this way
would mean permanent disgrace. Whether for humanitarian or political reasons, he clearly did not want to condemn her to death without giving her ample opportunity to recant.[29] To Dulcitius the notion of wishing to die for
one's faith would have seemed incomprehensible. Why would one insist on
having just one god, when there was room in the world for many? The Greek
officials in Palestine could not understand the behavior of the Maccabees; in
AD 178 the Roman philosopher Celsus claimed that Christians "offer their

bodies to be tortured and crucified to no purpose"; he called them "mad," recounting, "they deliberately rush forward to arouse the wrath of an emperor or a governor, which brings upon them blows and tortures and even death."[30]

By the end of the century, Christianity had become the established faith in the Roman world, and pagan rites and sacrifices had been declared illegal; now it was the pagans who were persecuted. Hypatia of Alexandria, who was murdered in AD 415, was not exactly a martyr, because she did not die as a "witness" to her faith; but we may well ask whether her death was to some extent caused by her being a woman. In a memorable passage, Gibbon makes it clear that the Christians behaved in an even more brutal fashion than the Romans who had persecuted Irene in Thessalonica. Speaking of Cyril, the patriarch of Alexandria, Gibbon writes: "He soon prompted, or accepted, the sacrifice of a virgin who professed the religion of the Greeks."[31] In his account of Hypatia's death, Gibbon stresses the rationality and education of the pagan woman and the violent passions and ignorance of her murderers; he also adds details of sexual sadism: they stripped her naked, they scraped her flesh from her bones with sharp oyster-shells. The biography of Hypatia in the ancient encyclopedia known as the *Suda* says simply that "she was torn to bits by the Alexandrians, and her mutilated body was scattered through the city" (D166 Adler = *WLGR*3 451). In this biography, it is not even clear that the murder was committed at the patriarch Cyril's instigation. Other Christians, particularly a reader in the church named Peter, were involved. It was a period of civil unrest in general and pogroms against Jews.[32]

Certainly Hypatia's gender would have given her particular notoriety, if only because it was very unusual for a woman to be a practicing philosopher, though there had been others in the past, usually relatives of male philosophers. But unlike those predecessors, she had remained a virgin; and, on occasion, she openly denied her femininity. She taunted an admirer with a Platonic homily that used as its object one of her sanitary towels;[33] according to her biography, "she threw a rough cloak (a *tribon*, like a man's) about herself and went forth through the centre of town and gave lectures in public about Plato or Aristotle or the works of some other philosophers to those who wanted to listen." Women in Hellenistic and Roman times could certainly go out alone, but only in order to go shopping, visiting, or to a festival, and not to give lectures.

The third-century BC philosopher Hipparchia was criticized for going around dressed like her husband and attending dinner parties with him;

when she got the better of a male philosopher in a discussion about logic, he tried to pull off her cloak (*himation*, Diogenes Laertius 6. 97 = *WLGR³* 217). But even in the relative freedom of the late Republic, Amasia Sentia, who pleaded her own defense before a court in 77 BC, was called "androgyne"; and Gaia Afrania, who brought lawsuits herself around the same time, was regarded as a "monster" (Valerius Maximus 8. 3 = *WLGR³* 178). Hypatia's biography relates that "when she was going out as usual a large crowd of bestial men, truly roughnecks, who knew no respect for the gods or the wrath of men, [the designation *theriodeis* suggests that they were hermits or monks],[34] seized the philosopher and brought a great pollution and disgrace on their fatherland." Certainly for Hypatia, as for Antigone, being a woman made her more visible and more vulnerable to criticism; but gender is only a contributing factor and not the central reason why they were put to death. We should not forget that Hypatia was not simply an educated woman but a mathematician; geometry and astronomy were confused by the ignorant with astrology. Like Irene, who was discovered with books and documents of a secret nature, Hypatia would have been suspected of being a sorceress.[35]

Although there is no way for us to know exactly what happened to Hypatia, the Christians who attacked her may have been more concerned about her political influence than about her philosophical ideas or status as a female. The *Suda* biography reports of the patriarch Cyril:

> When he passed by Hypatia's house, he saw that there was a large crowd in front of the door, made up of both men and horses, some approaching, some going away, and some waiting there. He asked what the gathering was and why there was commotion in front of the house, and learned from his followers that the philosopher Hypatia was now giving a lecture and that this was her house. And when he learned this he was very upset, and soon planned her murder, the most unholy of all murders.

According to this account, Cyril's motive is not misogyny, but envy: Hypatia was not only drawing large crowds, possibly away from his sermons, but crowds of rich men—that is why he was upset to see horses as well as men in front of her door, since only the very rich could afford to own horses, or in fact had the leisure to listen to lectures. It is interesting to note that, in this account, Cyril does not resent her worship of the old gods (i.e., being a pagan) so much as her influence over important people, the very men whose support he needed for his church.[36]

Thus, far more than a struggle of women against men, I now see in the documents we have been discussing a conflict between rational humane understanding and ignorant irrational insistence in which neither sex has a monopoly in either category: the end of the *Antigone* clearly shows that Creon was wrong to insist that his niece be buried alive for disobeying his orders; the Roman magistrates who examined the Christian martyrs at least gave them a chance to go free if they would perform what would have seemed to the Romans a trivial act of allegiance to the emperor, which most Romans would have done as readily as Americans would recite the Pledge of Allegiance to the Flag; the aristocrat Synesius of Cyrene, who later became a Christian and a bishop, studied with Hypatia, but uneducated and brutal men took her life. The biography in the *Suda* does not state specifically whether her murderers were pagan or Christian or that they particularly resented women who behaved in an unconventional way, but it does indicate that they had no regard for the law or for traditional culture.

It is only in popular legends about women saints that sexuality becomes the dominant issue. In narratives about later female saints who adopted men's dress, attention is carefully drawn to the sexuality the women are trying to deny. Hilaria, according to a sixth-century Coptic account of her life, dressed like a man in order to be accepted as a monk; she was known as Hilarion the eunuch, because "her breasts were not as those of all women; . . . she was shrunken by ascetic practices nor was she subject to the curse of women."[37] Some who thought her a man accused her of having had sexual relations with her own sister, whom she had cured of a devil. On her death-bed she revealed her true identity to the abbot of her monastery.[38] For Thecla, mentioned in the second-century AD *Acts of Paul*, as for Hipparchia and Hypatia, adopting a man's dress indicated that she had adopted a man's way of life and did not wish to be treated like a woman. After returning home to Iconium, "she went away to Seleucia, and after enlightening many with the word of God she slept a noble sleep" (43 = *WLGR*[3] 444).[39] But by the fifth century, Thecla's sexuality was thought to have been the actual cause of her death.[40] Pagan doctors, put out of business by her healing of the sick, hire thugs to rape her. They tell the men: "This virgin happens to be sacred to the great goddess Artemis. If she asks the goddess for anything, the goddess listens to her because she is a virgin and all the gods love her . . . If you can rape her, the gods and Artemis won't listen to her about the sick." The "evil men . . . stood like lions at her grotto and banged on the door." But Thecla knows why they have come, and as they seize her she prays to God to save her, and "not allow the violation of my maidenhood, which I have guarded till now in your name"; the rock opens just enough to allow her to pass through, and closes again behind her.[41] If the author of this story had been better informed about Artemis, he would have realized that although she required her attendants in myth and in cult to be virgins, she did not grant them any special powers of healing. Only in Christianity does celibacy confer a superior status. But it is perhaps ironic that the new importance accorded to virginity imparts to the lives of Christian female martyrs an emphasis on sexuality that was at most tangential in the pagan world.

Misogyny

If Greek men were not afraid of Greek women and did not fail to give credit to women's accomplishments even in areas ordinarily reserved for men, then why did they still remain wary of women in general and continue to deprive them of full citizenship rights? In recent times it has been tempting to assume that a principal reason was men's fear of women's sexuality; some critics have even suggested that men were repelled by the appearance of the female genitalia, and so were compelled to turn for pleasure to their own sex.[1] But if this was the reason, the Greeks themselves did not say so; in fact, extant Greek literature, most particularly in the narratives of traditional myth, contains little that resembles the explicit descriptions of lovemaking in modern novels, and Greek philosophers said so little about practical sexuality that Michel Foucault, commenting on his own *Histoire de la Sexualité*, could state that "the Greeks weren't interested in sex."[2]

Since it is Aristotle who, in his *Politics* states explicitly that "the male is superior and the female inferior, the male ruler and the female subject" (1254b 13–15), we might profitably begin by trying to discover why he considers inferiority of the female to be a state of nature (1260a 11). Here Aristotle offers no direct explanation, perhaps because he assumed that no serious argument would be proposed. But it is clear from the text that he has made certain assumptions about women's behavior. In Sparta, where women were given greater freedom than in Athens, "the women live with every licentiousness and luxury" (1269b 22–23); Spartan women's insulting behavior towards other women, he claims, had caused the downfall of many tyrannies (1314b 27–28). Aristotle advises that "it is an aid to chastity" if women are married when they are older, around eighteen years of age, because "young women are more licentious in regard to intercourse" (1335a 23–25). Presumably, then, women in the best-run governments must be kept under control because they are by nature incapable of sufficient moral restraint; or, to put it the other way round, women are morally unreliable, in regard both to sexual behavior and financial expenditure.

In this chapter I should like to examine how Aristotle in the fourth century BC came to accept the "fact" of women's moral inferiority. I will try to show that, before Christian times, Greek literature was concerned not with the physical effects of passion but with the effects of passion on reason, judgment, and, accordingly, on action. Both men and women can be victims of passion, but women are portrayed as being more readily susceptible to the effects of passion (even) than men, and thus inevitably are considered to be potentially more dangerous. At the end of this chapter I will explore why it is that, in our own reading of Greek texts, we stress the references to signs of gender that the Greeks themselves seem to have regarded as incidental. I suggest that it is because an emphasis on women's physical vulnerability was introduced into Western literature from Christian doctrine and the mythology of the early centuries of the Christian era.

In order to determine what men thought about women with whom they had some kind of permanent relationship, that is, wives, rather than *hetairai* or prostitutes, we must rely primarily on the portrayal of the effects of passion in epic and drama; comedy and amusing epigrams provide explicit information about various homosexual and heterosexual practices but principally in extramarital relations or extraordinary situations, like the women's withdrawal of their sexual favors in Aristophanes' *Lysistrata*—a tactic that was, even though Foucault and others say that Greek men weren't interested in sex, highly successful.

I will begin, then, at the beginning, with the story of Pandora. When Prometheus tricked Zeus and stole fire for man, according to the poet Hesiod in the *Works and Days*, Zeus then devised "a big trouble" for Prometheus and the men of the future (56); he ordered Hephaestus to mix earth and water, "and to put in the voice and strength of a human being (*anthrōpou*) and to make her a maiden's fair and lovely shape, in appearance like the deathless goddesses." Zeus orders Athene to teach the creature handiwork; Aphrodite pours golden *charis* ("sex appeal") about her head, and cruel desires and limb-devouring cares; Hermes puts in a bitch's mind and a thieving nature (60–68). The Graces and Persuasion give her jewelry, the Seasons a crown of flowers, and Athena dresses her; then Hermes names her "Pandora" because all the gods gave her a gift (*dōron*). She is sent as a "headlong trap" to Epimetheus ("Afterthought"), Prometheus' brother, who doesn't realize until it is too late that he has got hold of something evil (68–89). The woman opens the large jar she is carrying and scatters troubles and diseases around the earth; "she devised for men sorrowful trouble" (95). In this account, sexual appeal is only one reason why Pandora at first seems to Epimetheus to be something other than the evil that she is. Hermes was ordered to put into her a "bitch's mind and a thieving nature," and in fact he gives her "lies and cunning words and a thieving nature on the orders of Zeus the thunderer." She brings trouble to mankind (*anthrōpoisi*) not because of her sexuality but because she is a bitch —not exactly what we mean by the term, but as the Greeks thought of dogs: shameless, amoral, without judgment.[3]

In the *Works and Days* Hesiod does not say that all other women are like Pandora. But in his other epic, the *Theogony*, when Zeus sees that Prometheus has given him the bones rather than the meat of the sacrificial victim, he orders Hephaestus to make a nameless female creature "from whom is descended the race of women. They live as a great pain to mortal men (*andrasi*); they are helpers in times of plenty but not in cruel poverty" (591–93). He then compares women to the lazy drones in a beehive and adds:

> so Zeus made women for mortal men, partners in harsh deeds. But he gave another evil in place of a good; the man who escapes marriage and the evil that women work and does not wish to marry comes to cruel old age in want of someone to care for his old age [presumably, a son] and though he does not lack the means of life during his lifetime, when he is dead the heirs of a vacant inheritance divide up his substance. But for the man who has a share in marriage and has a good and intelligent wife, for him steadfast evil is set against good; but if a man encounters a mischievous sort of wife, he lives with unending pain in his heart, and the evil has no cure. (*Theogony* 600–612)

Like the archetype created by the gods, Pandora's descendants are beautiful to look at but destructive, a "headlong trap" (589). Pandora's daughters are also economically detrimental: they do no work; they wish to share abundance but not poverty.[4] Even a woman "equipped with intelligence" (*areruian prapidessi*, 608) is only partly able to offset evil with good; the "mischievous sort" (*atarteroio genethles*) brings unending pain and incurable evil.

Implicit in the *Theogony's* characterization of the woman from whom the race of women is descended and in the portrait of Pandora in the *Works and Days* is the notion that a woman's physical beauty conceals from the man who wants her, plus the son he cannot have without her, her power to do him harm. Her desirability itself is not the only problem; the real trouble is caused by the presence in women of evil intent, which emerges later as openly destructive behavior; she releases diseases upon the world, she consumes a man's livelihood. Semonides, in his satire on women, points out the same discrepancy between appearance and true nature; a beautiful woman is like a mare: she does not do any housework but tends to her own appearance: "a woman like her is a fine sight for others, but for the man she belongs to she proves a plague (*kakon*), unless he is some tyrant or king" (tr. Lloyd-Jones, *WLGR*³ 57). In the same way, he uses the simile of the sea to describe another woman's nature: "She has two characters (*du' en phresin noei*) . . . just as the sea often stands without a tremor, harmless, a great delight to sailors, in the summer season; but often it raves, tossed about by thundering waves. It is the sea that such a woman most resembles in her temper; like the ocean, she has a changeful nature" (7. 27, 37–42).

It is this power to seem good but to bring or think evil that makes the goddess Aphrodite so potentially harmful, not her sexual attraction alone. Aphrodite, like Pandora, is not born in an ordinary way but "grows up" (*eth-rephthē*) in the foam (*aphrōi*) surrounding the severed genitals of the god Heaven (*Theogony* 191–200): "Eros (Passion) accompanied her and beautiful Desire when she was born and first went into the company of the gods . . . maiden's soft voices and smiles and deceptions (*exapatas*), sweet pleasure, love, and gentleness" (201–6). The pleasures that come from sexual passion are sweet; but deception is potentially harmful, as Sappho says in her prayer to Aphrodite: "Aphrodite on your intricate throne, deathless, daughter of Zeus, weaver of plots (*doloploke*), I beg you, do not tame my heart with pain or with anguish, but come here" (fr. 1. 1–4). Aphrodite, because she is a weaver of plots, can bring anguish even to a woman in love, though Sappho's suffering, unlike the man's in Hesiod's *Theogony*, does not result from want of food or money, but from "cruel anxiety" and the possibility that she may not get what she wants, unless Aphrodite chooses to fight on her side (25–28 = *WLGR*³ 1).

The idea that Aphrodite can serve as an ally in a war for a woman's affections may derive from the myth of Helen, who, in Sappho's words, "far surpassed other people in beauty, left behind the best of husbands, and went to Troy. She sailed away and did not remember at all her daughter or her beloved parents, but [Aphrodite] led her astray" (fr. 16. 5–11 = *WLGR*³). Sappho tells the story in a poem that describes her feelings about "Anactoria who is no longer near" (15–16), whose lovely step and brilliant glancing of her face she longs to see; but in her account of Helen's adultery Sappho chooses to emphasize not Helen's sexual attributes but simply her beauty and the way Aphrodite "led her astray," so that she forgot all normal family ties and loyalties. It is the power of passion to affect one's mind, to cause one to do the opposite of what one wants or should do, that makes the works of Aphrodite a subject for song and story. As Semonides says at the end of his satire on women, also with Helen in mind:

> Each man will take care to praise his own wife and find fault with the others; we do not realize that the fate of all of us is alike. Yes, this is the greatest plague (*kakon*) that Zeus has made, and he has put round us a fetter that cannot be broken. Because of this some have gone to Hades fighting for a woman. (112–18)

The point is that men can easily be deceived about their character; as Hesiod says, "for a man wins no prize better than the good woman, nor any horrider than the bad one" (*Works and Days* 702–3).

There is no more powerful statement of the power of passion to alter man's judgment than the *Homeric Hymn to Aphrodite*. The hymn tells the story of how, after Aphrodite had led aside Anchises' mind (*parek noon ēgage*, 36) so that he fell in love with mortal women, Zeus got even with her by casting "into Aphrodite herself the desire to join in love with a mortal man" (45–46), so that she could not boast that she was superior to all the other gods and goddesses. Aphrodite goes to considerable trouble to deceive the young man Zeus has chosen for her, Anchises, who is "like to one of the immortals in appearance" (55). She goes to her shrine in Cyprus to bathe; she dresses carefully and then assumes the form and appearance of an unmarried maiden, "lest he be afraid of her when he perceived her [as a goddess] in his eyes" (82–83). He addresses her respectfully, as if she were a goddess in disguise, or a nymph, but she assures him that she is a mortal woman, names her parents and says that Hermes snatched her away while she was dancing for Artemis and brought her here to be his wife; she asks only that he take her "as a virgin and without experience in love" (133–34) to show to his father and mother. He is so overcome by the desire she casts into him (143) that he refuses to wait; "not even if who shoots from afar Apollo himself sent forth from his silver bow his cruel arrows at me—then I would be willing, woman like the immortal goddesses, having gone onto your bed to go down into the halls of Hades" (151–54).

The poet's comment, after he describes how Anchises removes the clothes Aphrodite so carefully put on, makes it clear that he is closer to a complete change of fortune than he imagines: "and then with the will of the gods and fate, the mortal slept with the deathless goddess, not knowing clearly [what he did]" (166–67). Immediately afterwards, Aphrodite herself reveals the consequences of his actions to him, but without the blandishments with which she had persuaded him, quite untruthfully, that she was not a goddess: "Wake up, son of Dardanus; why are you sleeping so soundly? And tell me if I seem to you to resemble the girl that you first saw with your eyes?" (177–79). "He woke up, and when he saw her he was afraid and turned his eyes aside and covered his fair face with his cloak"; he reminds her that she lied to him and begs her not to "let me live strengthless among men, but have pity on me. For a man is not healthy in life who has slept with the immortal goddesses" (188–90). If Anchises means here that he is afraid that he will henceforth be impotent, he does not say so explicitly, though he could easily have done so.[5] It is more likely that he has in mind what happened to Endymion, who, after intercourse with the goddess Selene (the Moon), fell into an eternal sleep, undying and ageless, or Tithonus, who lived forever, but as an old man who could not move his limbs. As Aphrodite herself says in the hymn: "I wouldn't choose that you live like that among the immortals and survive for all time" (238–40). Instead Anchises is to receive the son Aphrodite will bear to him when the son (Aeneas) is four years old, but Zeus will strike Anchises with lightning if he reveals "or boasts in his foolish heart that he has had intercourse with garlanded Aphrodite" (286–87). But Aphrodite too has been saddened and shamed by the experience:

> I will be greatly disgraced among the deathless gods for the rest of time because of you; before this the gods were afraid of my soft voice and plotting, with which I used to join all the gods to mortal women. My mind subdued them all. But I shall no longer have the power to boast of this since I have been greatly deceived, miserably, indescribably. I have wandered out of my mind, and got a child beneath my girdle because I went to bed with a mortal. (247–55)

Like Anchises, she was deceived and led astray, "out of her mind," by a desire that at first seemed beautiful but then brought pain: "His name shall be Ae-

neas because of the cruel (*ainon*) pain I have because I fell into a mortal's bed"
(198–99).

In tragic poetry describing the mistakes in judgment that lead to destruction, the metaphors of violence are used to characterize both sexual passion
and *atē*, the delusion that leads men to destruction, because in Sophocles'
words, "evil (*kakon*) seems good to the man whose mind the god is leading toward *atē*" (Sophocles, *Antigone* 622–23). Passion (*erōs*), says the chorus in the
Antigone, speaking of Haemon's love for his fiancé, Antigone, is "unconquered
in battle"; it travels beyond sea and land; no mortal or immortal can escape it,
and "he who has it is mad (*memēnen*)"; passion makes "the minds of the just
unjust to their disgrace" (791; cf. Sophocles, *Trachiniae* 441–44). Or, as the
chorus of Euripides' *Hippolytus* describes it after they have learned of Phaedra's passion for her stepson: "Eros, Eros, who distil desire upon the eyes; you
bring sweet pleasure in the souls of those whom you attack . . . no missile of
fire or of the stars is so powerful as the arrow of Aphrodite that Zeus' son
Eros shoots from his hands" (525–34).

In both these passages, as in the *Homeric Hymn to Aphrodite*, the females
themselves do not want to cause trouble. Rather, the problem is the passion
they inspire in others and the destructive actions the passion brings about. If
women are blamed, as they often are by the people whose lives are affected by
passion—whether their own or someone else's—it is because women's minds
seem particularly vulnerable to these destructive emotions. If Clytemnestra
will give all women, even good ones, a bad name, as the soul of Agamemnon
claims in the *Odyssey* (24. 192–202), it is because, unlike the faithful Penelope, who had a "good intelligence" (*agathai phrenes*), Clytemnestra "devised
shameful deeds." When Nestor tells the story to Telemachus, he too keeps
the emphasis on her mind: "Many times Aegisthus charmed Agamemnon's
wife with his speeches. At first Clytemnestra did not do a shameful deed, for
she had a good intelligence" (*phresi agathēisi, Odyssey* 3. 264–66). But Aegisthus sent away the bard whom Agamemnon had left to watch over her, and
"with her consent took her to his house" (272). Agamemnon, in his account of
the murder, continues to complain not of her sexual behavior but of her evil
intentions:

> Clytemnestra with her treacherous mind (*dolomētis*) killed Cassandra near me. I
> fell to the ground, raising my hands and throwing them as I died about the
> sword. But she—the bitch (*kynōpis*)—stood off, and did not trouble as I went

to Hades to shut my eyes with her hands or to close my mouth. So there is nothing more cruel or disgraceful (doglike, *kynteron*) than a woman who plans such deeds in her mind. (*Odyssey* 11. 422–28)

The inspiration for the character of Clytemnestra in the *Oresteia* derives directly from these passages: in the *Oresteia*, as in the *Odyssey*, nothing much is said about her love affair with Aegisthus; the emphasis is, rather, on revenge and justice. But since Aeschylus departs from Homer by making Clytemnestra, rather than Aegisthus, the primary killer, he places particular emphasis on her ability to plan and to think. Her speeches to the chorus and to Agamemnon, when she persuaded him against his better judgment to walk on the tapestries, provide evidence of her skill in saying "much to serve the time" (*pollōn kairiōs eirēmenōn*, 1372), something less than the whole truth, and it is this ability to say one thing with great effectiveness while meaning another that enables Clytemnestra to take both the chorus and Agamemnon off their guard. She herself calls attention to her intelligence; she understands the way the beacon system works better than the chorus does, and she complains that they, in doubting her account, treat her as if she were a young girl (277).

It is because of this command of her intelligence and emotions that the guard at the beginning of the play speaks of her "woman's man-counseling heart" (*androboulon kear*, 11), and she herself continually reminds the chorus that it is because she knows more than other women (348, 590–93), not because she has become "masculinized" or has "rebelliously" rejected the responsibilities of the household to assume a man's role in the outside world of politics.[6] In defending her action to the chorus (and audience), she speaks of Agamemnon as an enemy and emphasizes Agamemnon's sacrifice of their daughter, Iphigenia, and his infidelity to her with Cassandra and other women, in order to give some justification for her revenge. Understandably, she says nothing direct about her relationship with Aegisthus, merely calling him her "faithful friend" (1436), and does not describe in detail how she intends to live with him, in a normally structured household, as we discover her doing in the next play, the *Libation Bearers*.

By concentrating on individual words and metaphors, modern scholars have tended to emphasize sexual elements in the play.[7] But in using the language of the hunt to describe the murder, Aeschylus is not implying that Clytemnestra has become a man—the goddess Artemis, after all, delights in the hunt and in killing—but that she has used traps along with force, like a hunter. How else indeed could she have killed Agamemnon quickly, except with a sword? When Clytemnestra discovers in the *Libation Bearers* that Orestes has returned, she asks for a "man-slaying axe" (*androkmēta pelekun*, 889), not because she wants (by symbolic equation) to acquire a *phallos*, but in order to defend herself, now that Aegisthus is dead.

When in that play the chorus of libation bearers speaks of the women "monsters inimical to mortals" who have murdered male relatives, they are not concerned that women have killed men but that women have killed members of their own families and by treachery: Althaea killed her son Meleager by putting the log that was "his fellow in age" into the fire; Scylla, "the shameless one," murdered her father, Nisus, "as he drew breath in sleep" (620); Clytemnestra, in a "daring deed plotted by a woman's mind," "against your husband like an enemy you did go" (626–27); the women of Lemnos murdered their husbands, "first among crimes." Revenge by the sword will come to all these murdering women, as Clytemnestra herself says soon after in the play: "by guile shall we perish, just as we slew by guile" (888). The dream that Clytemnestra sent libations to avert—in which she thought that she had given birth to a snake, and wrapped it in swaddling clothes, and put it to her breast, and it drew forth blood with the milk—emphasizes both that her death will come as a surprise and that she will have been its origin. Modern interpreters have assumed that the snake suggests Orestes' maleness and that Clytemnestra in baring her breast before him is appealing to his instincts as a man (896–98).[8] But when in the *Iliad* Hecuba bares her breast to Hector, before he engages Achilles in single combat, it is to remind him of his obligation (*aidōs*) to his mother (22. 79–82). No one has suggested, presumably, that Hecuba is trying to seduce Hector, because Hecuba did not dream of giving birth to snakes, and of course Hector is planning to kill not her but Achilles. But nonetheless, as we have seen in the *Libation Bearers*, *aidōs* for a mother is a powerful deterrent, and Orestes hesitates when Clytemnestra makes the gesture.[9]

The "wrathful hounds" (924) that Clytemnestra threatens to send against Orestes, who are the goddesses known as the Erinyes that pursue him in the final play of the trilogy, have seemed in Freudian terms to represent qualities that Greek men found frightening in female anatomy.[10] But in Aeschylus' drama *Eumenides* it is not just Orestes and Apollo who find them repulsive but the old priestess who discovers them inside the temple. She does not think that they resemble women or even the Gorgons that she has seen in paintings of the story of Perseus; they appear to be diseased, unclean, and not dressed in the white clothes women are supposed to wear when in a divine precinct (Plautus, *Rudens* 279–81): "these appear wingless, black, altogether hateful in their ways; and they snore with a blast unapproachable, and from their eyes they drip a loathsome liquid. And their attire is such as one should not bring near to the statues of the gods or the houses of men" (51–56). Apollo tells them to go where they belong, to the sites of murder or castration, or mutilation such as the Persians practice. The Erinyes themselves claim only to want to drive their victims mad, with a song "maddening the brain, carrying away sense, destroying the mind" (329–30, 342–43), in order to cause their victims to destroy themselves as *erōs* or *atē* might in other contexts. Their contention, that the child is of the same blood as his mother because he was nourished by her during pregnancy (606–8), is countered by Apollo with the statement that "she who is called the child's mother is not its begetter, but the nurse of the newly sown conception. The begetter is the male, and she as stranger for a stranger preserves the offspring, if no god blights its birth" (658–61).

Apollo's argument has been considered evidence that a deep-seated misogyny was inherent in Athenian civilization, but it is important to remember that the god is speaking here as a character in a play in a context where he is acting as an advocate for a person accused of matricide; had Orestes been accused of killing his father to avenge his mother, Apollo might well have said what Aeschylus has the Erinyes say about the primacy of maternal blood ties. The role of the female in conception, of course, was not clearly understood; opinions varied about whether the female seed present in the menstrual fluid contributed to the appearance and character of the child.[11] But no Athenian audience would have believed that Apollo's argument was conclusive, any more than they would have considered practical the advice of the woman-hating Hippolytus, when he suggested that men ought to be able to buy "the seed of children" and not produce the human race from women (Euripides, *Hippolytus* 618–24). In fact, the jury in Aeschylus' drama casts the same number of ballots for Apollo as for the Erinyes, and it is only because Athena, who was born from Zeus without a mother, casts her vote for Apollo that Orestes is acquitted.

Does the outcome, then, represent a defeat of female values, which in the play are associated with darkness, pollution, madness and death, in favor of a more enlightened and rational order associated with male values? Not really, because the Erinyes and the ghost of Clytemnestra are not the only representatives of female nature; the maiden Athena is female too, and it is significant that she is able to persuade the Erinyes to use their considerable powers to preserve human life, rather than to destroy it. When the Erinyes threaten to "discharge poison from their heart upon the land, and after that a canker, blasting leaves and children" (782–85 / 810–15), Athena, in dissuading them, speaks of their powers as if they were mental rather than physical: "Do not discharge upon this land the words of an idle tongue" (829–31), "[do not] hurl against my country incentives to shed blood, harmful to the hearts of young men, maddening them with a fury not of wine" (858–60). In return for a shrine, sacrificial offerings, and a seat near the house of Erechtheus on the Acropolis, they promise to protect the city of Athens, her people, and her harvest. They leave the orchestra of the theatre accompanied by an escort of children and women and a company of aged women, the people who are most in need of protection because of their weakness and vulnerability.

Significantly, it is because of their celibacy that the Erinyes, who now take the name of Eumenides ("those with good will"), will be able to serve as protectors of the young, whom they had previously been pleased to destroy. Virgin goddesses often play the role of protectress. The maiden Artemis,[12] who demands the sacrifice of Agamemnon's daughter Iphigenia, is "kindly to the helpless young of savage lions and delightful to the breast-loving whelps of all beasts that roam the wild" (Aeschylus, *Agamemnon* 140–43). She protects not only the young but women in childbirth, and women's wombs in general; the maiden Hecate in Boeotia in Hesiod's day was worshipped as *kourotrophos*, nurse of the young (*Theogony* 450–52). Like Athena, because Aphrodite cannot "persuade or deceive" her, these goddesses can be trusted in ways that women subject to Aphrodite's powers to alter judgment cannot. That sexually active goddesses are not trusted with the care of the young has been taken as further evidence of Greek men's fear of women's sexuality, but it is their vulnerability to emotion that makes them dangerous, not the shapes of their bodies. The goddesses who abstain from the works of Aphrodite have less need to resort to plots and deceptions; like Artemis and Athena in their hymns, they simply go about their business, and join from time to time the company of the other gods.

It is no accident that the women in tragedy who help enact the wishes of the gods are virgins: Antigone, who cares for her father Oedipus and buries her brother Polynices, and Electra, who helps Orestes avenge the death of their father Agamemnon. To them may be contrasted one of Aphrodite's most destructive victims, Medea. Because of Medea's love for Jason, she betrayed her father, helped to lure her brother to his death, and brought about the deaths of Jason's uncle, again through guile, of his prospective bride and her father, and finally of her own and Jason's children. As Euripides reminds us, her very name means "planner and deviser" (*bouleuousa kai technōmenē*, cf. *mēdomai*, "devise").[13] That her gifts were used for evil is the work of Aphrodite and her son Eros. As Jason says, Aphrodite, not Medea, is responsible for his success (526–28). Modern critics have cited this statement as an example of his callousness and insincerity, but the choruses of the *Antigone* and the *Hippolytus* also blame Eros for the problems they are witnessing. In Euripides' *Trojan Women*, Helen argues to Menelaus (930–31), unpersuasively at first (1038), that Aphrodite, not she herself, is to blame for her elopement with Paris.[14] Even Penelope in the *Odyssey* 23. 222–24 says "a god" drove Helen to do it: "before that time she had not allowed folly (*atē*) to settle in her heart." As the chorus of the *Medea* says, after Jason leaves: "Erōtes (passions) coming in excess do not bring glory or virtue to men; if Cypris [Aphrodite] would come in moderation, no other goddess would be so welcome. Never, O Queen, may you let loose from your golden bow an inescapable arrow that you have anointed with desire" (627–33). They state conditionally the idea that Cypris might come in moderation, since it is unlikely ever to happen.

The Greeks, far more than we, concentrate on the moral consequences of passion, and even in the third century BC it was still associated with *atē*, the delusion that leads to destruction: "Cruel Eros, great pain, great harm to men; from you come destructive strife and lamentation and wailing and other boundless sorrows that come with these; Eros, may you rise up against my enemies' children, as you threw hateful *atē* into Medea's heart" (Apollonius of Rhodes, *Voyage of the Argo* 4. 445–49). Celibate goddesses are not only more trustworthy because their judgment is unaffected by Aphrodite and the delusion of passion; like Demeter when she comes to Eleusis disguised as an old nurse, they are freed from all responsibilities connected with reproduction and so are able to look after the young and those who need them. Demeter, after Persephone has been taken from her, disguises herself as an old woman, past child-bearing and the works of Aphrodite, so that she is able, both because of her experience with children and her present lack of involvement with men, to serve as a nurse for the son of a king, Demophoön (*Homeric*

Hymn 2. 202–4). She tells the baby's mother, in a speech that sounds like an incantation, "I know a strong antidote against the root-cutter [i.e., poisoner]; I know the good cure for painful attack" (229–30). But like Hecate, who can, if she wishes, easily take away the fisherman's catch (Hesiod, *Theogony* 443), Demeter can withdraw her protection at a moment's notice. When challenged by the baby's mother for putting her child in the fire, Demeter gets angry, puts the baby on the ground (251–55), and leaves. Still mourning for her lost daughter, she "made a most dreadful year on the earth that sustains mortals, a very vicious (*kynteron*, doglike) year, when the earth sent up no seed, for the goddess Demeter had hidden it" (302–7). This withdrawal of her favor, however, is not so capricious as Aphrodite's desire to sleep with Anchises, because it adheres to a recognized code, which men and gods both will know how to follow: in return for honor and respect—which includes accepting what the gods give, however strange it may seem, like putting one's only son into the fire—the gods will give their support to men. The Erinyes/ Eumenides in the *Oresteia* behave like Demeter in the hymn; all were goddesses connected with the regions below the earth, with death as well as with life. According to the traveler Pausanias, Demeter was also worshipped as "Erinys" in Arcadia, because of her anger (*Description of Greece* 8. 25. 5–6, cf. 8. 42).[15]

For mortal women, who did not have the power to vent their wrath on the world as did the Erinyes, the honors and rewards of chastity were greatly reduced. Epitaphs lament that young girls died before they could be married, and Electra in Sophocles' drama complains that she is not allowed to marry because her son might avenge Agamemnon's death (164–65, 187, 961–96). There was, however, some advantage in remaining celibate if it permitted access to a priesthood or temple service. The rewards of these positions varied, depending on the wealthy residents of the precinct, and most of the positions were hereditary, within aristocratic kinship groups (*phratries*), if not within families. In all periods for which we have information, temple service was virtually always temporary; an office would usually be held only for a year or two.[16] In most cases the duties of the attendants did not require residence; a woman might serve several deities at the same time. Virgin priestesses were required primarily by virgin goddesses. In myth, at least, if a priestess of Artemis lost her virginity, the goddess became angry: when Comaetho, a priestess, and Melanippus used Artemis' sanctuary "as a bridal chamber," Artemis' wrath destroyed the people; the earth bore no crops, and there were unusual diseases and inexplicable deaths (Pausanias 7. 19. 2). To prevent a recurrence of the problem, at the sanctuary of Singing Artemis near Mantinea in Arcadia, a woman "who had finished with intercourse" was substituted for the virgin priestess (Pausanias 8. 5. 12). Old peasant women were chosen for the position of Pythia at the temple of Apollo at Delphi, because, being too old for intercourse with mortal men, they were ready to serve as the "bride" of the god (Herodotus 1. 182; cf. Thriae in *Homeric Hymn* 4. 552–61).[17] But, since virgins and celibates also served that most unchaste of goddesses, Aphrodite, it seems that celibacy must have had a practical as well as a ritual function. The doctor Soranus in his *Gynaecology* recommends perpetual virginity, because women who have been prevented from intercourse by law or service to the gods, and girls who have been guarded in legal virginity "are less susceptible to diseases because they have lighter menstrual periods and put on weight because they are spared the complications that result from ordinary life" (1. 32). For widows, there would have been financial benefits and opportunity for public honor and service: "I was priestess of Demeter, and before that of the Cabeiroi, sir, and then of Dindymene [Cybele], I the old woman whom now the dust covers, the supervisor of many young women. I had two sons who in my happy old age closed my eyes in death" (Callimachus, *Epigr.* 48 G-P = 40Pf. = *AP* 7. 728, third century BC).

But, whereas in the cults of the Greek Olympians celibacy seems primarily to have served a practical function, in the early Christian Church (and after) it came to be considered explicitly superior to being sexually active, and that is where, rather than in the pagan Greek world, I believe, the notion originated that a woman's body, rather than her mind, is vulnerable and potentially shameful. The notion that virginity (or celibacy) brings one closer to God appears first in the New Testament in the epistle of St. Paul to the Christian community at Corinth:

> The unmarried or celibate woman (or man) cares for the Lord's business; her aim is to be dedicated to him in body as in spirit; but the married woman cares for worldly things; her aim is to please her husband. In saying this I have no wish to keep you on a tight rein. I am thinking simply of your own good, for what is seemly, and of your freedom to wait upon the Lord. (I Corinthians 7:34–35)

The unmarried and widows of whatever age should not marry, though, he advised:

if they cannot control themselves, they should marry, better to marry than to burn with vain desire (8–9) ... If, however, you do marry, there is nothing wrong in it; and if a virgin marries, she has done no wrong. But those who marry will have pain and grief in this bodily life and my aim is to spare you. (28)

In this community of Greek Christians there would have been nothing unfamiliar about the idea that celibacy freed one for service; but it is a new idea that such service, instead of being a privilege available to a few aristocratic girls or widows, might be available to all women, at any stage in their lives.

However, this universal opportunity for service offered to women of all ages and classes within the Christian community did not guarantee them a place in the hierarchy of the Church. At Corinth, a woman like Phoebe might be a ministrant (*diakonos*) and a hostess (*prostatis*) for many people, including Paul himself (I Romans 16:1), but he states explicitly:

women should not address the meeting. They have no license to speak, but should keep their place as law directs. If there is something that they want to know, they can ask their own husbands at home. It is a shocking thing that a woman should address the congregation (*lalein en ekklesiai*). (I Corinthians 14:35–36)

Thus, while man and woman are equal before God, or "in the Anointed one, Jesus" (Galatians 3:28), on earth, following Jewish custom, man takes precedence.[18] As the writer of the First Epistle of Timothy puts it, "a woman must be a learner, listening quietly and with due submission. I do not permit a woman to be a teacher (*didaskein*) nor must woman domineer over man, but she should be quiet" (2:11–12). He explains, echoing Paul's own interpretation of the Old Testament story (Genesis 2:4–4:24), that women must be restrained because they are by nature morally inferior: "for Adam was created first, and Eve afterwards, and it was not Adam who was deceived (*epatēthē*), it was the woman who, yielding to deception (*exapatētheisa*) fell into sin" (2:13–15). Paul himself describes the serpent's deception as mental corruption, glossing "deceived" (*exapatētheisa*) with "corrupt your minds" (*phtharei to noēmata*) (II Corinthians 11:3), but by the second century the serpent's deception had become full-fledged seduction. In the Protevangelium of James, when Joseph discovers that his betrothed, Mary, is pregnant, he asks: "Has the story of Adam been repeated in me? For as Adam was absent in the hour of his prayer and the serpent came and found Eve alone and deceived and defiled her (*emiainen autēn*), so also has it happened to me" (13:1, PBodmer 27).

The notion of inherent female inferiority is present, though not as physically explicit, in the teaching of Paul. He did not approve of women in Corinth attending services, praying, or prophesying, without wearing a veil (I Corinthians 11:1–15). Pagan philosophers also approved of sobriety in women's dress, but the Christian teachers differ from the pagans in not imposing similar restrictions on men. Even the oriental cults that offered Christianity such strong competition had rules of chastity for both men and women, though women, as in the pre-Christian era, had by their nature more susceptibility to pollution by blood. For example, in the cult of Men Tyrannus at Sounion in the third century AD, "purity" for men meant being "cleansed of garlic, pork and women"; for women, it required waiting "seven days after [her menstrual period], having washed completely, and ten days after a funeral, and forty days after a miscarriage [or abortion, *phthora*]" (*SIG* 3633).[19] But in early Christian doctrine, because of the danger to themselves and to the men around them that derived from their sexuality, women had a greater need for celibacy than men, and it offered them not only an opportunity to serve (and be supported by) the community but also a means of redemption. In the apocryphal Acts of Paul, a popular document of the late second century AD that was translated from Greek into Syriac, Coptic, Ethiopic, and Latin, several of Paul's beatitudes are concerned with chastity for men and women, but he ends with specific advice for women: "Blessed are the bodies of virgins, for they shall be well pleasing to God, and shall not lose the reward of their purity" (3:5–6).[20] Later, being a widow (I Timothy 3:3–15; Titus 2:3) or a virgin became virtual offices within the Church.[21] In epitaphs, whereas pagan virgins were said to have been carried off by Death if they died before marriage, Christian virgins were said to have married Christ, as in this inscription for a thirteen-year-old girl:[22]

> Here Maria has entrusted to the lamps of the saints her body; chaste, serious, wise, kind, gentle and quiet, whose high birth brought her fame in life, but by pleasing the god she surpassed the honor of her descent. For she did not choose marriage with a mortal, but in her love of virginity, an eternal marriage and with Christ sought eternal light, which is enclosed by no boundary. (CIL V. 6734 = CE 782)[23]

Mary, Jesus' mother, is mentioned first in Mark, the earliest gospel, only after Jesus is grown up, and she seems to have several additional sons (3:31). But in Matthew's gospel she is the virgin bearer of the divine child (Matthew

1:18–25; cf. Luke 1:26–38). In Matthew, it is necessary for her to be a virgin so that the Old Testament prophecy can be fulfilled: "The virgin will conceive and bear a son" (1:23).[24] But by the second half of the second century AD, in the apocryphal Protevangelium of James, Mary is discovered to be a virgin also *after* Jesus is born. The midwife proclaims to Salome, the daughter of King Herod, who happens to be standing outside the cave where Jesus was born: "I have a new sight to tell you; a virgin has brought forth and her nature (*physis*) is not altered" (19:3). Salome refuses to believe, and tests with her finger, and her hand falls off, consumed by fire, only to be miraculously restored when she acknowledges the power of God and touches the child (20:1–3).

The importance of chastity in Paul's teaching is reinforced in the apocryphal Acts of Paul by the story of the virgin Thecla.[25] The account of Thecla's adventures bears closer resemblance to an ancient pagan novel than to the doctrinal and often unexciting narratives of the canonical gospels. Thecla was engaged to a man named Thamyris, but she was so inspired by the teaching of Paul that she rejected Thamyris (in the plot of a pagan novel, the heroine would simply be separated from her fiancé by circumstantial events). Thamyris accuses Paul of sorcery and has him first imprisoned and then thrown out of the city of Iconium. Thecla is condemned to be burned; she is brought in naked, but makes the sign of the cross and the fire does not burn her; God sends an earthquake and thunderstorm, and so Thecla is saved. She immediately goes to Paul and offers to follow him wherever he goes, her hair cut short, that is, in disguise as a boy. He allows her to follow him, reluctantly, since she is "comely" and subject to temptation. In Antioch, she is immediately pursued by another suitor, Alexander, but she resists him and makes fun of him. Alexander gets angry and has her condemned to be eaten by wild beasts, but a lioness licks her feet, and then Tryphaena, a rich woman who has lost her own daughter, adopts her. Alexander recaptures Thecla and consigns her again to the beasts, but the lioness defends her, and all the women in the audience take her side. She is thrown into a pit full of water to be devoured by seals [*sic*], but she uses the water to baptize herself. Finally, she is bound by her feet to bulls (like Dirce in the pagan myth). When Tryphaena faints in reaction to this, Alexander gives the order to have Thecla freed; the governor and all the women recognize the power of God. Thecla leaves Antioch, dressed as a man, and searches for Paul in Myra; when she finds him, he sends her forth to teach.

The author of the Acts of Paul makes no reference to what Paul said to the

Corinthians about women keeping silent in meetings, though he seems familiar with other aspects of Paul's doctrines, the Acts of the Apostles, and the first three gospels. It would seem that Thecla had proved herself to be beyond temptation, because of her courage and resistance to men, and had become enough like a man to be able to do a man's work. She returns to her hometown, Iconium, and discovers that her fiancé Thamyris is dead but her mother is alive, which she takes as a sign of the power of God: "And when she had borne this witness she went away to Seleucia, and after enlightening many with the word of God she slept with a noble sleep" (3:7–43). The story does not so much do credit to women as express the Church's restrictive and demanding notions about female conduct, as contrasting it with pagan adventure stories makes clear.[26] Perpetual chastity is now the goal of the courageous heroine, rather than marriage. Thecla not only dresses like a man to ward off male advances, but she behaves like a man in other respects, rewarding her mother and then her surrogate mother, Tryphaena, with preaching instead of affection, and leaving them both behind in order to go on with her work.

The Acts of Paul demonstrate more clearly than any doctrinal document how distant the notion of Christian celibacy is from the pagan. Before the Christian era, no pagan celibate, even if she served for an extended term, like the Vestal Virgins in Rome, needed to be ashamed of her femininity. In the fourth century BC the female philosopher Hipparchia adopted men's clothing, like two of Plato's female pupils (Diogenes Laertius 3. 46).[27] Hipparchia was married to the philosopher Crates, had intercourse with him in public, and went with him to dinner parties, like a *hetaera* (D.L. 6. 96–98). But by the fourth century AD, after pagan philosophers had become as ascetic as Christians, the philosopher Hypatia of Alexandria chose to remain a virgin. When one of her pupils fell in love with her, she displayed and threw before him one of the rags she used as a sanitary napkin, and said: "You are in love with this, young man, not with [the Platonic ideal of] the Beautiful" (*Suda* 644. 12 ff. = Damascius fr. 102 Zintzen). Like Thecla and the third-century Christian martyrs Perpetua and Irene, Hypatia—at least according to this anecdote—believed that in order to carry on with her work it was necessary to deny her femininity.[28]

It is the early Christians, rather than the ancient Greeks, who first became conscious of, even obsessed with, the dangers of women's physical sexuality; and it is from them rather than Aeschylus, Euripides, or Plato that the fear of women's bodies (rather than their minds) ultimately derives.

EPILOGUE

If there ever was a time when women ruled the civilized world, or even served as the central focus of a civilized society, Greek myth does not record it. Such societies, to the extent that they are imagined, are depicted as barbarians, like the Amazons or Lycians. The myths portray with sympathy the life of young women and their fear of marriage and the separation from their own families that it will bring. But at the same time, myth portrays marriage and motherhood, with all the difficulties they involve, as the conditions most women desire, and in which women can be best respected by society and happiest in themselves. On occasion, myths show women advising male rulers and even taking over some of their responsibilities; when faced with serious moral decisions, these women take courageous action, even at the cost of their own lives, and win admiration. But other myths warn of women's ability to deceive men and betray their trust, particularly in the effect of sexual passion on their minds. What the myths themselves seem not to describe, at any time or place, is the possibility of true independence for women, apart from their families or society as a whole. There are in myth no successful communities of women apart from men, or conditions in which women continuously dominated over the other members of society.

Why did the Greeks fail to imagine that a Greek society could exist in which men and women would prefer to share those responsibilities, or where women might fight and govern, while men performed the traditional duties of the wife at home? Was it the result of a deliberate repression?[1] Were they afraid that organized groups of women might destroy them, as the daughters of Danaus killed their husbands on their wedding night in what (according to Eva Keuls) was "the most, perhaps one of the most widely dramatized motifs in Greek culture."[2] Yet once again, if we look directly at the surviving dramatic representation of the myth and not simply at a summary of the story, Aeschylus does not seem to be advocating or even describing patriarchal repression or stratification. The Danaids have fled to Argos with their father to escape cousins who wish to marry them against their will. Whether the girls object to their suitors personally or to men in general is not clear, but in either case, they have not only their father's support but his guidance: "our father Danaus, advisor and leader, arranger of pieces on the board" (*Suppliant Women* 11–12). The king of Argos, although reluctant to involve himself in a war, offers them sanctuary. Although they themselves express a general fear of men, "May I never become in any way subject to the power of males! (*arsenōn*) (392–93), their father and the king both behave honorably and are sympathetic to their plight. The play thus seems to be concerned not with male-female conflict in general but with a particular case of a disputed marriage and the issues of justice that derive from it.

In fact, Greek men may not have been so much concerned with repressing women as with protecting them, in a world where women from a physical point of view were far more vulnerable than they are today. Oedipus, observing that his daughters have done more on his behalf than his sons, comments that in Egypt "the men sit at home and work at the loom while their wives go outside and provide the means of life" (Sophocles, *Oedipus at Colonus* 340–41), as if it were unreasonable to expect women to support and care for their aged fathers when men were available. He means his remarks as a compliment; he fully appreciates what his daughters have done for him:

> My sons, who ought to have struggled for me, run the household at home like girls, but you instead of them work on my behalf; [Antigone], from the time she ceased to be a child and developed her full strength, has always been a wanderer with me, poor thing, an old man's guide. Often in the wild woods without food, barefooted, journeying, exhausted by heavy rain and heat, miserable, she thinks of secondary importance the comforts of home, so her father can have sustenance. (342–52)

Oedipus does not doubt Antigone's ability to look after him, or her loyalty to him; he questions only whether it is right, while her brothers are alive, for her to live this sort of life.

If Greek men wished to repress Greek women through their mythology, why do their two most important epics, the *Iliad* and the *Odyssey*, describe a war fought over a woman? If it were only their own honor they had set out to defend, after the Trojans had been punished they would have allowed Menelaus to kill or repudiate Helen; instead Homer tells how Menelaus brought her back to Sparta, and shows her peacefully and happily employed in her traditional role. The poet Stesichorus was said to have been struck blind for writing about Helen's elopement with Paris, and in consequence told the story that a phantom had represented her at Troy, while she herself was in Egypt (192–93 *PMGF*).

How did Helen, the woman who had caused the deaths of so many at Troy (Semonides 7. 116–17; Aeschylus, *Agamemnon* 687–90), contrive to be appreciated even by those who had suffered most on her account? It was because both she and Menelaus thought the gods were responsible for what happened to her. When Paris was asked to make his fateful judgment about which of the goddesses was most beautiful, he chose Aphrodite in preference to the much more powerful Athena and Hera because Aphrodite offered to give him the most beautiful woman in the world, who happened to be Helen. As we have seen, when, in the *Iliad*, Helen is reluctant to go to Paris, Aphrodite threatens her with harsh punishment if she does not obey (3. 399–417).[3]

In Euripides' drama the *Trojan Women*, when Menelaus comes to take Helen away after the fall of Troy, she says to him in her own defense that Paris came to Sparta in the company of a great goddess (940–41). She concludes her speech by stating:"If you think you can control the gods, it is ignorance on your part to harbor such a wish" (964–95). In modern productions of the play, Helen is usually portrayed as doing her best to appeal sexually to Menelaus, but in the original drama the emphasis is completely on her rhetoric. If Menelaus decides not to kill Helen but instead to bring her home to Sparta, we must accept that he could not discount the force of her argument about the power of the gods. Also neither he nor anyone else could forget that she was the daughter of Zeus, the most powerful of the gods, whose disfavor no one would want to incur. It is because of that connection, not because of any particular virtue on his part, that Menelaus after his death will go to dwell in the Elysian Fields (*Odyssey* 4. 563–64).

As modern readers who do not believe in the power of the ancient gods, we are inclined to prefer the rationalistic arguments put forth in the *Trojan Women* by Hecuba, who denies that the myth of the Judgment of Paris could be true. In her view Helen, not the gods, is responsible for her own actions: "Don't call the goddesses ignorant in order to cover up your own immorality; you will not persuade the wise" (981–82). How could Aphrodite have brought Helen from Sparta to Troy when she was sitting quietly in heaven? Paris was strikingly handsome: "Your mind when it saw Paris was transformed itself into (*epoiēthē*) Aphrodite. All foolishness among mortals is Aphrodite, and the name of the goddess rightly begins with thoughtlessness (*aphrosynē*)" (988–90).

The argument that proper gods could not encourage immoral behavior had been made by philosophers before and during Euripides' lifetime. Euripides tends to put such statements into the mouths of characters at moments of crisis in their lives, because they cannot believe that the gods have allowed the disasters in which they find themselves to have happened. After he discovers that, in a fit of madness, he has killed his wife and children, Heracles states that he does not consider himself to be the son of Zeus (*Heracles Mad* 1264). He asks who could worship a cruel goddess like Hera (1307–8). He denies that such traditional myths could be true: "For a god, if he is truly a god, needs nothing. These are the miserable tales of poets" (1345–46). But the audience knows that Hera sent the goddess Lyssa to drive Heracles insane, and it is only because Athena intervenes that he comes to his senses.[4] Even though he does not seem to be aware of it, the gods are in control, and they do not need to abide by the codes of behavior that he or any other mortal wishes to create for them.

In the *Iliad* and the *Odyssey*, Helen's most impressive quality is a direct intelligence.[5] Perhaps because she is the daughter of a god, she is able to recognize a god when she sees one. Helen sees through Aphrodite's disguise when she appears to her as an old woman (*Iliad* 3. 396–98). She objects to the way the goddess has treated her, carrying her off to please any man she wishes to favor; she tells Paris that she wishes he had been killed by Menelaus, "who is superior to you in strength and hand and spear" (3. 431); she tells Priam that she wishes that she had died before she came to Troy with his son, "leaving behind the people I know and my late-born child and my dear friends" (3. 174–75). She speaks the last speech in the *Iliad*, lamenting over Hector's dead body, again regretting that Paris took her to Troy and describing Hector's kindness to her—a gentleness that Homer describes also in the scene with Hector's family in *Iliad* 6, in contrast to his effectiveness as a warrior. No one doubts her sincerity.

In the *Odyssey*, home once more in Sparta, she is the model wife. Her daughter and Menelaus' son by a slave girl, Megapenthes, are being married on the same day (*Odyssey* 4. 3); apparently she would have approved of the advice Euripides has Andromache give to Hermione about going along with one's husband in his love affairs and nursing his bastard children, so that she might do nothing to displease him (*Andromache* 221–25).[6] When she enters the room, she is compared to Artemis (*Odyssey* 4. 123), but like Penelope and other model wives she begins to work in wool.[7] She shares her husband's sorrows (184) but gives Menelaus and his guests an elixir, *nepenthe*, to make them happy (220–21). She speaks of her time in Troy with the same regret she expressed in the *Iliad*:

> The other Trojan women wept [when Odysseus secretly entered Troy and killed many Trojans], but I rejoiced, for already my heart had turned to go back home, and I lamented my delusion (*atē*), which Aphrodite gave me, when she led me there away from my dear homeland, and made me take myself from my child and my bridal chamber and my husband, who lacked nothing, neither in intelligence nor appearance. (259–64)

It is this clever and dignified Helen who in Euripides' *Trojan Women* manages to persuade Menelaus not to kill her. That she survives despite her husband's initial hostility is not so much a testament to the powers of Aphrodite, as Hecuba alleges (1051), as a tribute to her ability to marshal traditional lines of argument. To the Greeks, as we have seen, what makes women appealing and dangerous is not just their beauty or sexuality, but their intelligence.

Abbreviations

AP	*Anthologia Palatina*
ARV²	*Attic Red-Figure Vase-Painters*, 2nd ed. (Beazley 1963)
CE	*Carmina Latina Epigraphica* (Buecheler and Lommatzsch 1897–1926)
CIL	*Corpus Inscriptionum Latinarum*
CMG	*Corpus Medicorum Graecorum*
D-K	*Die Fragmente der Vorsokratiker* (Diels and Kranz 1960–64)
FGE	*Further Greek Epigrams* (Page 1981)
FGrHist	*Die Fragmente der griechischen Historiker* (Jacoby 1923–)
Garl.Phil.	*The Garland of Philip* (Gow and Page 1968)
G-P	*The Greek Anthology: Hellenistic Epigrams* (Gow and Page 1965)
IG	*Inscriptiones Graecae* (1873–)
ILS	*Inscriptiones Latinae Selectae* (Dessau 1979–80)
Kaibel	*Epigrammata Graeca* (Kaibel 1878)
KRS	*The Presocratic Philosophers* (Kirk, Raven, and Schofield 1983)
L	*Oeuvres complètes d'Hippocrate* (Littré 1839–61)
LGPN	*A Lexicon of Greek Personal Names* (Fraser and Matthews 1987)
LIMC	*Lexicon Iconographicum Mythologiae Classicae* (Ackermann and Gisler 1981–99)
LSCG	*Lois sacrées des cités grecques* (Sokolowski 1969)
M-W	*Fragmenta Hesiodea* (Merkelbach and West 1967)
PCG	*Poetae Comici Graeci* (Kassel and Austin 1983–)
Peek	*Griechische-Versinschriften* (Peek 1955)
Pf.	*Callimachus* (Pfeiffer 1949-53)
Pleket	*Texts on the Social History of the Greek World*, vol. 2, *Epigraphica* (Pleket 1969)
PMGF	*Poetarum Melicorum Graecorum Fragmenta* (Page and Davies 1991)
POxy	*The Oxyrhynchus Papyri* (Grenfell and Hunt 1898–)
SB	*Sammelbuch griechischer Urkunden aus Ägypten* (Preisigke et al. 1915–)
SEG	*Supplementum Epigraphicum Graecum* (1923–)
SIG	*Sylloge Inscriptionum Graecarum* (Dittenberger 1915–24)
Supp.Hell.	*Supplementum Hellenisticum* (Lloyd-Jones and Parsons 1983)
TGrF	*Tragicorum Graecorum Fragmenta* (Snell and Kannicht 1986–)
W	*Iambi et Elegi Graeci* (West 1971)
WLGR³	*Women's Life in Greece and Rome*, 3rd ed. (Lefkowitz and Fant 2005)

Notes

Preface to Second Edition

1. *Die Töchter des Zeus: Frauen im alten Griechenland,* tr. Holger Fliessbach and Axel Haase (Munich: C. H. Beck Verlag, 1992); *Gynaikes ston Elliniko Mytho,* tr. Amalia Megapanou (Athens: Castaniotis, 1993).

2. Anon., *Wisconsin Bookwatch* (April 1991): 3; B. Bainbridge, *The Observer* (11/30/86): 21. Other reviews: M. Beard, *The Guardian* (8/8/86); L. Bowman, *Favonius* 1 (1987): 55; A. Brien, *New Statesman and Society* (6/24/88): 41; H. Brumberger, *Literaturbericht Griechisch. Anregung* (*Zeitschrift für Gymnasialpädagogik* 42. 2 (1996): 122–23; G. Clark, *JACT Review* (2nd series) 1 (1987): 21, *JACT Review* 9 (1991): 17; S. G. Cole, *Religious Studies Review* 14. 2 (1988): 153–54; J. deLuce, *Choice* 24. 5 (1/87): 755; R. Hawley, *Classical Association News* 12/89: 8–9; J. Cahill, *Phoenix* 43 (1989): 165–69; P. Jones, *The Times [of London]* 8/7/86; E. Keuls, *AHR* 93 (1988): 394–95; H. King, *TLS* 12/19/86, p. 1430; P. Properzio, *CW* 81.1 (1987): 56–57; J. Rusten, *Washington Book Review* (May 1987): 18–19; W. Schuller, *Frankfurter Allgemeine Zeitung* (11/30/92): 10; R. P. Sonkowsky, *The Key Reporter* (Spring 1989): 5; A. J. L. van Hooff, *Mnemosyne* 42.3–4 (1989): 503–4; Y. Vernière, *REG* 1987: 149–50; P. Walcot, *Greece and Rome* 34 (1987): 105–6.

3. Lefkowitz and Fant 1982, 1992, 2005. All references in this book are to the third (2005) edition.

4. Rusten 1987, 19.

5. Hawley 1989, 9.

6. Cf. Beard 1986, Cole 1988, 153–54, Keuls 1988, 394–95.

7. See below, ch. 7.

8. Cahill 1989, 166.

9. Sawyer 1996, 91–116.

Preface to the First Edition

1. The story of the death of Great Pan (*pan megas*), as told by Plutarch (*Moralia* 419b–d), follows the pattern of miracle reports in the New Testament; Wicker 1975, 158–59. Originally it may have been an aetiological myth explaining the ritual lament for "the all-great" (*pammegas*) Thamuz (i.e., Adonis); Brenk 1977, 96n.11.

2. Burkert 1979, 30.

3. DuBois 1982, 103; Goldhill 1984a, 197.

4. Lévi-Strauss 1955, 91–92; Segal 1982, 180–85.

5. Burkert 1983, 173–77.

6. Cf. Slater 1968, 283–84; Simon 1978, 250; Segal 1982, 189–204.

Chapter 1. Princess Ida and the Amazons

1. Wells 1978, 1–5; Auerbach 1978, 4–7.

2. Glasscock 1975, 313.

3. Chesler 1972, 286.

4. Diner 1965, xiv–xv.

5. Cf. French 1985, 72: " . . . the fundamental nature of patriarchy is located in stratification, institutionalization, and coercion. Stratification of men above women leads in time to stratification of classes: an elite rules over people perceived as 'closer to nature,' savage, bestial, animalistic . . . ."

6. Diner 1965, 127–28.

7. Bachofen 1967, 147.

8. Pembroke 1967.

9. Below, ch. 13.

10. Merck 1978, 101; Jacoby 1949, 895, and now esp. Blok 1995, passim.

11. See also Hoelscher 1973; Thomas 1976; Francis 1980.

12. Merck 1978, 103; Boardman 1982.

13. Cantarella 1981, 33–34.

14. Pembroke 1967, 1–18.

15. How and Wells 1912, i. 134; Pembroke 1967, 29.

16. Pembroke 1965, 218–47; Vidal-Naquet 1981, 190.

17. Pembroke 1967, 20.

18. Ibid., 34.

19. Bamberger 1973, 268.

20. Ibid., 280.

21. Cf. also Merck 1978, 108.

22. *LIMC* I 1981, 636–43, s.v. Amazones (P. Devambez).

23. Kleinbaum 1983, 118.

24. David 1976, 130, 148, 151.

25. Wiseman 1979, 143–53.

26. Jacoby 1949, 75.

27. Bachofen 1967, 150–51.

28. Campbell 1967, l–liii; Cantarella 1983, 14–21.

29. On Bachofen's influence see esp. Cantarella 1983, 7–36, and the materials collected in Heinrichs 1975, 331–443.

30. Bachofen 1967, 658–61; below, ch. 13.

31. Millett 1970, 111–15.

32. Winnington-Ingram 1983, 123–27.

33. Lloyd-Jones 1971/1983, 4.

34. Winnington-Ingram 1983, 127.

35. Zeitlin 1978, 165–66.

36. Parker 2005, 275; for etymology, see Chantraine 1983, I:261.

37. Lloyd-Jones 1971/1983, 73; Parker 1983, 30n.66.

38. Simon 1978, 250; Zeitlin 1982, 136.

39. Cf. duBois 1982, 103; Tyrrell 1984, 42, 102, 113.

40. Cf. Tyrrell 1984, 59.

41. Leach 1969, 85–112.

42. Henry James, *The Bostonians*, 1886, ch. 17.

43. Heilbrun 1979, 157.

44. Surely the motive for making this distinction is not mere protectionism, as Heilbrun alleged, writing as Cross 1985, 52–53, 98.

45. Humphreys 1983, 79–130.

46. Cole 1981, 219–45.

47. *Supp.Hell.* 401; *WLGR*³ 10.

48. *WLGR*³ 217.

49. Peek 1955, no. 1881; *WLGR*³ 42.

50. See below, ch. 12.

Chapter 2. The Powers of the Primeval Goddess

1. See ch. 3.

2. West 1997, 276–83.

3. Pritchett 1958, 31; text and translation in Dalley 1989, 228–77.

4. See Guerney 1961, 190–92.

5. See also Clay 2003, 129–38.

6. In the *Works and Days* Hesiod calls this creature Pandora (80–82). See below, chs. 7 and 13.

Chapter 3. The Heroic Women of Greek Epic

1. See below, chs. 7 and 12.

2. Scholia to *Iliad* 6. 434b2. 1–2, Erbse II, p. 204.

3. Ibid., 6. 491. 2–4, II, p. 214.

4. Ibid., 6. 433–39. 3–4, II, p. 203.

5. Ibid., 6. 491. 1–2, II, p. 214.

6. Ibid., 6. 433. 1–6, II, p. 204.

7. Pomeroy 1975a, 16–19.

8. See below, ch. 11.

9. On a boy's need for a male protector, see Finley 1978, 125–26.

10. See also below, ch. 10.

11. Griffin 1980, 97–98.

Chapter 4. Chosen Women

1. Pickard-Cambridge (1968, 265) accepts Plat., *Gorg.* 502d–e as evidence for the presence of women in the fourth-century BC theatre, but the dramatic date of the dialogue is the fifth century BC. As Pickard-Cambridge observes (263–64), Aristophanes' jokes about audiences are too particular to be taken as positive evidence one way or the other (cf. Wilson 1982, 157–61).

2. Reading *tis an genoiman;* see Lefkowitz 1981b, 86–87.

3. Lefkowitz 1981b, 14–15; King 1983, 114; King 1998, 75–80.

4. West 1985, 1–30.

5. E.g., Slater 1968, 11–12.

6. West 1985, 119–20.

7. Cf. *Odyssey* 11.248–50; Maas 1973c, 66–67.

8. The papyrus text's *autoisieron*, 'it was not holy for them' (*POxy* 1611 fr. 1), is probably corrupt and should refer only to the maiden (Kakridis 1947, 77–80); Vergil includes Caeneus, changed back to female form, as a victim of *durus amor* along with Phaedra, Procris, Eriphyle, and Dido. Caeneus was the subject of a tragedy by Ion and comedies by Araros and Antiphanes (cf. Maas 1973b, 65). The antiquarian Aulus Gellius (9. 4. 15), to show that the story of Caeneus was not simply a myth, cites Pliny the Elder (*Natural History* 7. 36–37), who says he saw in Africa a woman who had changed into a man on the day of his marriage. Pliny mentions two other cases, and Diodorus Siculus several more (32. 10); the poet Euenus chooses for the subject of an epigram (*AP* 9. 75 = *Garl.Phil.* 2310 G-P) another case of wedding-night discovery.

9. E.g., Pomeroy 1975b, 109.

10. *WLGR*[3] 32; Knox 1978, 312.

11. Slater 1968, 297–301; Girard 1977, 44; Foley 1981, 143; Zeitlin 1982, 131.

12. As Albert Henrichs has observed (1984, 231–34), the notion that ritual has a primarily social function is relatively modern: "Dionysus has been so drastically uprooted from his original Greek habitat and transplanted to modern regions where blood is more plentiful than wine that he might not survive. Can Dionysus be saved?"

13. Zeitlin 1982, 136.

14. Garland 1985, 29.

15. Lefkowitz 1981b, 1–11.

16. Pomeroy 1985, 120, 154.

17. See ch. 13.

18. Matthew 1:23; Harvey 1973, 19.

19. See also Pindar, *Pythian* 9. 18–28.

Chapter 5. Seduction and Rape

1. See Gould 1989, 64.

2. Such confrontations are a typical Herodotean device for conveying abstract ideas; whether they have any historical basis is another question; cf. S. West 1991, 151.

3. Although the point of such rationalization is to give human beings full responsibility for their actions, Flory (1987, 25–28) conjectures that Herodotus may be making fun of rationalizing historians such as Hecataeus. For contemporary criticism of myths of seduction by gods see Eur., *Heracles* (1341–46), with precedents in Xenophanes (21A32. 24–25 I 122 D-K), Antiphon the sophist (87B10 II p. 340 D-K, cf. Anaxagoras 59B12 II p. 37). See Lefkowitz 1991, 239–46.

4. Cf. *Il.* 3. 401, where Helen asks Aphrodite where she will take her next; Paris' gift from Aphrodite was "painful lust" (*machlosynē*, 24. 30). On a skyphos in the Museum of Fine Arts (Boston 13. 186), Paris leads her off by the wrist (see below, ch. 6), in the presence of Aphrodite and Peitho (holding a flower, see n.38); cf. Buxton 1982, 45–46.

5. Aristarchus, an ancient commentator on Homer, preferred to understand the line as meaning that the struggles and groans were undertaken by the Greeks on behalf of Helen (i.e., as an objective rather than subjective genitive). Cf. Kirk 1985, 153.

6. *Contest of Homer and Hesiod* 224–46 Allen; see Lefkowitz 1981a, 7.

7. Keuls 1985, 50.

8. Forbes Irving 1990, 69.

9. Zeitlin 1986, 122–51.

10. Apollodorus 3. 14. 2, s.v. *Areōs pagos* (I 348 Adler); cf. Parker 1983, 378.

11. Cf. Demosthenes *Against Aristocrates* 23. 53, 55 where motive is not a factor; if a man kills someone having intercourse with his wife or mother or sister or daughter, or with a concubine kept for the purpose of bearing legitimate children, the homicide is justifiable.

12. Cf. esp. Harris 1990, 370–77, with addendum by Brown 1991, 533–34, *contra* (e.g.) Carey 1989, 80.

13. See also *kartei damassaito*, "deflower," ii. 10–11. The phrase *kartei oiphein* is "forthright," but *oiphein* as a term for intercourse is perhaps not quite so offensive as Attic *binein*, cf. Bain 1991, 72–74.

14. Sealey 1990, 71–74.

15. Cf. the discussion in Lonsdale 1993.

16. On the importance of the contact of the eyes, cf. Buxton 1982, 84, 112–13, and on the meeting of the glances of male and female on vase paintings depicting erotic pursuit, Sourvinou-Inwood 1991, 69. Cf. also NY 06.1021.149/ARV 523, 2, characterized by Keuls 1985, 50 as "Poseidon and Hermes on a raping expedition together"; see ch. 6. Also the Niobid painter's Boreas and Oreithyia, fig. 7.

17. Cf. the story of Demeter Fury at Thelpusa in Arcadia. Poseidon wanted to have intercourse with Demeter, who turned herself into a mare; when he saw that she had tricked him, he turned himself into a stallion and mated with her (Paus. 8. 25. 5).

18. On the translation of *porphyreos* as "dark, shining" rather than "purple" see Schrier 1979, 316–22.

19. Like eye contact (cf. n.16), the touching of hands is a sign of consensual intimacy. Cf. Sourvinou-Inwood 1991, 68–69.

20. Cf. also one of the few surviving lines from Aeschylus' *Amymone*. Amymone, one of the Danaids, had gone out to look for water, and was about to be raped by a satyr when she was rescued by Poseidon, who says: "you are fated to be my partner, and I am fated to be your partner (*TGrF* fr. 13).

21. There is no question that the males enjoyed these erotic encounters; cf. Dioscurides' epigram about how as the result of being in Doris' "garden" he has become "immortal" (*AP* 5. 55 = 1484 G-P; cf. Schrier 1979, 309–12).

22. Here I follow the text of Lloyd-Jones 1971, 599–603.

23. *Epist. Aeschines* 10. 4–5 Blass; Oakley and Sinos 1993, 15. Cf. Trenkner 1958, 133–34; Schwegler 1913, 16–17; for analogous rites of passage see Nilsson 1913, 365.

24. It is not "rape" (cf. Bremer 1975, 274), as Burnett 1970, 85–86 noted, rightly; cf. also Burnett 1962, 95–96, unfairly criticized by Michelini 1987, 269n.166.

25. On the gesture, see esp. Jenkins 1983, 139–40.

26. See above, ch. 4.

27. Or like Polydora, whose husband Borus raised her son by the river Spercheus as his own, *Iliad* 16. 175–77, or Evadne, whose father wisely inquired from the oracle of Delphi about his daughter's pregnancy and so learned that the child was Apollo's (Pindar, *Olympian Ode* 6. 35–57). But other women were less fortunate, such as Alope (murdered by her father after he discovered she had borne a son by Poseidon), Leucothoe (buried alive by her father), and Danae (confined in a brazen tower, see below in this chapter).

28. See Burnett 1962, 94.

29. Apparently this was a story told by Simonides in one of his poems, 563 *PMGF* = schol. *Il.* 9. 557–58 II 518–19 Erbse.

30. Some aspects of her suffering are vividly described in Sophocles' *Tyro*; cf. frs. 658, 659 *TGrF.*

31. Cf. Forbes Irving 1990, 69: "in myth women are continually punished for being raped [*sic*]," listing Leucothoe, Psamathe, Alope, Arne, Danae, along with Aura, Pelopeia, and Taygete, who commit suicide.

32. Cf. Lloyd-Jones 1982, 161 = 1990a, 78.

33. Cf. *Il.* 24. 524–33, and Macleod 1982, 133.

34. There are some problems with the text, but the general sense is clear; cf. Griffith 1983 ad loc.

35. Although Griffith 1983 ad loc. thinks here *tis* means virtually the same thing as *ti*, it is probable that the chorus has metamorphosis in mind, cf. Lefkowitz 1981b, 97.

36. In the case of most ordinary marriages, transfer to her husband's home would not require the bride to sever ties with her mother. Cf. Sourvinou-Inwood 1991, 73–74.

37. Cf. Tyrrell and Brown 1991, 106–7.

38. In vase painting, a flower held in a woman's hand represents this moment of erotic "ripeness;" cf. Sourvinou-Inwood 1991, 65.

39. Cf. Faraone 1990, 236–37.

40. Cf., e.g., Whallon 1980, 57: "[Cassandra's] mood is not of post-coital tristesse, but of non-orgiastic inadequacy."

41. Cf. Soph., *Trachiniae* 141–52, esp. 147–50: a young woman leads "an untroubled life in pleasure until she is called a woman instead of a girl (*anti parthenou gyne*) and takes on her share of worries in the night, because she is afraid for her husband and children."

42. In his tirade against women, Hippolytus uses the dowry as evidence that women are evil: "her father offers a dowry to settle her elsewhere, in order to be rid of the evil" (Eur., *Hipp.* 627–29).

43. The right choice seems to have been made by a father in a lost comedy (fr. 1000 *PCG* VIII = 13–26 = *WLGR*[3] 38, tr. H. Lloyd-Jones), for his daughter says of her husband, "he is all that I wished with regard to me, and my pleasure is his pleasure, father."

44. E.g., Lefkowitz 1981b, 93; Zeitlin 1986, 123.

45. Cf. esp. Jenkins 1983, 142.

46. This story may also have been included in the Hesiodic *Catalogue of Women*, cf. fr. 128 M-W).

47. See above, ch. 4.

48. Cf. Fraenkel 1962, II 555: "but from the beginning it is not merely brute force which is here at work; with all her resisting Cassandra is susceptible to the power of the god's *charis*." But does she resist at first, or only at the last moment, since it is not simply the *ergon aphrodision* (cf. Semonides, fr. 7. 48 W), but *ergon teknōn* that is involved? For wrestling as a metaphor for sexual activity, see Poliakoff 1982, 104–7.

49. Cf. the meadow where Phaedra hopes to find rest (and Hippolytus, cf. Bremer 1975, 278) and the beautiful setting on the banks of the Ilissus that is the site of Plato's *Phaedrus* 229b; cf. Parry 1989, 22.

50. Bühler 1960; translation in Gow 1953, 128–32.

51. Cf. Snyder 1989, 93–97; Stehle 2001, 190–96.

Chapter 6. "Predatory" Goddesses

In the preparation of this chapter I owe thanks especially to D. von Bothmer and M. Kilmer; to the referees and editors of *Hesperia* for specific improvements and corrections; to E. R. Knauer, B. Ridgway, and C. Sourvinou-Inwood for advice and encouragement; and to C. Gentilesco for editorial assistance.

1. See also the Hebrew tradition about the origin of the giants known as the Nephelim: "the gods saw that the daughters of humans were attractive, and they took wives from whoever they chose . . ." (Genesis 6:4); West 1997, 117.

2. On the tradition that Medea was immortal, see Pindar, *Pythian Odes* 4. 11; Braswell 1988, 76.

3. The myth of Circe may have its origins in Near Eastern epic: Ishtar in the Gilgamesh epic turns two of her lovers into animals (*Gilg.* VI. ii. 26, iii. 7); see West 1997, 408 and note 14. The myths about Eos and her lovers may have influenced the characterization of Calypso, Circe, and Aphrodite (see Boedeker 1974, 64–84; Friedrich 1978, 39–43).

4. The myth of Aphrodite and Adonis came to Cyprus and Asia Minor from the cult of Ishtar and Thammuz in Syria; Page 1955, 127. On the identification of Aphrodite with Ishtar, see Burkert 1992, 20, 97–98. The union of Demeter and Iasion takes place in a plowed field, like the ritual marriage of the goddess Inanna to the king of Sumer. One king is even called Dumuzi, the name of her divine spouse; see Frymer-Kensky 1992, 50–57.

5. On Selene and Endymion, see Apollonius of Rhodes (*Argonautica* 4. 57); the story may come from Musaeus' *Theogony* (cf. Epimenides 3B2 I 33 D-K; see *FGrHist* IIIb Suppl. I, 575). Another of Selene's mortal lovers was the Eleusinian ruler and hierophant Eumolpus, by her the father of Musaeus (Philochorus 328 *FGrHist* F208 = schol. Ar. *Ran.* 1033).

6. In the catalogue of vases in Kaempf-Dimitriadou 1969, 76–109, there are 147 scenes with Eos and her lovers as opposed to 116 depicting Zeus and his lovers (60 with women and 56 with Ganymede). Boreas and Oreithyia is the next most popular subject with 56, then Poseidon and his lovers with 40.

7. Both myths were portrayed in the akroteria of the Athenians' temple at Delos; Robertson 1975, 356.

8. *LIMC* III 1986, 759–75, s.v. Eros (C. Weiss).

9. Kaempf-Dimitriadou 1969, 47–53.

10. Ibid., 57; Vermeule 1979, 162–78; *LIMC* III 1986, 779, s.v. Eos (C. Weiss); see also n.47 below.

11. Stewart 1995, 74–77; cf. Zeitlin 1986, 150, quoting Dover 1978, 88: "pursuit is the role prescribed for the male, flight for the female," but these categories apply only to mortals.

12. Stewart 1995, 86; see also Zeitlin 1986, 150.

13. Stewart 1995, 86.

14. Osborne, 1996, 65–77.

15. Osborne 1996, 67–68, 76; cf. also Frontisi-Ducroux 1996, 83: "a scenario terrifying to Greek men."

16. Cf. West 1966, 486: "[Eos] was one of the most predatory of goddesses," and Friedrich 1978, 41: "Dawn is rapacious in her way."

17. E.g., Osborne 1996, 72: "just as behind every man there is a satyr restrained only by social protocols, so behind every woman there is an Eos: Female desire can be rampant, too."

18. See esp. the perceptive remarks of Vermeule 1979, 121; see also Stehle 1990, 94; Sourvinou-Inwood 1991, 49.

19. For further discussion, see above, ch. 5; and Harrison 1997, 188.

20. Cf. Keuls 1985, 50, who speaks of Zeus and Hermes going on a "raping expedition."

21. See above, ch. 4.

22. Osborne 1996, 67.

23. Robson 1997, 81, who also cites the myth of Artemis' companion Polyphonte (Antoninus Liberalis 21), who fell in love with a bear: her two huge sons became savage cannibals.

24. See esp. Ridgway 1999, 93–94.

25. Shapiro 1992, 61; Calame 1999, 67. Even Danae's lap is covered by her cloak and dress when she receives the shower of gold from Zeus, as in a kalyx krater from Cerveteri in St. Petersburg ST 1723 = ARV^2 360, 1: 1648 = $LIMC$ III 1986, 327, no. 1, pl. 1, s.v. Danae (J.-J. Maffre). Nonetheless, Stewart 1995, 87, suggests that by mid-century, "in polite society, these images were simply no longer acceptable; in effect they had all but become pornography."

26. Clay 1989, 159: "not force but persuasion and guile constitute the secret tools of successful seduction." Dougherty (1993, 140–41, and 1998, 270), in her discussion of Apollo's abduction of Cyrene emphasizes the "violence" of Pindar's agricultural metaphors; but cf. Bremmer 2000, 102–3.

27. Cf. Clay 1989, 158, 175.

28. Shapiro 1992, 66; Kilmer 1997, 132; and, about attitudes in general, Kilmer 1990, 270; and Kilmer 1993, 200.

29. Berlin, Staatliche Museen, F 2352, from Nola = ARV^2 1107, 1 = $LIMC$ III 1986, 762, no. 104, s.v. Eos (C. Weiss) = Kaempf-Dimitriadou 1969, 85, no. 104.

30. On the power of the gaze, see (in general) Robertson 1975, 214; Buxton 1982, 51, 112–13, 214 n.86; Sourvinou-Inwood 1991, 69; Padel 1992, 62–63. On the erotic gaze, see Reeder 1995, 125–26; Frontisi-Ducroux 1996, 82–84; Sutton, 1997/1998, 35.

31. Bell krater by the Christie Painter, Baltimore Museum of Art, 1951.486 = ARV^2 1048.27 = $LIMC$ III 1986, 762, no. 99, s.v. Eos (C. Weiss) = Kaempf-Dimitriadou 1969, 85, no. 110 = Reeder 1995, 401–2, no. 131 (C. Benson). Compare the bell krater from Cumae (Paris, Cab. Méd. 423 = ARV^2 1055, no.72 = $LIMC$ III 1986, 762, no. 100, s.v. Eos [C. Weiss] = Kaempf-Dimitriadou 1969, 185, no. 112), where a winged Eos, approaching from the left, reaches out towards a fleeing Cephalus (identified by an inscription), who holds two spears over his left shoulder; a companion, behind Eos, is running away.

32. Paris, Cab. Méd. 846 = ARV^2 1050, 1 = $LIMC$ III 1986, 768, no. 182, s.v. Eos (C. Weiss) = Kaempf-Dimitriadou 1969, 90, no. 173.

33. For examples, see esp. Sutton 1992, 27; Sutton 1997/1998, 32–39; also the scene on the fragment of a loutrophoros in the Ashmolean Museum, Oxford University, inv. no. 1966.888 = $LIMC$ III 1986, 905, no. 639c, pl. 646, s.v. Eros (A. Hermary et al.) = Reeder 1995, 168–69, no. 25.

34. Baltimore, Walters Art Museum, 48.2034 = ARV^2 509, 1657 = $LIMC$ III 1986, 765, no. 139, s.v. Eos (C.Weiss) = Kaempf-Dimitriadou 1969, 87, no. 130 = Reeder 1995, 399–401, no. 130 (C. Benson).

35. Cf. Eos catching Cephalus on a Nolan amphora by the Niobid Painter in the Rijksmuseum in Leiden (PC 78 = ARV^2 605, 58 = $LIMC$ III 1986, 761, no. 77, pl. 77, s.v. Eos [C. Weiss] = Kaempf-Dimitriadou 1969, 83, no. 83), and on a pelike by the Niobid Painter, formerly in Königsberg (Univ. F 162 = ARV^2 603,44 = $LIMC$ III 1986, 761, no. 76, pl. 76, s.v. Eos [C. Weiss] = Kaempf-Dimitriadou 1969, 83, no. 81).

36. Boston, Museum of Fine Arts, 95.28, from Vulci = ARV^2 482, 816 = $LIMC$ III 1986, 769, no. 201, pl. 201 s.v. Eos (C. Weiss) = Kaempf-Dimitriadou 1969, 90, no. 179.

37. On the gesture, see Jenkins 1983, 139–40; Oakley and Sinos 1993, 32.

38. New York, Metropolitan Museum of Art, 28.167 = ARV^2 890, 175; 1673 = $LIMC$ V 1990, 549, no. 44, pl. 44, s.v. Hyakinthos (L. and F. Villard) = Kaempf-Dimitriadou 1969, 81, no. 53 = Shapiro 1992, 70–72, Fig. 3.10.

39. Brunswick, Maine, Bowdoin College Museum of Art, 1908.003, from Athens = ARV^2 606, 68 = $LIMC$ III 1986, 137, no. 56, pl. 56, s.v. Boreas (S. Kaempf-Dimitriadou) = Kaempf-Dimitriadou 1969, 107, no. 364.

40. On Athena as *pompos*, see Sinos 1993, 80–83. On Herodotus 7. 189, cf. How and Wells 1912, vol. II, 215; $LIMC$ III 1986, 134, s.v. Boreas (S. Kaempf-Dimitriadou). There is a rationalized version of the myth in Plato's *Phaedrus* 229c–d.

41. $LIMC$ VIII 1997, 969, no. 213, s.v. Persephone (G. Güntner) = Andronikos 1994, 59–69, pls. 19–26. Cf. Cohen 1996, 119–21.

42. The narcissus in this myth is a "miraculous flower"; see Richardson 1974, 144.

43. Athens, National Archaeological Museum, 13119, from Athens = ARV^2 1656

= *LIMC* III 1986, 135, no. 9, pl. 9, s.v. Boreas (S. Kaempf-Dimitriadou) = Kaempf-Dimitriadou 1969, 105, no. 343.

44. Ferrara, Museo Archeologico Nazionale di Ferrara, 9351, from Spina = *ARV²* 880, 12 = *LIMC* IV 1988, 157, no. 44, pl. 44, s.v. Ganymedes (H. Sichtermann) = Kaempf-Dimitriadou 1969, 79, no. 34. For similar scenes, see a lekythos from Novoli in Taranto, Mus. Naz., 54383 = *ARV²* 556, 108 = *LIMC* IV 1988, 156, no. 30, s.v. Ganymedes (H. Sichtermann) = Kaempf-Dimitriadou 1969, 77, no. 8, and an oinochoe (with Zeus approaching Ganymede from the right) in Basel, H. A. Cahn 9 = *ARV²* 874, 3 = *LIMC* IV 1988, 157, no. 41, pl. 41, s.v. Ganymedes (H. Sichtermann) = Kaempf-Dimitriadou 1969, 79, no. 31.

45. Madrid, Museo Arqueológico Nacional, 11158 = *ARV²* 649, 45 = *LIMC* III 1986, 773, no. 268, pl. 268, s.v. Eos (C. Weiss) = Kaempf-Dimitriadou 1969, 92, no. 194.

46. St. Petersburg, State Hermitage Museum, B 682 = *ARV²* 391 = *LIMC* III 1986, 773, no. 267, s.v. Eos (C. Weiss) = Kaempf-Dimitriadou 1969, 92, no. 193 = Vermeule 1979, 167, fig. 17.

47. Vermeule 1979, 166. If the painting had some relevance to death, one would expect to find it on a lekythos rather than a rhyton; cf. Kaempf-Dimitriadou 1969, 57.

48. Zeus granted immortality to Ganymede and to his sons Herakles and Polydeukes; the latter generously shared his immortality with his half-brother Castor. Aphrodite made Cephalus' son Phaethon a "bright divinity" (*daimona dion*, Hes., *Theog.* 991), but this is a status more like that of hero, because he is confined to one place as "the secret keeper of her temple" (Nagy 1979, 192); no sexual relationship is implied (Stehle 1990, 96).

49. Kurtz and Boardman 1971, 144–45; see *LIMC* III, 1986, 779, s.v. Eos (C. Weiss). Vermeule 1979, 163, cites only Heraclitus (below, n.52) in support of her claim that "Eos the Dawn goddess carried off the dead on 'the wings of the morning' or to motivate the event by simple sexual attraction or love." The notion of flying to God on the wings of the morning derives from Psalm 139: 9–10 (King James Version).

50. Sourvinou-Inwood 1995, 337–46; cf. Garland 1985, 54–59. In Etruria in the first half of the fifth century, mirrors depicting the goddess Thesan (Eos) carrying her dead son Memnon were popular. As De Puma 1994, 187, suggests, "she, like her mortal devotees, has had to bow to a power stronger than the king of the gods."

51. *LIMC* III, 1986, 779, s.v. Eos (C. Weiss).

52. As Athenaeus has Plutarch say at his learned symposium: "Whom do the goddesses abduct?" (*anarpazousin*); on the translation, cf. Bremmer 2000, 103. "Is it not the most beautiful ones? And these are the ones they live with: Eos with Cephalus and Clitus and Tithonus, Demeter with Iasion, Aphrodite with Anchises and Ado-

nis" (xiii. 566d). See also Heraclitus, *Allegoriae* = *Quaestiones Homericae* 68; Kaempf-Dimitriadou 1969, 57.

53. Vatican City, Musei Vaticani, 12241 = *LIMC* III 1986, 795, no. 30, pl. 30, s.v. Eos = Thesan (R. Bloch) = De Puma 1994, 181–82, pl. 16.7.

54. Once J. Rhodes = *ARV*² 987,5 = *LIMC* III, 1986, 773, no. 269, pl. 269, s.v. Eos (C. Weiss) = Kaempf-Dimitriadou 1969, 92, no. 199.

55. Paris G 123 = *ARV*² 435,94 = *LIMC* IV 1988, 157, no. 52, pl. 52, s.v. Ganymedes (H. Sichtermann) = Kaempf-Dimitriadou 1969, 79, no. 39.

56. *LIMC* IV 1988, 157, no. 56, pl. 66, s.v. Ganymedes (H. Sichtermann) = Kaempf-Dimitriadou 1969, 79, no. 40 = Dover 1978, 92 and pl. 1; see also Robertson 1975, 277 and pl. 60: "the Greeks saw honour, not shame, in the youth's having a god for a lover."

57. On the fragment, see Lloyd-Jones 1971, 414–17; above, ch. 5, and below, ch. 9.

58. Cf. *LIMC* IV 1988, 78–80, nos. 22–75, s.v. Europe (M. Robertson) for a list of red-figure vases showing Europa riding: "bull generally galloping, often over sea."

59. Europa's story was told in poems (now lost) by Eumelus, Stesichorus, and Bacchylides; see Campbell 1991, 3; Bühler 1968, 25–26.

60. In Moschus' poem Europa is ready for marriage, and she responds without hesitation to the bull's approaches. Similarly, in fourth-century vase paintings, Danae is shown looking upward, with her breasts bare, collecting the golden rain in her lap, as on a bell krater from Boeotia in the Louvre (Paris CA 925 = CVA pls. 44, 1–45 = *LIMC* III, 1986, 328, no. 9, pl. 9, 335, s.v. Danae (J.-J. Maffre).

61. To speak of this abduction as "bestial rape" (Robson 1997, 74, 77) seems extreme. There is no suggestion that Zeus remained in bull form after he took Europa to Crete. Even in Moschus' poem, where the bull is extraordinarily affectionate, they leave before they have any erotic contact, with Europa (as in many vase paintings) sitting on the bull's back, holding the bull's long horn in one hand, and grasping the hem of her chiton in her other hand, to keep it from dipping into the sea, while the cloth on her shoulders billows out like a sail (Moschus, *Europa*, 108–30).

62. Bell krater by the Berlin Painter (Tarquinia RC 7456), *ARV*² 206, 126 = *LIMC* IV, 1988, 77, no. 2, pl. 2, s.v. Europe (M. Robertson). Kurtz 1983, 102, observes that this vase "represents an earlier stage in the story" than the Berlin Painter's depiction of Europa on the bull's back (Oxford 1927.4502 = *ARV*² 210.172 = *LIMC* IV 1988, 79, no. 41, s.v. Europe [M. Robertson]). Bühler 1968, 54: "Europe mit weit ausschreitenden Füssen neben dem Stier herläuft."

63. Kilmer 1997, 128.

64. Keuls 1985, 51.

65. Frontisi-Ducroux 1996, 88.

66. The story was told in the lost cyclic epic *Epigonoi* (fr. 5 Bernabé); for details, see Kearns 1989, 177.

67. Hom., *Il.* 24.525–26: "so the gods have allotted for unfortunate mortals, to live in sorrow; but they are free from cares." Cf. Macleod 1982, 133: "the gods, who in this book show their pity for men and demand that men pity each other, also will human suffering and never share in it."

68. See esp. Sourvinou-Inwood 1991, 47–50.

69. Cf. Verg., *Aen.* 2.648–49. According to Hyginus, *Fab.* 94, the lightning bolt killed him. On other variants of the story, see Austin 1964, 247–48.

70. Cf. Calame 1999, 67.

71. For examples, see Reeder 1995, 352–57, nos. 111–13; in general, see Kaempf-Dimitriadou 1969, 28–30.

72. For examples, see Reeder 1995, 358–61, nos. 114–16; Burn 1987, 52.

73. The author of the *Homeric Hymn to Apollo* sets aside obscure local myths of Apollo's abductions of mortal women and concentrates instead on how the god founded his shrine at Delphi; Clay 1989, 56. But cf. the emphasis in Stewart 1995, 76, "the Homeric hymn to Apollo recounted the god's progress from insatiable womanizer to panhellenic deity."

74. Cohen 1996, 130, sees Helios' statement as a "dubious consolation," and the promise of marriage as an authorization of violence.

75. Cf. Dougherty 1993, 144–45.

76. E.g., Rabinowitz 1993, 197–201; cf. Stewart 1995, 80 and fig. 1, but see above, ch. 5.

77. Above, ch. 5 at n.24, which Cohen 1996, 134 n.39, sees as "another authorization." Cf. Rabinowitz 1993, 201–2.

78. Danae says to Zeus in Aesch., fr. 47a.784–85 *TGrF,* "you have the [responsibility] for the greater fault, but I have paid the whole [penalty]." Cf. the fate of Antiope, who was abducted by Zeus (schol. Ap.Rhod. 4.1090, 304–5 Wendel) but forced to expose her twin sons, and then was imprisoned and tortured. In Eur., *Antiope* fr. 208N = fr. 33 Kambitsis, Antiope observes: "if the gods have abandoned me and my twin sons, there is a reason for it; for some people are unfortunate, and others fortunate." Cf. note 67, above.

79. Cf. Clay 1989, 171.

80. Cf. how Odysseus is afraid that intercourse with Circe will make him "weak and unmanned" (*Od.* 10.341); Clay 1989, 182–83.

81. *LIMC* VII 1994, 269, s.v. Peleus (R. Vollkommer).

82. Reeder 1995, 299–300; cf. Sourvinou-Inwood 1991, 66.

83. Louvre G 373: *ARV*² 573, no. 9; *LIMC* III, 1986, p. 239, no. 29, pl. 189, s.v. Cheiron (M. Gisler-Huwiler).

84. Rehm 1994, 20. British Museum B 298: *LIMC* VII 1994, p. 260, no. 117, s.v. Peleus (R. Vollkammer); Oakley and Sinos 1993, p. 87, fig. 67.

85. As Sourvinou-Inwood observes (1991), 66, the iconography of Peleus' capture of Thetis differs completely from scenes of other abductions.

86. Berlin, Staatliche Museen, F 2279, from Vulci = ARV^2 115.2 and 1626 = LIMC VIII 1997, 8, no. 13, pl. 13 = Reeder 1995, no. 106, 341–43. On the wrestling hold, see Poliakoff 1987, 40.

87. Dover 1978, 95–96 and pl. R 196: a–b; Stewart 1995, 81–82; Sutton 1997/1998, 30. The name Peithinos is unique; Pape and Benseler 1911/1959, 1154; LGPN 2, 365.

88. Of the Eos vases listed by Kaempf-Dimitriadou 1969, there are 15 lekythoi, but 44 amphoras, 30 kraters, 28 drinking cups, 16 hydriai, 6 stamnoi, and 6 oinochoai.

89. Sutton 1997/1998, 31. Also see above, n.7, on the placement of the Eos-Cephalus and Boreas-Oreithyia myths on the akroteria of the Athenians' temple at Delos; the terra-cotta statue of Zeus and Ganymede at Olympia may have been an akroterion; cf. Robertson 1975, 277, cited above in n.56.

90. Euripides, Alc. 1149–53; And. 1284–88; Hel. 1688–92; Ba. 1388–92, and a different first line, Med. 1415–19. If the lines were added later by actors, it was in order to please a public who liked such sententiae; Barrett 1964, 417. According to Roberts 1987, 56, and Dunn 1996, 24–25, the lines are pro forma ritual; but cf. Lefkowitz 1989, 80–82.

Chapter 7. The Last Hours of the Parthenos

1. Lefkowitz 1981b, 41–47.

2. Cf. Pomeroy 1994, 268–69.

3. See above, ch. 5.

4. On the ritual purpose of such sacrifices, cf. esp. Versnel 1980, 145.

5. Some of these effects are noted in other Hippocratic treatises, e.g., Prorrheticon 2. 30. 34 (headaches); de Mulierum Affectibus 127. 4, 127. 19, de Natura Muliebri 3. 4, Superfetatione 34. 1 (hysteria).

6. This seems to have been the plot of a play by Aeschylus, the Xantriae or possibly the Semele; cf. Lloyd-Jones 1971, 567–68.

7. E.g., IG I^2 1014 = CEG 24; AP 7. 486, 489, 490, 649; above, ch. 9.

8. Kearns 1989, 57; cf. O'Connor-Visser 1987, 197–99.

9. See above, ch. 3.

10. Kearns 1990, 338–44.

11. Reeder 1995, 356–57 and fig. 113 = LIMC I (1981) 744 no. 21, s.v. Amymone. Cf. Buxton 1982, 84, 112–13; Sourvinou-Inwood 1991, 69; above, ch. 6.

12. See also above, chs. 5 and 6.

13. Lloyd-Jones 1982, 161–62 = Lloyd-Jones 1990a, 78–79.

14. The translations of Sophocles and of Aeschylus' *Agamemnon* in this chapter are by Hugh Lloyd-Jones.

15. See below, ch. 12; Wilkins 1990, 177–94.

16. Burkert 1983, 65–67; Gantz 1993, 598–60.

17. Gantz 1993, 659.

18. See the scholion Euripides' *Hecuba* 573. 2, I 53–54 Schwartz = Eratosthenes 241 *FGrHist* F 14; Pindar, *Pyth.* 4. 240, 9. 123–24; Burkert 1985, 76. Collard 1991, 161, mistakenly conflates the two practices, cf. Burkert 1983, 5n.16.

19. Athenaeus 13. 590e = Hypereides, fr. 178 Kenyon = *WLGR*³ 288.

20. Kearns 1989, 58–59; Pearson 1907, xix; Wilkins 1993, 104–5, and see below ch. 12.

21. Wilkins 1993, 104–5.

22. Kearns 1989, 166–67.

23. See Wilkins 1993, 112.

24. Scholion to Plat. *Symp.* 208d, pp. 63–64 Greene.

25. Foley 1985, 40.

26. *WLGR*³ 27B; see also below ch. 12.

27. According to Demaratus 42 *FGrHist* F4 the demand was made by Persephone, but according to Hyginus fab. 46. 238 it was Poseidon.

28. Brulé 1987, 31–32; Kearns 1989, 59–63, 201–2; Mikalson 1991, 93–94; on the connection of the Erechtheides with this cult, see Parker 1987, 212n.66.

29. See Connelly 1996, 53–80, esp. 79–80.

30. Burkert 1983, 63–64; Lloyd-Jones 1990b, 312–13.

31. London 1897. 7–27. 2; Maas 1973a, 42; cf. Gantz 1993, 658; Harder 1993, 180n.16.

32. See the Hippocratic treatises *On the Diseases of Young Girls*, VIII 468 L = *WLGR*³ 349 (also above, ch. 4) and *On Double Pregnancies* 34. 1 VIII 504–7 L; and now esp. Dean-Jones 1994, 50–51.

33. Aristotle cites a line from Euripides' *Telephus* (fr. 719 *TGrF*) as what "the poets say" (*Politics* A 2 p. 1252b8); see also Eur., *Andromache* 665, *Helen* 276, *Orestes* 115; Hall 1989, 197; Harder 1993, 238n.136.

34. Cf. Loraux 1987, 34, 48.

35. E.g., Foley 1982, 170: "Ironically, the ideal bride and the ideal sacrificial victim become one, as the education for marriage provides the transition to voluntary death."

Chapter 8. Women in the Panathenaic and Other Festivals

1. E.g., Tyrrell and Brown 1991, 114–15.

2. Humphreys 1983, xiii.

3. See Satyrus' *Life of Euripides* F 6. fr. 39 col. x–xi Schorn, and the ancient life of Euripides T A. 102–7 *TGrF*.

4. The saying became proverbial. Cf. Menander, Monostichos 344 Jäkel; *AP* 10. 107; Arrian, *Anabasis* 1. 26. 2, *Cynegetica* 35. 1.

5. Graham 1981, 314; also Arrigoni 1985, xxi–xxiii; Sinclair Holderman 1985, 299–330; Connelly 2007.

6. See Calame 1977, 151n.211.

7. Pearson 1907 146; Calame 1977, 235–36; Parker 1987, 192.

8. Parker 1987, 192.

9. Perhaps the presentation of the *peplos* is the significant moment that is portrayed in the central action of the east frieze of the Parthenon; Smarczyk, 1984, 550n.15; Simon, 1983, 66–67; Connelly 1996, 60.

10. Ziehen 1949, 460.

11. Musti 1982, 364.

12. Parke 1977, 38–39; Deubner 1932, 31; on the making of the *peplos*, see esp. Barber in Neils et al. 1992, 112–17.

13. Simon 1983, 60 and pl. 22.1.

14. Henderson 1987, 155; see now Parker 2005, 218–48.

15. Shares of meat are distributed as follows: *prytaneis*, 5 shares; *árchōtes* 3; *tamiai* of Athena and *hieropoioi*, 1; *strategoi* and *taxiarchoi*, 3; participants in the procession and *kanephoroi*, "as customary" (*IG* II² 334. 11–1; Jacoby on 328 *FGrHist* F 8).

16. Frazer 1898, II 387 on Pausanias 1. 29. 16; Pseudo-Plutarch, *Lives of the Ten Orators* 844d.

17. Demetrius of Phaleron 228 *FGrHist* F 5, Pollux III. 55 s.v. *skiadophoros*, schol. Ar., *Av.* 1551; Simon 1983, 65; Smarczyk 1984, 551.

18. Robertson 1983, 242; B. Nagy 1979, 361; also now Parker 2005, 227–28.

19. Contrast Loraux 1981, 47–49.

20. Robertson 1983, 280.

21. See also below, ch. 10.

22. Schol. Aristophanes, *Eq.* 566c p. 142 Jones-Wilson; Wycherley 1978, 71.

23. Loraux 1993, 48–49; on the various versions of this myth, see Hollis 1990, 226–31.

24. Kearns 1989, 139, 161.

25. Robertson 1983, 241–88.

26. Cf. how in second-century AD Ephesos, the Kouretes reenacted the birth of Artemis as a "vital contribution to the very existence of the Greek city" under Roman rule; Rogers 1991, 145.

27. In the Hesiodic *Aegimius* (the earliest version of the story), Thetis dipped Achilles in a basin of water (fr. 300 M-W); cf. Livrea 1973, on Apollon. 4. 816.

28. Parker 1991, 8.

29. Parker 1987, 196–97.

30. Parker 1983, 196n.40; cf. Shapiro 1986, 135. On the birth of a monster child as a form of salvation, see Kearns, 1990, 323–26.

31. Wilamowitz-Moellendorff 1926, 87.

32. E.g., *IG* II/III² 11907 = 548 Peek, 12067 = 1387 Peek. The circumstances of death, outside of battle, are not usually described in fifth-century inscriptions, but fourth-century inscriptions also make explicit the importance of ordinary domestic virtues; see Humphreys 1983, 93, 121. For some poignant Hellenistic examples, see *WLGR³* 363–68.

33. Contrast the protestations of Loraux 1987, 1–5.

34. Vernant 1980, 50.

35. Richardson 1974, 27; Zeitlin 1989, 159; Parker 1991, 9–10.

36. Suda *s.v. kourotrophos gē*, I 3 p. 167 Adler; Simon 1983, 69; *LIMC* IV 1988, 922–51, *s.v.* Erechtheus (U. Kron).

37. Sometimes Erechtheus and Erichthonius are identified (e.g. Parker 1987, 193–94), but in Euripides' *Ion*, 999–1009, Erichthonius is a snakelike figure, like Cecrops, distinct from Erechtheus; cf. Wilamowitz-Moellendorff 1926, 131–32; Robertson 1985, 254–58.

38. See Lloyd-Jones 1990a, 269; Sissa and Detienne 1989, 241–42.

39. Lycurgus thought that childbearing was the most important function of free women; see Xenophon *Respublica Lacedaemoniorum* 1. 4.

40. Cf. what Iphigenia says to Clytemnestra, as an argument in favor of her self-sacrifice: "you bore me for all the Hellenes, not for yourself alone" (1386) (below, ch. 12). Statements such as these seem to argue strongly against an ambiguous role or virtual nonexistence of women in Athenian life, as formulated by Brulé 1987, 135, and Loraux 1993, 10–11.

41. According to the writer of Athenian history Phanodemos, 325 *FGrHist* F 4 (cited by Photios *s.v. parthenoi*), the eldest two daughters, Protogeneia and Pandora, offered themselves as sacrifice when their country was invaded by Boeotia (*sic*); in Euripides' *Ion*, Creusa explains that when Erechtheus sacrificed Creusa's sisters she was spared because she was still an infant (279–80).

42. Unfortunately, the reference to the sacrificed daughter's cult in *IG* II² 1262. 52 does not specify its location, but according to Phanodemus (325 *FGrHist* F 4) and the comic poet Phrynichus (fr. 32 *PCG*), the daughters were sacrificed on the hill Hyacinthus at Sphendonae; cf. Kearns 1989, 201.

43. Cf. Loraux 1987, 46.

44. *IG* II² 3453 = *WLGR³* 399A is probably its base; cf. Lewis 1955, 5.

45. Henderson 1987, xxxviii–xxxix.

46. Contrast Loraux 1981, 47, who imagines that Euripides may be commenting on the savagery involved in the sacrificing of virgins on behalf of armies of men: "ex-

pose to the judgment of the spectators these armies of men who find their salvation in the blood of virgins"; and Kearns, 1990, 337–44, who goes to some length to explain the apparent paradox of girls' being chosen as role models for males, e.g., because of the transsexual nature of ephebic puberty rites (331).

47. Kearns 1990, 331.

48. Zuntz 1955, 30; cf. Pearson, 1907, xxvii: "this [Athenian] sense of justice springs from a conspicuous devotion to religion"; and Mikalson 1991, 233.

49. Cf. Fraenkel 1962, on Aesch., *Ag.* 1297.

50. E.g., Menoeceus in Eur., *Phoenissai* 998–1005; cf. above, ch. 7.

51. Wycherley 1978, 63–64; but see *Suda* L 262, according to which it is located "in the middle of the Ceramicos."

52. Curiously, no surviving Athenian poetry tells the story of Codrus; see Wilamowitz-Moellendorff 1893, ii. 130. On the modes chosen for self-sacrifice, see Versnel 1980, 140n.2, 155n.1.

53. Connelly 1996, 53–80.

54. Contrast Parke 1977, 56: "the participants would not need to [participate in the Panathenaia] with religious feeling, nor would they be expected to acquire any personal merit or spiritual reward from their performance." But for the Greeks, all public festivals, such as athletic competitions, secular as they may seem to us, were religious in character.

55. E.g., the Eleusinian priestess who ca. 176 AD initiated Marcus Aurelius and Commodus is led by the goddess away from every kind of sorrow to the isles of the blessed: "she brought her a death sweeter than sleep, far better than that of the Argive heroes" (*IG* II^2 3632. 12–6); cf. Richardson 1974, 311.

56. A rule-proving exception: the initiation of the Emperor Hadrian, "who lavishes the cities with his boundless wealth (*ploutos*), and above all these the famous land of Cecrops" (*IG* II^2 3575 = Kaibel 863. 11–12); cf. Richardson 1974, 317.

57. On aspects likely to be inauthentic, see Parke 1977, 87.

58. The significant political aspect of the festival is not discussed by Kraemer 1992, 27.

59. Contrast the absurdly selfish prayer to Demeter and Persephone offered by the woman impersonated by Euripides' relative, who asks that they send her daughter a rich husband or a stupid one (289–91).

60. Cf. Sissa and Detienne 1989, 251–52, despite the reservations of Loraux 1993, 247–48.

Chapter 9. Women without Men

1. Poliakoff 1982, 104–5; Bernardini 1983, 113–14.

2. Frazer 1921, 2. 67.

3. Fraenkel 1962, iii. 555.

4. Bremmer 1985.

5. Vase paintings concentrate on the moment of interception and depict rapes by gods of young men, like Zeus and Ganymede, or Eos and Cephalus (see ch. 6), as well as the rapes by gods of women (ch. 5).

6. Kannicht 1969, ii. 342–43; on other possible interpretations of the speech, see Foley 1993, 60.

7. E.g., Moschus 2. 79–107.

8. The poet of the *Catalogue* concentrates on the compensation given to Europa's father (fr. 141. 1–6). Similarly, when Zeus carried off Ganymede to be his lover, he gave the boy's father, Tros, some of the swift horses that carried the immortals (*Homeric Hymn* 5. 207–17).

9. Campbell 1964, 86.

10. See also above, ch. 7.

11. Richardson 1974, 226.

12. Ibid., 161.

13. Ibid., 316–17.

14. Hansen 1983, no. 89; Kurtz 1975, 56, pl. 42.1.

15. Hansen 1983, no. 24 = *WLGR*[3] 273; Humphreys 1983, 153; Gressmair 1966, 63–75.

16. Cf. Euripides, *Iphigenia at Aulis* 461; *Medea* 985; Sophocles, *Antigone* 654, 816; Euripides, *Hecuba* 416, 612; Kurtz and Boardman 1971, 161.

17. Cf. Euripides, *Heracles* 480–82; Lattimore 1962, 193.

18. Gressmair 1966, 75–77.

19. *WLGR*[3] 13 = *AP* 7. 490; Lattimore 1962, 194n.62; cf. *FGE* 678ff.

20. Lefkowitz 1981b, 1–10.

21. Winnington-Ingram 1982, 247–49.

22. Wiersma 1984, 54–55.

23. Lloyd-Jones 1983, 144–47, warns against believing that any particular character or the chorus represents the poet. Vellacott (1975, 6–8), however, insists that conjectures about Euripides' meaning must be made in order to protect the poet's "integrity," even though that allows modern readers to add a considerable element of subjectivity.

24. Cf. Vellacott 1975, 163–66.

25. Wiedemann 1983, 163–70.

26. Tr. Lloyd-Jones 1975; cf. Menander *Dyscolus* 381–89.

27. Cf. the poet Nossis, judging a picture on the grounds of verisimilitude: "If your little watch-dog saw you, she would wag her tail, and think she saw the mistress of her house" (*AP* 9. 604 = 2815 G-P = *WLGR*[3] 20); also *AP* 6. 353–54; Erinna *AP* 6. 352 = 1796 G-P. But men also admire verisimilitude, e.g., Theocritus, *Idylls* 1. 55–56.

28. On the Thesmophoria see now esp. Parker 2005, 270–83. Zeitlin 1982, 144–

47, by a series of ingenious associations, deduces that the rites represent a formalized and temporary return to a matriarchal state. Yet, when women band together, as in Aristophanes' *Lysistrata*, it is for the salvation of the community; they wish to return to their men and their normal lives (below, ch. 11). One wishes we knew more about Pherecrates' comedy *Tyrannis*, where some kind of temporary gynaecocracy may have been involved (*PCG* VII 175).

29. Richardson 1974, 26–28; Foley 1993, 63. On the advantages of mystery cults for the present lives of worshipers, see Burkert 1987, 20.

30. Richardson 1974, 214.

31. Cf. Pherecrates fr. 181 *PCG*.

32. Detienne 1977, 109–10, and see now Parker 2005, 283–89.

33. Calame 1977, ii. 69–70.

34. Above ch. 4.

35. It seems particularly significant that the Pythia, although a priestess of a male god, Apollo, is female, since gods usually have priests of the same sex as themselves; Latte 1940, 15; Burkert 1985, 117.

Chapter 10. Wives

1. Gould 1980, 39–42.

2. Pomeroy 1985, 20.

3. Sappho's descriptions of love and loss seem to offer little grounds for Pomeroy's claim (1975b, 52) that "the lyric poems of the female writers of the Archaic Age give us the happiest picture of women in Greek literature." Pomeroy's account of these writers is singled out for comment and splendidly garbled by French (1985, 143), in a paragraph that illustrates the risks involved in writing about the ancient world without knowledge of its languages or history: "The great Sappho had students, at least one of whom, Erinna, wrote poetry that her male contemporaries considered as good as Homer's. A group of women poets called the 'nine Earthly Muses' were viewed as the best poets of their age." Not only did Sappho (sixth century BC, Lesbos) and Erinna (fourth century BC, Telos) live at different times and places; the "nine Muses that Earth bore" were never seen together; they were only listed together in an epigram by the first-century BC poet Antipater of Thessalonica (*AP* 9. 26 = 19 *Garl. Phil.*): Praxilla, Moero, Anyte, Sappho (whom Antipater calls "the female Homer"), Erinna, Telesilla, Corinna, Nossis, and Myrtis. No ancient critic that I can discover compares Erinna to Homer.

4. Wives are frequently compared to Penelope on grave inscriptions (Peek, no. 165, pp. 163–64).

5. For example, Smith 1960, 127–45.

6. Gould 1980, 56–58.

7. The word I have translated as "attraction" is "breezes" in the Greek, a term that denotes a sudden, powerful sensation.

8. Lloyd-Jones 1964, 28 = Lloyd-Jones 1990b, 106. The quoted passage may be from a lost play of Menander; see Handley 2006, 23–25.

9. Sandbach 1972, 328–30.

10. See also Pasion's will in Demosthenes 45. 28 = $WLGR^3$ 78; Aristotle's will in Diogenes Laertius 5. 11–61 = $WLGR^3$ 79. Cf. also the concept of *patria potestas* in Roman law (Treggiari 1982, 34–44).

11. Gould 1980, 50; Cole 1981, 234.

12. Thesleff 1965, 151–54.

13. See now Hamel 2003, 104–6.

14. Gould 1980, 50n.85.

15. Humphreys 1983, 104–18.

16. Cf. Euripides, *Alcestis* 288–89.

17. Pomeroy 1985, 89–90.

18. SBX. 10756; Pomeroy 1981, 308–9.

19. All quotations of the "*Laudatio Turiae*" are from the translation of Wistrand 1976; cf. Gordon 1977, 7–12; Horsfall 1983; and Mazzolani 1982.

20. Ciccotti 1985, 8.

21. Lefkowitz 1981b, 32–40.

22. Cf. "Turia" 1. 30: "Why should I mention your domestic virtues, chastity, obedience, compatibility, industry in working wool, religion without superstition, sobriety of attire, modesty of appearance?" (Lefkowitz 1981b, 28–29). The unique *domiseda* occurs in *CIL* VI. 11602 (Comfort 1960, 275).

23. Horsfall 1982.

24. Lattimore 1962, 277–80.

25. Bloch 1963, 193–218.

26. Bloch 1945, 199–244.

27. E.g., *ILS* 4154.

28. Cf. Brown 1972, 172–73.

Chapter 11. Influential Women

1. Wiesen 1976, 199–212.

2. de Ste. Croix 1981, 24–25.

3. Lacey 1968, 54–55, 80–81; on Antigone as a moral agent, see Foley 2001, 172–200.

4. Foley 1975, 36; Sorum 1982, 206; O'Brien 1977, xiii–xxx.

5. Sorum 1982, 207.

6. Heilbrun 1973, 9.

7. Foley 1975, 33–36.

8. Heilbrun (1973, 10) cites an unidentified verse translation: "But to defy the State—I have no strength for that." The Greek says only "Do you intend to bury him, when Creon has forbidden it?" (Sophocles, *Antigone* 47).

9. According to Plutarch (*Moralia* 259d), Mithridates (first century BC) decreed that the corpse of his enemy Poredorix be left unburied, but when the guards arrested a woman burying the body, Mithridates permitted her to complete the burial and gave her clothes for the corpse, "probably because he realized that the reason behind it was love."

10. Campbell 1964, 193–94, 168–69; Alexiou 1974, 22.

11. On the gendering of voices in tragedy, see Foley 2001, 15.

12. Humphreys 1983, 106; Lacey 1968, 148–49.

13. Alcmena refuses to sleep with her husband Amphitryon until he has avenged her brothers' deaths (*Shield* 15–17); Intaphernes' wife chooses to have her brother spared rather than her husband (Herodotus 3. 119. 6); and Althaea brings about the death of her son Meleager because he killed her brothers (*Bacchylides* 5. 136–44). The "illogicality" (in modern terms) of Antigone's argument and its similarity to the Herodotean passage have caused scholars to question its authenticity (e.g., Winnington-Ingram 1980, 145n.80); but cf. Lefkowitz 1981b, 5n.8; Humphreys 1983, 67.

14. Daube 1972, 6–7; Blok 2001, 106.

15. Humphreys' claim (1983, 62) that "the heroines of fifth-century BC tragedy are different [from the heroines of epic, like Andromache]: they are agents in their own right, acting in opposition to men or as substitutes for them" fails to take account of the crucial distinction between right and wrong action. Althaea, for example, is listed first in a catalogue of evil women by the (female) chorus of Aeschylus, *Libation Bearers* 603 ff.

16. Jacob 1963, 290; Jebb 1900, xlii.

17. Cf. Aeschylus, *Libation Bearers* 585 ff.

18. Euripides' *Melanippe the Wise*, fr. 482 *TGrF*. According to the Aristophanes scholia, the play provided later writers with many quotations both for and against women (e.g., frs. 497–99, 502, 503 *TGrF*).

19. Annas 1981, 181–85; cf. Adam 1963, I 345.

20. Redfield 1978, 160, by analyzing the condition of Spartan women in terms of the artificial polarities of *oikos* and *polis*, suggests that "we can see the Spartan policy as a somewhat extreme enactment of general Greek ideas"; but surely Aristotle regarded it as anomalous, and ultimately self-destructive. On women's status in the polis, see Gould 1980, 46.

21. Cartledge 1981, 86–89.

22. See above, ch. 10.

23. See Plutarch, *Gracch.* 2. 19; Cicero, *Brut.* 58. 211; Seneca, *de Cons.* 16; Tacitus, *Dial* 28; Valerius Maximus 4. 4 praef. = *WLGR*[3] 258–60.

24. The second-century AD traveler Pausanias saw a statue of Telesilla in Argos (ii. 20. 8–10). See also the male poets Solon of Athens and Tyrtaeus of Sparta, both of whom were assumed to have been generals, perhaps because of the hortatory stance they adopt in their poems (Lefkowitz 1981b, 38, 42). In part, the story of Telesilla appears to be an aetiology of the annual Argive festival of Impudence (*hybristika*), one of several Greek rituals involving transvestism and role change (Burkert 1985, 259, 440n.53). Cf. how an Argive woman was celebrated for killing king Pyrrhus when he attacked the city in 271 BC (Stadter 1965, 52).

25. Stadter 1965, 101–3.

26. Schaps 1977, 323–30.

27. See also Pleket 15 = *WLGR³* 191; *CIL* viii. 23888 = *WLGR³* 199; Van Bremen 1981, 223–41.

28. Thesleff 1965, 151.

29. Pomeroy 1985, 17–30.

30. Cantarella 1981, 113–14. Callimachus (in Catullus' translation, 66. 25–26) may have been alluding to how she helped assassins dispose of her first husband, Demetrius (her mother's lover, whose presence kept her mother in power), so that she could marry Ptolemy (Justin 26. 3).

31. Berenice II also won chariot races at Olympia; see *WLGR³* 203A.

32. Macurdy 1932, 130–36.

33. See above, ch. 10.

34. Cf. Pomeroy 1985, 24–28; Macurdy 1932, 202–5. Cleopatra's daughter Cleopatra Selene issued coins in her own name, but they showed her husband Juba on the reverse; Macurdy 1932, 225.

35. Pomeroy 1985, 119–20.

36. Above, ch. 10; cf. Balsdon 1962, 204–5.

37. Ciccotti 1985, 24–26.

38. Lentulus' wife probably was Sulpicia, wife of Cornelius Lentulus Cruscello; Valerius Maximus 6. 6. 3; *RE* IV (1901) 1384.

39. Balsdon 1962, 51.

40. All translations from Latin texts not otherwise credited are by Maureen B. Fant.

41. Balsdon 1962, 47–48.

42. Millar 1977, 546–48.

43. Macurdy 1932, 205.

44. Balsdon 1962, 142, 160.

45. Antonina is alleged to have got her husband Belisarius' life spared through Theodora's intervention (Procopius, *Secret History* 4). Perhaps one reason why Theodora's contemporaries (like Cleopatra's) disliked her is that she often seemed to function, literally as well as figuratively, as co-ruler; oaths, for example, were sworn to Jus-

tinian and Theodora jointly (Gibbon 1854/1994, IV 40); see also her speech in the Hippodrome (Browning 1971, 112).

46. Warner 1976, 285–86.

Chapter 12. Martyrs

1. Henrichs 1984, 198–208.

2. Lloyd-Jones 1983, 89.

3. Translations from the *Agamemnon* are by H. Lloyd-Jones 1983.

4. Q14 Fontenrose 1978 = nos. 361, 362, Parke and Wormell 1956.

5. The passage from *Iliad* 18. 98–99 about Achilles' choice is also cited by Plato in defense of Socrates' decision not to alter his behavior even at the risk of execution, *Apology* 28c–d.

6. Cf. 1236–37.

7. See above, ch. 7.

8. See Aeschylus, *Agamemnon* 140–44; Lloyd-Jones 1983, 100–101.

9. According to the ancient commentary on Aristophanes, *Frogs* 67.

10. Zuntz 1955, 81–88.

11. See above, ch. 7.

12. Cf. Aristodemus (above, n.4), who murders his daughter by stabbing her in the chest and in the stomach, to show that she wasn't pregnant (Pausanias 4. 13. 2).

13. Above, chs. 7 and 9.

14. Lebek 1985, 7–8.

15. Lloyd-Jones 1983, 88–89, and above, ch. 8.

16. Above, chs. 7 and 11.

17. Above, ch. 10.

18. Musurillo 1972; Rader 1981; and see esp. the more recent Salisbury 1997, which contains a detailed analysis of the historical context of Perpetua's martyrdom.

19. Dodds 1965, 47–53; Lefkowitz 1981b, 53–54.

20. Translations of the *Acts of the Christian Martyrs* are by H. Musurillo 1972.

21. Lefkowitz 1981b, 54–58.

22. In 310 BC two hundred children from the best families were sacrificed when Carthage was besieged, and three hundred other children "who were suspect" also volunteered (Diodorus Siculus 20. 14. 5; Burkert 1980, 105n.2, 121n.1).

23. Henrichs 1980, 205, 196nn.3, 4; Stager and Wolff 1984, 42–44.

24. See also Musurillo 1972, no. 22.

25. Hroswitha, Latin text, ed. K. Strecker (Leipzig 1906); English translation by L. Bonfante (New York 1979).

26. Meeks 1983, 102.

27. Benko 1985, 114, 129.

28. In Apuleius' *Metamorphoses*, Lucius the Ass is afraid to have intercourse with a

murderess because of the contagion he might incur from her (*scelerosae mulieris contagio macularier*, 10. 29, 34).

29. Lanata 1973, 220.

30. Origen, *Against Celsus* 8. 65; Stewart 1984, 124.

31. Gibbon 1854/1994, II 945–46.

32. Rist 1965, 214–25; Dzielska 1995, 83–88.

33. Schanzer 1985, 62–63.

34. Rist 1965, 222.

35. Ibid., 216; Dzielska 1995, 91–92.

36. Dzielska 1995, 87–89.

37. Drescher 1947, 75.

38. Ibid., 80. See also Patlagean 1976, 597–623.

39. Hennecke 1964, 364.

40. The later account clearly refers to the grotto and relics of the fourth-century cult of Theclas in Seleucia described by the Spanish nun Egeria in *Itinerarium* 2–5 (= *WLGR*[3] 450A).

41. *Acts of Paul and Thecla*, last section of codex G, in Lipsius 1891, 271–72; Dagron 1978, 48–49.

Chapter 13. Misogyny

1. Walcot 1984, 46; Keuls 1985, 125–26; Henriques 1964, 45–46.

2. Dreyfus and Rabinow 1983, 229.

3. Cf. Semonides fr. 7. 12–20 with Lloyd-Jones 1975, note on 1. 12.

4. Hesiod (*Works and Days* 373–74) warns against the woman who wiggles her hips in order to get a man to let her poke into his granary, which also suggests that men did not always give women enough to eat (West 1978, 251). Cf. Arthur (1973, 47), who imagines that the poets' complaints are "part of the bourgeois polemic against aristocratic luxury." But it is hard to see why the poets ought to be considered bourgeois; see de Ste. Croix (1981, 60–62) on the meaning of Marx's terminology and the difficulty of applying it to the ancient world.

5. In the *Iliad*, Achilles' tutor was cursed by his father, because he slept with the father's mistress. The curse was that he should never have a son of his own (9. 554–56). For speculation that the myth of Anchises reflects fear that intercourse with a goddess will cause impotence, cf. Devereux 1982, 33.

6. Goldhill 1984b, 42. Cf. Foley 1981, 151.

7. See Zeitlin 1978; Humphreys 1983, 41; Tyrrell 1984, 93–100; and Goldhill 1984b, 33, 195, and esp. 283, where he uses bewildering psycho-babble to characterize the trilogy as a complex meditation on symbolism of the primal scene.

8. Tyrrell 1984, 110–11; Devereux 1976, 183–203.

9. See above, ch. 3.

10. Slater 1968, 189; Tyrrell 1984, 111–12.

11. Lefkowitz 1981b, 21; Humphreys 1983, 41.

12. At *Agamemnon* 140, I follow the reading *ha kala*, "the beautiful one," a traditional epithet of Artemis; see Barrett 1964, 170.

13. Page 1938, 102.

14. See also below, Epilogue.

15. Richardson 1974, 258.

16. See Connelly 2007, 17–18.

17. Cf. Latte 1940, 9–18.

18. Parvey 1974, 125–28; Fiorenza 1983, 226–36.

19. Cf. the Cyrene cathartic inscription, *SEG* IX. 72 = *LSCG* Suppl. 115; Parker 1983, 332–51.

20. See above, ch. 12.

21. Humphreys 1983, 47.

22. On epitaphs for young pagan women who died before marriage, see ch. 7.

23. Cf. Diehl 1967, no. 1699 = *CIL* XI: 1. 1491 = *CE* Suppl. 352.

24. See above, ch. 4.

25. Hennecke 1964, ii. 353–64. In the apocryphal Acts of Peter, when Agrippa's concubines and his wife Xanthippe refuse to sleep with him because they have taken the Christian vow of purity, Peter is executed (33–36); Hennecke 1964, 316–18.

26. Patlagean 1976, 597–623; cf. Dagron 1978, 38–39; Davies 1980, 58–61; MacDonald 1983, 34–53.

27. Diogenes Laertius lists "Lastheneia of Mantinea and Axiothea of Phlius, who is reported by Dicaearchus to have worn men's clothes" (3. 46). According to *POxy* 3656, one of them, probably Lastheneia, studied philosophy first with Plato, then with Speusippus (Diogenes Laertius 4. 2), and then with Menedemus; according to Aristophanes the Peripatetic, "she was pretty and full of unaffected charm."

28. See above, ch. 12.

Epilogue

1. French 1985, 72; Keuls 1985, 324.

2. Keuls 1985, 337–38.

3. See above, ch. 3.

4. Lefkowitz 2003, 167.

5. See also Worman 2001, 36–37.

6. See above, ch. 10.

7. Lefkowitz 1981b, 26, 28.

References

Ackermann, H. C., and J.-R. Gisler, eds. 1981–99. *Lexicon Iconographicum Mythologiae Classicae.* Zurich.

Adam, J. 1963. *The Republic of Plato*, ed. 2. Cambridge.

Adler, A. 1967. *Suidae Lexicon.* Leipzig.

Alexiou, M. 1974. *The Ritual Lament in Greek Tradition.* Oxford.

Andronikos, M. 1994. *Vergina*, vol. 2, *The Tomb of Persephone.* Athens.

Annas, J. 1981. *An Introduction to Plato's Republic.* Oxford.

Arrigoni, G. 1985. *Le donne in Grecia.* Rome.

Arthur, M. 1973. "Early Greece: origins of the Western attitude toward women," *Arethusa* 6:7–58.

Auerbach, N. 1978. *Communities of Women: An Idea in Fiction.* Cambridge, Mass.

Austin, R. G. 1964. *P. Vergili Maronis Aeneidos Liber Secundus.* Oxford.

Bachofen, J. J. 1967. *Myth, Religion, and Mother Right: Selected Writings*, tr. R. Mannheim. Princeton.

Bain, D. 1991. "Six Greek verbs of sexual congress," *Classical Quarterly* 51:51–77.

Balsdon, J.P.V.D. 1962. *Roman Women: Their History and Habits.* London.

Bamberger, J. 1973. "The myth of matriarchy." In *Women, Culture, and Society*, ed. M. Z. Rosaldo and L. Lamphere, 263–80. Stanford.

Barrett, W. 1964. *Euripides: Hippolytos.* Oxford.

Beazley, J. D., ed. 1963. *Attic Red-Figure Vase-Painters*, ed. 2. Oxford.

Benko, S. 1985. *Pagan Rome and the Early Christians.* London.

Bernardini, P. A. 1983. *Mito e attualità nelle odi di Pindaro.* Rome.

Blass, F. 1908. *Aeschinis Orationes.* Leipzig.

Bloch, H. 1945. "The last Pagan revival in the West," *Harvard Theological Review* 38: 199–244.

———. 1963. "The Pagan revival in the West at the end of the fourth century." In Momigliano 1963, 193–218.

Blok, J. 1995. *The Early Amazons: Modern and Ancient Perspectives on a Persistent Myth.* Leiden.

———. 2001. "Virtual voices: towards a choreography of women's speech in classical Athens." In Lardinois and McClure 2001, 95–116.

Boardman, J. 1982. "Heracles, Theseus, and Amazons." In *The Eye of Greece*, ed. D.C. Kurtz and B. Sparkes (Festschrift M. Robertson), 1–28. Cambridge.

Boedeker, D. D. 1974. *Aphrodite's Entry into Greek Epic*, Mnemosyne Supplement 32. Leiden.

Braswell, B. K. 1988. *A Commentary on the Fourth Pythian Ode of Pindar.* Berlin.

Bremer, J. M. 1975. "The meadow of love and two passages in Euripides' *Hippolytus*," *Mnemosyne* 28: 268–80.

Bremmer, J. 1985. "La donna anziana." In *Le donne in Grecia*, ed. G. Arrigoni, 275–98. Bari.

———. 2000. "Founding a city: the case of Cyrene." In *La fundación de la Ciudad: mitos y ritos en el mundo antiguo*, ed. P. Azara, R. Mar, E. Riu, and E. Subías, Arquitext, 12:101–9. Barcelona.

Brenk, F. E. 1977. *In Mist Appareled: Religious Themes in Plutarch's* Moralia *and* Lives. Leiden.

Brown, P. 1972. *Religion and Society in the Age of Augustine.* London.

Brown, P. G. M. 1991. "Athenian attitudes to rape and seduction," *Classical Quarterly* 41:533–34.

Browning, R. 1971. *Justinian and Theodora.* New York.

Brulé, P. 1987. *La fille d' Athènes.* Centre de Recherches d'Histoire Ancienne, vol. 76. Paris.

Buecheler, F., and E. Lommatzsch. 1897–1926. *Carmina Latina Epigraphica.* Leipzig.

Bühler, W. 1960. *Die Europa des Moschos: Text, Übersetzung und Kommentär*, Hermes Einzelschriften, vol. 13. Wiesbaden.

———. 1968. *Europa.* Munich.

Burkert, W. 1966. "Kekropidensage und Arrhephoria," *Hermes* 94: 1–25.

———. 1979. *Structure and History in Greek Mythology and Ritual*, Sather Classical Lectures 47. Berkeley.

———. 1980. "Glaube und Verhalten," in *Le Sacrifice dans l'Antiquité, Entretiens Hardt* 27:91–125.

———. 1983. *Homo Necans*, tr. P. Bing. Berkeley.

———. 1985. *Greek Religion: Archaic and Classical*, tr. J. Raffan. Oxford: Basil Blackwell.

———. 1987. *Ancient Mystery Cults.* Cambridge, Mass.

———. 1992. *The Orientalizing Revolution: Near Eastern Influence in the Early Archaic Age.* Cambridge, Mass.

Burn, L. 1987. *The Meidias Painter.* Oxford.

Burnett, A. P. 1962. "Human resistance and divine persuasion in Euripides' *Ion*," *Classical Philology* 57:89–103.

———, ed. and tr. 1970. *Euripides: Ion.* Englewood Cliffs, N.J.

———. 1971. *Catastrophe Survived.* Oxford.

Buxton, R. G. A. 1982. *Persuasion in Greek Tragedy: A Study of Peitho.* Cambridge.

Calame, C. 1977. *Les choeurs de jeune filles en Grèce archaïque*. Filologica e critica 20, vol. 2, *Alcman*. Rome.

———. 1999. *The Poetics of Eros in Ancient Greece*. Princeton.

Cameron, A., and A. Kuhrt. 1983. *Images of Women in Antiquity*. London.

Campbell, J. 1967. "Introduction" to Bachofen 1967: xi–lvii.

Campbell, J. K. 1964. *Honour, Family, and Patronage*. Oxford.

Campbell, M. 1991. *Moschus, Europa*, Altertumswissenschaftliche Texte und Studien, vol. 19. Wiesbaden.

Cantarella, E. 1981. *L'ambiguo malanno*. Rome (= 1987. *Pandora's Daughters*, tr. M. B. Fant. Baltimore).

———. 1983. "Johann Jacob Bachofen." In J. J. Bachofen, *Introduzione al diritto materno*. Rome 1983.

Carey, C., ed. 1989. *Lysias: Selected Speeches*. Cambridge.

Cartledge, P. 1981. "Spartan wives: liberation or license," *Classical Quarterly* 31: 84–105.

Chantraine, P. 1983. *Dictionnaire étymologique de la langue grecque*. Paris.

Chesler, P. 1972. *Women and Madness*. New York.

Ciccotti, E. 1985. *Donne e politica negli ultimi anni della Repubblica Romana*, ed. E. Cantarella (*Antigua* 33). Naples.

Clay, J. S. 1989. *The Politics of Olympus: Form and Meaning in the Major Homeric Hymns*. Princeton.

———. 2003. *Hesiod's Cosmos*. Cambridge.

Cohen, A. 1996. "Portrayals of abduction in Greek art: rape or metaphor." In Kampen 1996, 117–35.

Cole, S. G. 1981. "Could Greek women read and write?" In Foley 1981, 219–46.

Collard, C. 1991. *Euripides: Hecuba*. Warminster.

Comfort, H. 1960. "Some inscriptions near Rome," *American Journal of Archaeology* 64:273–76.

Connelly, J. B. 1996. "Parthenon and *Parthenoi*: a mythological interpretation of the Parthenon frieze," *American Journal of Archaeology* 100:53–80.

———. 2007. *Portrait of a Priestess*. Princeton.

Craik, E. M., ed. 1990. *"Owls to Athens": Essays for Sir Kenneth Dover*. Oxford.

Cross, A. 1985. *Sweet Death, Kind Death*. New York.

Dagron, G. 1978. *Vie et miracles de Sainte Thècle*. Subsidia Hagiographica 62. Brussels.

Dalley, S., ed. and tr. 1989. *Myths from Mesopotamia: Creation, the Flood, Gilgamesh, and Others*. Oxford.

Daube, D. 1972. *Civil Disobedience in Antiquity*. Edinburgh.

David, T. 1976. "La position de la femme en Asie Centrale," *Dialogues d'Histoire Ancienne* 2:129–62.

Davies, S. 1980. *The Revolt of the Widows*. Carbondale, Ill.

Deacy, S., and K. F. Pierce, eds. 1997. *Rape in Antiquity*. London.

Dean-Jones, L. A. 1994. *Women's Bodies in Classical Greek Science*. Oxford.

Delcourt, M. 1959. *Oreste et Alcmeon*. Paris.

De Puma, R. D. 1994. "Eos and Memnon in Etruscan mirrors." In *Murlo and the Etruscans: Art and Society in Ancient Etruria*, ed. R. D. De Puma and J. P. Small, 180–89. Madison.

Dessau, H., ed. 1979–80. *Inscriptiones Latinae Selectae*. Chicago.

de Ste. Croix, G. E. M. 1981. *The Class Struggle in the Ancient Greek World*. London.

Detienne, M. 1977. *The Gardens of Adonis*, tr. J. Lloyd. London.

Deubner, L. 1932. *Attische Feste*. Berlin.

Devereux, G. 1976. *Dreams in Greek Tragedy*. Berkeley.

———. 1982. *Femme et mythe*. Paris.

Diehl, E. 1967. *Inscriptiones Latinae Christianae Veteres*, suppl. J. Moreau and H.-I. Marrou. Dublin.

Diels, H., and W. Kranz, eds. 1960–64. *Die Fragmente der Vorsokratiker*. Berlin.

Diner, H. 1965. *Mothers and Amazons: The First Feminine History of Culture*, ed. and tr. J. P. Lundin. New York.

Dittenberger, W. 1915–24. *Sylloge Inscriptionum Graecarum*, ed. 3. Leipzig.

Dodds, E. R. 1965. *Pagan and Christian in an Age of Anxiety*. Cambridge.

Dougherty, C. 1993. *The Poetics of Colonization: From City to Text in Archaic Greece*. New York.

———.1998. "Sowing the seeds of violence: rape, women, and the land." In *Parchments of Gender: Deciphering the Bodies of Antiquity*, ed. M. Wyke, 267–84. Oxford.

Dover, K. J. 1978. *Greek Homosexuality*. Cambridge.

———. 1988. "Greek homosexuality and initiation." In *The Greeks and Their Legacy*, 115–34. Oxford.

Dowden, K. 1989. *Death and the Maiden*. London.

Drescher, J. 1947. "Three Coptic legends." In *Annales du service des antiquités d' Égypte*, cahier 4. Cairo.

Dreyfus, H. L., and P. Rabinow. 1983. "On the genealogy of ethics." In *Michel Foucault*, ed. 2. Chicago.

duBois, P. 1979. "On horse/men, Amazons, and endogamy," *Arethusa* 12:35–49.

———. 1982. *Centaurs and Amazons: Women and the Pre-history of the Great Chain of Being*. Ann Arbor.

———. 1988. *Sowing the Body*. Chicago.

Dunn, F. M. 1996. *Tragedy's End: Closure and Innovation in Euripidean Drama*. New York.

Dzielska, M. 1995. *Hypatia of Alexandria*, tr. F. Lyra. Cambridge, Mass.

Erbse, H. 1969–83. *Scholia Graeca in Homeri Iliadem*. Berlin.

Faraone, C. A. 1990. "Aphrodite's *Kestos* and apples for Atlanta," *Phoenix* 44:219–43.

Finley, M. I. 1978. *The World of Odysseus*, rev. ed. New York.

Fiorenza, E. S. 1983. *In Memory of Her*. New York.

Flory, S. 1987. *The Archaic Smile of Herodotus*. Detroit.

Foley, H. P. 1975. "Sex and state in ancient Greece," *Diacritics* 5.4:31–36.

———, ed. 1981. *Reflections of Women in Antiquity*. New York.

———. 1982. "Marriage and sacrifice in Euripides' *Iphigenia at Aulis*," *Arethusa* 15:159–80.

———. 1985. *Ritual Irony: Poetry and Sacrifice in Euripides*. Ithaca.

———, ed. 1993. *The Homeric Hymn to Demeter*. Princeton.

———. 2001. *Female Acts in Greek Tragedy*. Princeton.

Fontenrose, J. 1978. *The Delphic Oracle*. Berkeley.

Forbes Irving, P. F. 1990. *Metamorphosis in Greek Myth*. Oxford.

Fraenkel, E. 1962. *Aeschylus: Agamemnon*. Oxford.

Francis, E. D. 1980. "Greeks and Persians: the art of hazard and triumph." In *Ancient Persia: The Art of an Empire*, ed. D. Schmandt-Besserat. Malibu.

Frankfort, R. 1977. *Collegiate Women: Domesticity and Career in Turn-of-the-Century America*. New York.

Fraser, P. M., and E. Matthews, eds. 1987–. *A Lexicon of Greek Personal Names*. Oxford.

Frazer, J. G. 1898. *Pausanias' Description of Greece*. London.

———. 1921. *Apollodorus*. Loeb Classical Library. London.

French, M. 1985. *Beyond Power*. New York.

Friedländer, P., and F. Hoffleit. 1948. *Epigrammata*. Berkeley.

Friedrich, P. 1978. *The Meaning of Aphrodite*. Chicago.

Frontisi-Ducroux, F. 1996. "Eros, desire, and the gaze." In *Sexuality in Ancient Art*, ed. N. B. Kampen, 81–100. Cambridge.

Frymer-Kensky, T. 1992. *In the Wake of the Goddesses: Women Culture, and the Biblical Transformation of Pagan Myth*. New York.

Gallo, L. 1984. "La donna greca e la marginalità," *Quaderni Urbinati di Cultura Classica* 18:7–51.

Gantz, T. 1993. *Early Greek Myth: A Guide to Literary and Artistic Sources*. Baltimore.

Garland, R. 1985. *The Greek Way of Death*. Ithaca.

Gibbon, E. 1854/1994. *The History of the Decline and Fall of the Roman Empire*, ed. D. Womersley. London.

Girard, R. 1977. *Violence and the Sacred*, tr. P. Gregory. Baltimore.

Glasscock, J., ed. 1975. *Wellesley College 1875–1975: A Century of Women*. Wellesley.

Goldhill, S. 1984a. "Exegesis: Oedipus (R)ex," *Arethusa* 17:177–200.

———. 1984b. *Language, Sexuality, Narrative: The Oresteia*. Cambridge.

Gordon, A. E. 1977. "Who's who in the Laudatio Turiae," *Epigraphica* 39:7–12.

Gould, J. 1980. "Law, custom, and myth: aspects of the social position of women in Classical Athens," *Journal of Hellenic Studies* 100:38–59.

———. 1989. *Herodotus: Historians on Historians.* New York.

Gow, A. S. F. 1953. *The Greek Bucolic Poets.* Cambridge.

Gow, A. S. F., and D. L. Page. 1965. *The Greek Anthology: Hellenistic Epigrams.* Cambridge.

———. 1968. *The Garland of Philip.* Cambridge.

Graham, J. 1981. "Religion, women, and Greek colonization," *Centro Ricerche e Documentazione sull'Antichità Classica 'Atti* 11 (n.s. 1), 293–314. Rome.

Grenfell, B. P., and A. S. Hunt. 1898–. *The Oxyrhynchus Papyri.* London.

Gressmair, E. 1966. *Das Motiv der Mors immatura.* Innsbruck.

Griffin, J. 1980. *Homer on Life and Death.* Oxford.

Griffith, M., ed. 1983. *Aeschylus: Prometheus Bound.* Cambridge Greek and Latin Classics. Cambridge.

Guerney, O. R. 1961. *The Hittites.* Harmondsworth.

Hall, E. 1989. *Inventing the Barbarian: Greek Self-Definition through Tragedy.* Oxford.

Hamel, D. 2003. *Trying Neaira: The True Story of a Courtesan's Life in Greece.* New Haven.

Handley, E. 2006. "Dialogue with the night (PAnt 1.15 = PCG VIII 1084)," *Zeitschrift für Papyrologie und Epigraphik* 155:23–25.

Hansen, P. A. 1983. *Carmina Epigraphica Graeca.* Berlin.

Harder, R. E. 1993. *Die Frauenrolle bei Euripides.* Drama Beiheft 1. Stuttgart.

Harris, E. M. 1990. "Did the Athenians regard seduction as a worse crime than rape?" *Classical Quarterly* 40:370–77.

Harrison, T. 1997. "Herodotus and the ancient Greek idea of rape." In *Rape in Antiquity,* ed. S. Deacy and K. F. Pierce, 185–208. London.

Harvey, A. E. 1973. *A Companion to the New Testament.* Oxford/Cambridge.

Heilbrun, C. 1973. *Towards a Recognition of Androgyny.* New York.

———. 1979. *Reinventing Womanhood.* New York.

Heiler, F. 1977. *Die Frau in den Religionen der Menschheit.* Berlin.

Heinrichs, H. J. 1975. *Materialien zu Bachofens "Das Mutterrecht."* Frankfurt.

Henderson, J. 1987. *Aristophanes: Lysistrata.* Oxford.

Hennecke, E. 1964. *New Testament Apocrypha,* ed. W. Schneemelcher. Philadelphia.

Henrichs, A. 1980. "Human sacrifice in religion: three case studies," *Entretiens Hardt* 27:195–242.

———. 1984 "Loss of self, suffering, violence," *Harvard Studies in Classical Philology* 88:205–40.

Henriques, F. 1964. *Love in Action: The Sociology of Sex.* London.

Hoelscher, T. 1973. *Griechische Historienbilder des 5 and 4 Jahrhunderts*. Beiträge zur Archaeologie 6. Wiirzburg.

Hollis, A. S. 1990. *Callimachus: Hecale*. Oxford.

Horsfall, N. 1982. "Allia Potestas and Murdia: two Roman women," *Ancient Society* (Macquarie Univ.) 12.2:27–33.

———. 1983 "Some problems in the 'Laudatio Turiae,'" *Bulletin of the Institute of Classical Studies* 30:85–98.

How, W. W., and J. Wells. 1912. *A Commentary on Herodotus*. Oxford.

Humphreys, S. C. 1983. *The Family, Women, and Death*. London.

Jacob, H. E. 1963. *Felix Mendelssohn and His Times*. Englewood Cliffs, N.J.

Jacoby, F. 1923–. *Die Fragmente der griechischen Historiker*. Berlin.

———. 1949. *Atthis*. Oxford.

Jebb, R. C. 1900. *Sophocles: Antigone*, ed. 3. Cambridge.

Jenkins, I. 1983. "Is there life after marriage? a study of the abduction motif in vase paintings of the Athenian wedding ceremony," *BICS* 30:137–45.

Kaempf-Dimitriadou, S. 1969. *Die Liebe der Götter in der Attischen Kunst des 5. Jahrhunderts v. Chr. Antike Kunst*, vol. 11. Bern.

Kaibel, G. 1878. *Epigrammata Graeca*. Berlin.

Kakridis, J. T. 1947. "Caeneus," *Classical Review* 61:77–80.

Kambitsis, J. 1972. *L'Antiope d'Euripide*. Athens.

Kampen, N. B., ed. 1996. *Sexuality in Ancient Art: Near East, Egypt, Greece, and Italy*. Cambridge.

Kannicht, R. 1969. *Euripides Helena*. Heidelberg.

Kassel, R., and C. Austin, eds. 1983–. *Poetae Comici Graeci*. Berlin.

Kearns, E. 1989. *The Heroes of Attica*. BICS Supplement 57. London.

———. 1990. "Saving the city." In *The Greek City*, ed. O. Murray and S. Price, 321–44. Oxford.

Keuls, E. 1985. *The Reign of the Phallus: Sexual Politics in Ancient Athens*. Berkeley.

Kilmer, M. F. 1990. "Sexual violence: archaic Athens and the recent past." In Craik 1990, 261–77.

———. 1993. *Greek Erotica on Attic Red-Figured Vases*. London.

———. 1997. "Rape in early red-figured pottery: violence and threat in homo-erotic and hetero-erotic contexts." In *Rape in Antiquity*, ed. S. Deacy and K. F. Pierce, 123–41. London.

King, H. 1983. "Bound to bleed: Artemis and Greek women." In Cameron and Kuhrt 1983, 109–27.

———. 1998. *Hippocrates' Woman*. London.

Kirk, G. S. 1985. *The Iliad: A Commentary*, vol. 1, books 1–4. Cambridge.

Kirk, G. S., J. E. Raven, and M. Schofield, eds. 1983. *The Presocratic Philosophers*, 2nd ed. Cambridge.

Kleinbaum, A. W. 1983. *The War against the Amazons*. New York.

Knox, B. M. W. 1978. *Word and Action*. Baltimore.

Kraemer, R. 1992. *Her Share of the Blessings: Women's Religions among Pagans, Jews, and Christians in the Greco-Roman World*. New York.

Kurtz, D. C. 1975. *Athenian White Lekythoi*. Oxford.

———. 1983. *The Berlin Painter*. Oxford.

Kurtz, D. C., and J. Boardman. 1971. *Greek Burial Customs*. London.

Lacey, W. K. 1968. *The Family in Classical Greece*. London.

Lanata, G. 1973. *Gli atti dei martiri come documents processuali*. Milan.

Lardinois, A., and L. McClure, eds. 2001. *Making Silence Speak*. Princeton.

Latte, K. 1940. "The coming of the Pythia," *Harvard Theological Review* 33:9–18.

Lattimore, R. 1962. *Themes in Greek and Latin Epitaphs*. Urbana, Ill..

Leach, E. 1969. "Virgin birth." In *Genesis and Other Essays*. London.

Lebek, W. D. 1985. "Das Grabepigramm auf Domitilla," *Zeitschrift für Papyrologie und Epigraphik* 59:7–8.

Lefkowitz, M. R. 1981a. *The Lives of the Greek Poets*. Baltimore.

———. 1981b. *Heroines and Hysterics*. London.

———. 1989. "'Impiety' and 'atheism' in Euripides' dramas," *Classical Quarterly* 39 (1): 70–82.

———. 1991. "Commentary on Vlastos," *Proceedings of the Boston Area Colloquium in Ancient Philosophy* 5:239–46. Lanham, Md.

———. 2003. *Greek Gods, Human Lives*. New Haven.

Lefkowitz, M. R., and M. B. Fant, eds. 2005. *Women's Life in Greece and Rome*, ed. 3. Baltimore.

Lévi-Strauss, C. 1955. "The structural study of myth." In *Myth: A Symposium*, ed. T. Sebeok, 81–106. Bloomington.

Lewin, J. 1966. *Aeschylus: The House of Atreus*. Minneapolis.

Lewis, D. M. 1955. "Who was Lysistrata? Notes on Attic inscriptions (II)," *Annual of the British School at Athens* 50:1–36.

Lipsius, R. A. 1891. *Acta Apostolorum Apocrypha*, vol. 1. Leipzig.

Littré, M. P. E. 1839–61. *Oeuvres complètes d'Hippocrate*. Paris.

Livrea, E. 1973. *Argonauticon Liber Quartus*. Biblioteca di Studi Superiori 60. Florence.

Lloyd-Jones, H. 1964. "A fragment of new comedy: P. Antinoopolis 15," *Journal of Hellenic Studies* 84:21–34 (= 1990b, 94–114).

———. 1971. "Appendix," *Aeschylus*, vol. 2, ed. H. Weir Smyth, 325–603. Loeb Classical Library. Cambridge, Mass.

———. 1971/1983. *The Justice of Zeus*. Berkeley.

———. 1975. *Females of the Species*. London.

————. 1978. "Ten notes on Aeschylus, *Agamemnon,*" *Dionysiaca* (Festschrift D. L. Page), 45–61 (= 1990a 318–34). Cambridge.

————. 1982/1993. *The Oresteia.* Berkeley.

————. 1982. "Pindar," *Proceedings of the British Academy* 68:139–63 (= 1990a: 57–79).

————. 1983. "Artemis and Iphigenia," *Journal of Hellenic Studies* 103:87–102 (= 1990a: 306–30).

————. 1990a. *Academic Papers: Greek Epic, Lyric, and Tragedy.* Oxford.

————. 1990b. *Academic Papers: Greek Comedy, Hellenistic Literature, Greek Religion, and Miscellanea.* Oxford.

Lloyd-Jones, H., and P. Parsons, eds., 1983. *Supplementum Hellenisticum.* Berlin.

Lonsdale, S. 1993. *Dance and Ritual Play.* Baltimore.

Loraux, N. 1978. "Sur la race des femmes et quelques-uns de ses tribus," *Arethusa* 11: 43–85.

————. 1981. *Les enfants d'Athéna.* Paris.

————. 1987. *Tragic Ways of Killing Women,* tr. Arthur Forster. Cambridge, Mass.

————. 1993. *Children of Athena,* 2nd ed.. Princeton.

Maas, P. 1973a. "Aeschylus *Agam.* 231 ff. Illustrated." In *Kleine Schriften,* ed. W. Buchwald, 42. Munich.

————. 1973b. "Akusilaos über Kaineus." In ibid., 63–66.

————. 1973c. "De deorum cum feminis mortalibus concubitu." In ibid., 66–67.

MacDonald, D. R. 1983. *The Legend and the Apostle: The Battle for Paul in Story and Canon.* Philadelphia.

Macleod, C. W. 1982. *Homer, Iliad Book XXIV.* Cambridge.

Macurdy, G. H. 1932. *Hellenistic Queens.* Baltimore.

Mazzolani, L. S. 1982. *Una moglie.* Palermo.

Meeks, W. A. 1983. *The First Urban Christians.* New Haven.

Merck, M. 1978. "'The city's achievements, the patriotic Amazonomachy and ancient Athens." In *Tearing the Veil,* ed. S. Lipschitz. London.

Merkelbach, R., and M. L. West, eds. 1967. *Fragmenta Hesiodea.* Oxford.

Michelini, A. N. 1987. *Euripides and the Tragic Tradition.* Madison.

Mikalson, J. 1991. *Honor Thy Gods.* Chapel Hill.

Millar, F. 1977. *The Emperor in the Roman World, 31 B.C.–A.D. 337.* London.

Millett, K. 1970. *Sexual Politics.* New York.

Momigliano, A. 1963. *The Conflict between Paganism and Christianity in the Fourth Century.* Oxford.

Musti, D. 1982. *Pausania, guida della Grecia I: l'Attica.* Scrittori Greci e Latini. Rome.

Musurillo, H. 1972. *The Acts of the Christian Martyrs.* Oxford.

Nagy, B. 1979. "The naming of Athenian girls: a case in point," *Classical Journal* 74: 360–64.

Nagy, G. 1979. *The Best of the Achaeans*. Baltimore.

Neils, J., et al. 1992. *Goddess and Polis: The Panathenaic Festival in Ancient Athens.* Princeton.

Nilsson, M. P. 1913. *Griechische Feste von religiöser Bedeutung*. Stuttgart.

Oakley, J. H. 1995. "Nuptial nuances: wedding images in non-wedding scenes in myth." In Reeder 1995, 63–73.

Oakley, J. H., and R. H. Sinos. 1993. *The Wedding in Ancient Athens*. Madison.

O'Brien, J. V. 1977. *Bilingual Selections from Sophocles' Antigone*. Carbondale, Ill.

O'Connor-Visser, E.A.M.E. 1987. *Aspects of Human Sacrifice in the Tragedies of Euripides*. Amsterdam.

Osborne, R. 1996. "Desiring women on Athenian pottery." In Kampen 1996, 65–80.

Padel, R. 1992. *In and Out of the Mind: Greek Images of the Tragic Self*. Princeton.

Page, D. L. 1938. *Euripides: Medea*. Oxford.

———. 1955. *Sappho and Alcaeus*. Oxford.

———. 1981. *Further Greek Epigrams*. Cambridge.

Page, D. L., and M. Davies. 1991. *Poetarum Melicorum Graecorum Fragmenta*. Oxford.

Pape, W., and G. Benseler. 1911/1959. *Wörterbuch der Griechischen Eigennamen*, ed. 3. Graz.

Parke, H. W. 1977. *Festivals of the Athenians*. London.

Parke, H. W., and D. E. W. Wormell. 1956. *The Delphic Oracle*. Oxford.

Parker, R. 1983. *Miasma: Pollution and Purification in Early Greek Religion*. Oxford.

———. 1987. "Myths of early Athens." In *Interpretations of Greek Mythology*, ed. J. Bremmer, 187–214. London.

———. 1991. "The *Hymn to Demeter* and the *Homeric Hymns*," *Greece & Rome* 38:1–17.

———. 2005. *Polytheism and Society in Athens*. Oxford.

Parry, A. M. 1989. *The Language of Achilles and Other Papers*. Oxford.

Parvey, C. F. 1974. "The theology and leadership of women in the New Testament." In *Religion and Sexism*, ed. R. Ruether, 117–49. New York.

Patlagean, E. 1976. "L'Histoire de la femme déguisée en moine et l'évolution de la sainteté feminine à Byzance," *Studi Medievali* 17:597–623.

Pearson, A. C., ed. 1907. *Euripides: The Heraclidae*. Cambridge.

Peek, W. 1955. *Griechische Vers-Inschriften*. Berlin.

———. 1965. "Die Penelope der Ionerinnen," *Athenische Mitteilungen* 80:163–64.

Pembroke, S. 1965. "The last of the matriarchs: a study in the inscriptions of Lycia," *Journal of the Economic and Social History of the Orient* 8:217–47.

———. 1967. "Women in charge," *Journal of the Warburg and Courtauld Institutes* 30:1–35.

———. 1970. "Locres et Tarente," *Annales Économies, Sociétés, Civilisations* 25: 240–70.

Pfeiffer, R. 1949–53. *Callimachus*. Oxford.

Pickard-Cambridge, A. 1968. *The Dramatic Festivals of Athens*, 2nd ed., ed. J. Gould and D. M. Lewis. Oxford.

Pleket, H. W. 1969. *Texts on the Social History of the Greek World*, vol. 2, *Epigraphica*. Leiden.

Poliakoff, M. 1982. *Studies in the Terminology of the Greek Combat Sports*. Beiträge zur klassischen Philologie 146. Koenigstein.

———. 1987. *Combat Sports in the Ancient World*. New Haven.

Pomeroy, S. B. 1975a. "Andromaque: un exemple méconnu de matriarchat," *Revue des Études Grecques* 68:16–19.

———. 1975b. *Goddesses, Whores, Wives, and Slaves*. New York.

———. 1981. "Women in Roman Egypt." In Foley 1981, 303–22.

———. 1985. *Women in Hellenistic Egypt from Alexander to Cleopatra*. New York.

———. 1994. *Xenophon, Oeconomicus: A Social and Historical Commentary*. Oxford.

Preisigke, F., et al. 1915–. *Sammelbuch griechischer Urkunden aus Ägypten*. Strassburg and elsewhere.

Pritchett, J. B. 1958. *The Ancient Near East*. Princeton.

Rabinowitz, N. S. 1993. *Anxiety Veiled: Euripides and the Traffic in Women*. Ithaca.

Rader, R. 1981. "The martyrdom of Perpetua." In *A Lost Tradition: Women Writers of the Early Church*, ed. P. Wilson-Kastner, 1–32. Lanham, Md.

Redfield, J. 1978. "The Women of Sparta," *Classical Journal* 73:146–61.

Reeder, E. D. 1995. *Pandora: Women in Classical Greece*. Princeton.

Rehm, R. 1994. *Marriage to Death: The Conflation of Wedding and Funeral Rituals in Greek Tragedy*. Princeton.

Richardson, E. 1964. *The Etruscans*. Chicago.

Richardson, N. 1974. *The Homeric Hymn to Demeter*. Oxford.

Richlin, A., ed. 1992. *Pornography and Representation in Greece*. New York.

Ridgway, B. S. 1999. *Prayers in Stone*. Sather Classical Lectures, vol. 63. Berkeley.

Rist, J. M. 1965. "Hypatia," *Phoenix* 19:214–25.

Roberts, D. 1987. "Parting words: final lines in Sophocles and Euripides," *Classical Quarterly* 37:51–64.

Robertson, M. 1975. *A History of Greek Art*. Cambridge.

Robertson, N. 1983. "The riddle of the Arrhephoria at Athens," *Harvard Studies in Classical Philology* 87:241–88.

———. 1985. "The Origin of the Panathenaea," *Rheinisches Museum* 128:231–95.

———. 1988. "Melanthus, Codrus, Neleus, Caucon: ritual myth as Athenian history," *Greek, Roman, and Byzantine Studies* 29:201–61.

Robson, J. E. 1997. "Bestiality and bestial rape in Greek myth." In Deacy and Pierce 1997, 65–96.

Rogers, G. 1991. *The Sacred Identity of Ephesos*. London.

Rose, V. 1886. *Aristotelis Fragmenta.* Leipzig.

Salisbury, J. E. 1997. *Perpetua's Passion.* London.

Sandbach, F. H. 1972. *Menandri Reliquiae Selectae.* Oxford.

Sawyer, D. F. 1996. *Women and Religion in the First Christian Centuries.* London.

Schanzer, D. 1985. "Merely a Cynic gesture?" *Rivista di Filologia* 113:61–66.

Schaps, D. 1977. "The woman least mentioned," *Classical Quarterly* 27:323–30.

Schorn, S. 2004. *Satyrus aus Kallatis.* Basel.

Schrier, O. J. 1979. "Love with Doris." *Mnemosyne* 32:302–36.

Schwegler, C. 1913. *De Aeschinis quae feruntur epistolis.* Giessen.

Sealey, R. 1990. *Women and Law in Classical Greece.* Chapel Hill.

Segal, C. 1982. *Dionysiac Poetics and Euripides' Bacchae.* Princeton.

Shapiro, H. A. 1986. "The Attic deity Basile," *ZPE* 63:134–36.

———. 1992. "Eros in love: pederasty and pornography in Greece." In Richlin 1992, 53–72.

Shewring, W., tr. 1980. *The Odyssey.* Oxford.

Simon, B. 1978. *Mind and Madness in Ancient Greece: The Classical Roots of Modern Psychiatry.* Ithaca.

Simon, E. 1983. *Festivals of Attica: An Archaeological Commentary.* Madison.

Sinclair Holderman, E. 1985. "Le sacerdotesse: requisiti, funzioni, poteri." In Arrigoni 1985, 299–330.

Sinos, R. H. 1993. "Divine selections." In *Cultural Poetics in Archaic Greece: Cult, Performance, Politics,* ed. C. Dougherty and L. Kurke, 73–91. Cambridge.

Sissa, G. 1990. *Greek Virginity,* tr. Arthur Goldhammer. Cambridge, Mass.

Sissa, G., and M. Detienne. 1989. *La vie quotidienne des dieux grecs.* Paris.

Slater, P. 1968. *The Glory of Hera.* Boston.

Smarczyk, B. 1984. *Untersuchungen zur Religionspolitik und politischen Propaganda Athens im Delisch-Attischen Seebund.* Munich.

Smith, W. 1960. "The ironic structure in *Alcestis,*" *Phoenix* 14:127–45.

Snell, B., and R. Kannicht. 1986–. *Tragicorum Graecorum Fragmenta.* Göttingen.

Snyder, J. M. 1989. *The Woman and the Lyre.* Carbondale, Ill.

Sokolowski, F. 1969. *Lois sacrées des cités grecques.* Paris.

Sorum, C. E. 1982. "The family in Sophocles' *Antigone* and *Electra,*" *Classical World* 75.4:201–11.

Sourvinou-Inwood, C. 1991. *Reading Greek Culture.* Oxford.

———. 1995. *"Reading" Greek Death to the End of the Classical Period.* Oxford.

Stadter, P. 1965. *Plutarch's Historical Methods: An Analysis of De Mulierum Virtute.* Cambridge.

Stager, L., and S. R. Wolff. 1984. "Child sacrifice at Carthage: religious rite or population control?" *Biblical Archaeology Review* 10.1:30–51.

Stehle, E. 1990. "Sappho's gaze: fantasies of a goddess and young man," *Differences* 2.1:88–125.

———. 2001. "The good daughter: mothers' tutelage in Erinna's *Distaff* and fourth-century epitaphs." In Lardinois and McClure 2001, 179–200.

Stewart, A. 1995. "Rape?" In Reeder 1995, 74–90.

Stewart, Z. 1984. "Greek crowns and Christian martyrs," *Antiquité Paienne et Chrétienne* (memorial to A.-J. Festugière). *Cahiers d'Orientalisme* 10:119–24.

Sulimirski, T. 1970. *The Sauromatians*. Ancient Peoples and Places, no. 73. New York.

Sutton, R. F., Jr. 1992. "Pornography and persuasion on Attic pottery." In Richlin 1992, 3–35.

———. 1997/1998. "Nuptial Eros: the visual discourse of marriage in classical Athens," *Journal of the Walters Art Museum* 55/56:27–48.

Thesleff, H. 1965. *The Pythagorean Texts of the Hellenistic Period*. Abo, Finland.

Thomas, E. 1976. *Mythos und Geschichte*. Cologne.

Treggiari, S. 1982. "Consent to Roman marriage: some aspects of law and reality," *Classical Views* 26:34–44.

Trenkner, S. 1958. *The Greek Novella in the Classical Period*. Cambridge.

Tyrrell, W. B. 1984. *Amazons: A Study in Athenian Mythmaking*. Baltimore.

Tyrrell, W. B., and F. S. Brown 1991. *Athenian Myths and Institutions*. New York.

Van Bremen, R. 1983. "Women and wealth." In Cameron and Kuhrt 1983, 223–41.

Vellacott, P. 1975. *Ironic Drama*. Cambridge.

Vermeule, E. 1979. *Aspects of Death in Early Greek Art and Poetry*. Sather Classical Lectures, no. 46. Berkeley.

Vernant, J.-P. 1980. *Myth and Society in Ancient Greece*, tr. J. Lloyd. Atlantic Highlands, N.J.

———. 1991. *Mortals and Immortals*, ed. F. I. Zeitlin. Princeton.

Versnel, H. S. 1980. "Self-sacrifice, compensation and the anonymous gods." In *Le Sacrifice dans l'Antiquité, Entretiens Hardt*, vol. 27, 136–85. Vandoevres-Genève.

Vidal-Naquet, P. 1981. "Slavery and the rule of women." In *Myth, Religion, and Society*, ed. R. L. Gordon, 187–200. Cambridge.

Voigt, E. M. 1971. *Sappho et Alcaeus*. Amsterdam.

von Bothmer, D. 1975. *Amazons in Greek Art*. Oxford.

Walcot, P. 1984. "Greek attitudes towards women: the mythological evidence," *Greece and Rome* 31:37–47.

Warner, M. 1976. *Alone of All Her Sex: The Myth and Cult of the Virgin Mary*. London.

Wells, A. M. 1978. *Miss Marks and Miss Woolley*. Boston.

West, M. L. 1966. *Hesiod: Theogony*. Oxford.

———. 1971. *Iambi et Elegi Graeci*. Oxford.

———. 1978. *Hesiod: Works and Days*. Oxford.

————. 1985. *The Hesiodic Catalogue of Women*. Oxford.

————. 1997. *The East Face of Helicon: West Asiatic Elements in Greek Poetry and Myth*. Oxford.

West, S. 1991. "Herodotus' portrait of Hecataeus," *Journal of Hellenic Studies* 111: 144–60.

Whallon, W. 1980. *Problem and Spectacle: Studies in the* Oresteia. Heidelberg.

Wicker, K. O'B. 1975. "De defectu oraculorume." In *Plutarch's Theological Writings and Early Christian Literature*, ed. H. D. Betz, 131–80. Leiden.

Wiedemann, T. 1983. "Thucydides, women, and the limits of rational analysis," *Greece and Rome* 30:163–70.

Wiersma, S. 1984. "Women in Sophocles," *Mnemosyne* 37 (1978): 25–55.

Wiesen, D. 1976. "The contribution of antiquity to American racial thought." In *Classical Traditions in Early America*, ed. J. W. Eadie, 191–212. Ann Arbor.

Wilamowitz-Moellendorff, U. v. 1893. *Aristoteles und Athen*. Berlin.

————, ed. 1926. *Euripides: Ion*. Berlin.

Wilkins. J. 1990. "The state and the individual: Euripides' plays of voluntary self-sacrifice." In *Euripides, Women, and Sexuality*, ed. A. Powell, 177–94. London.

————. 1993. *Euripides: Heraclidae*. Oxford.

Wilson, N. 1982. "Two observations on Aristophanes' *Lysistrata*," *Greek, Roman and Byzantine Studies* 23:157–63.

Winnington-Ingram, R. P. 1980. *Sophocles: An Interpretation*. Cambridge.

————. 1982. "Sophocles and women," *Entretiens Hardt* 29:233–57.

————. 1983. *Studies in Aeschylus*. Cambridge.

Wiseman, T. P. 1979. *Clio's Cosmetics*. Leicester.

Wistrand, E. 1976. *The So-called Laudatio Turiae*. Studia Latina et Graeca. Gothoburgiensia 34. Goteborg.

Worman, N. 2001. "The voice which is not one: Helen's virtual guises in Homeric epic." In Lardinois and McClure 2001, 19–37.

Wycherley, R. E. 1978. *The Stones of Athens*. Princeton.

Zeitlin, F. 1978. "The dynamics of misogyny in the *Oresteia*," *Arethusa* 11:149–81.

————. 1982. "Cultic models of the female: rites of Dionysus and Demeter," *Arethusa* 15:129–55.

————. 1986. "Configurations of rape in Greek myth." In *Rape*, ed. S. Tomaselli and R. Porter, 122–51. Oxford.

————. 1989. "Mysteries of identity and designs of the self in Euripides' *Ion*," *Proceedings of the Cambridge Philological Society*, n.s. 35:144–97.

Ziehen, L. 1949. "Panathenaia." *RE* 36.2:457–93.

Zintzen, C. 1967. *Damascii Vitae Isidori Reliquiae*. Hildesheim.

Zuntz, G. 1955. *The Political Plays of Euripides*. Manchester.

Index

abduction of females by gods: characteristics of, 44–52, 56–69, 75–76, 78–79, 81, 84, 108; criteria for, 46–52, 84; distinguished from rape, 54–56, 72; enactment in weddings, 80–81; fear of, 63; gratitude for, 57–59, 65; resentment of, 61–65, 205n.78

abduction of men by goddesses and gods, 70; characteristics of, 73, 75–76, 77–79, 172–74, 203n.52; interpretations of, 71–72, 76, 80–81; as representations of death, 76

Adonia, 119

Adonis. *See* Aphrodite

adultery, 38–39, 117–18, 131

Aegisthus, xvii, 174–75

Aeschylus: *Europa*, 60, 77–78; *Oresteia*, 10, 48, 67, 90, 107, 121, 153–55, 175–78; *Prometheus*, 44, 63, 109, 188; *Suppliants*, 186–87

Aethra, 151

Afrania, 149, 165

Agrionia, xix

Agrippina, 2, 139, 151

Alcestis, 28, 125–28, 130

Alcman, *partheneion*, 120

Alcmena, 47, 84, 106, 124, 214n.13

Althaea, 176, 210n.15

Amasia Sentia, 165

Amazons, 1–12; breasts of, 3–5; foreignness of, 5–7, 186; modern interpretations of, 3; myths of, 2–6; nonexistence of, 7–8; sexuality of, 11; in South America, 7–8; wars against, 5, 8–9, 11

Amymone, 66, 79, 84, 198n.20

Anchises, 78, 172–73

Andromache: as advisor, 30–32; as model

wife, 29–35, 38, 129–30, 135, 143, 189–90; as survivor, 115–16, 158

Antigone: as daughter, 187; family curse on, xvii, 45, 50, 142, 174; on *nomoi*, 159–60; as sister, 139–42, 151, 178, 187; suffering of, 83, 85–86, 88; as woman, 159–60

Antiope, 59, 62–63

Antipoenus, daughters of, 157

Anyte, 113

Aphrodite (Cypris, Cytherea, Venus): and Adonis, 70, 119, 200n.4; birth of, 17, 171; character of, 23; deception by, 82, 171–74, 178; garden of, 99; gifts of, 169; power of, 38–39, 47, 120, 155, 179–81, 188–90

Apollonius of Rhodes, 7, 51, 121, 179

Aretaphila, 146, 148

aristocratic women, 95–97, 122, 130–31, 135–38, 161–64, 183

Aristodemus, 154

Aristophanes, 103, 105, 118–19, 144, 169

Aristotle, 132, 145, 147, 168

arrhephoroi, 96–99

Arria, 151

Arsinoe, 148

Artemis, beauty of: 190, 121; at Brauron, 96; in Ephesus, 166, 208n.26; as *parthenos*, 108, 120, 180; powers of, 91, 175–76, 178

Artemisia, 122, 139

Atalanta, 46, 83, 106, 120

atē (delusion), xvii, 45, 50, 52, 83, 87–88, 100, 142, 169–73, 174, 179, 190

Athena: in Athens, 10, 96–100, 103, 105, 177; and Erichthonius, 98–100; helping mortals, 62, 75, 189; as *parthenos*, 108; powers of, 120, 124, 169, 178

Athens, 95–105, 131

CREDITS

Acknowledgments of prior publication of chapters in earlier versions are due as follows: Chapter 1, *Times Literary Supplement* (Nov. 27, 1981), 1399–1401; Chapter 2, *The American Scholar* 58 (1989), 586–91; Chapter 3, *The American Scholar* 56 (1987), 503–18; Chapter 4, *The American Scholar* 54 (1985), 207–19; Chapter 5, *Consent and Coercion to Sex and Marriage in Ancient and Medieval Societies*, ed. A. E. Laiou (Cambridge: Harvard University Press, 1993), 17–37; Chapter 6, *Hesperia* 71 (2003), 325–44; Chapter 7, *Pandora's Box: Women in Classical Greece*, ed. Ellen Reeder (Princeton: Princeton University Press, 1995), 32–38; Chapter 9, *Greece and Rome* 30 (1983), 31–47; Chapter 10, *Images of Women in Antiquity*, ed. A. Cameron and A. Kuhrt (London: Routledge, 1983), 49–64; Chapter 11, *Worshipping Athena: Panathenaia and Parthenon*, ed. Jenifer Neils (Madison: University of Wisconsin Press, 1996), 78–91. Translations, unless otherwise noted, are my own.

Acknowledgments for permission to reproduce illustrations are due as follows: Figures 1 and 14, Antikensammlung, Staatliche Museen zu Berlin, Preussischer Kulturbesitz; Figure 2, Baltimore Museum of Art; Figure 3, Walters Art Museum, Baltimore; Figure 4, Museum of Fine Arts, Boston; Figure 5, Metropolitan Museum of Art, New York; Figure 6, Bowdoin College Museum of Art, Brunswick, Maine; Figure 7, Museo archeologico nazionale di Ferrara, Italy; Figure 8, Arqueológico nacional, Madrid; Figure 9, State Hermitage Museum, St. Petersburg; Figure 10, Musei Vaticani, Archivio fotografico; Figure 11, Soprintendenza archeologica per l'Etruria meridionale, Rome; Figure 12, Musée du Louvre, Paris; Figure 13, British Museum, London.